SACRAMENTO PUBLIC LIBRARY
3 3029 04434 8381

D0971707

MOTHER MILLETT

By the same author

Sexual Politics

The Prostitution Papers

Flying

Sita

The Basement

The Loony Bin Trip

The Politics of Cruelty

A.D., A Memoir

MOTHER MILLETT

Kate Millett

VERSO

London · New York

First published by Verso 2001

Verso
UK: 6 Meard Street, London W1F 0EG
USA: 180 Varick Street, New York NY 10014-4606
www.versobooks.com

Verso is the imprint of New Left Books

ISBN 1–85984–607–6

British Library Cataloguing in Publication Data
A catalogue record for this book is available from the British Library

Library of Congress Cataloging-in-Publication Data
A catalog record for this book is available from the Library of Congress

Typeset in Monotype Fournier by The Running Head Limited,
www.therunninghead.com
Printed and bound in Great Britain by Biddles Ltd, *www.biddles.co.uk*

Contents

Acknowledgments

I am very grateful to my friend Linda Kavars, who looked after the Farm during all my absences and made possible these visits with my mother.

Introduction

I began writing about my mother, little sketches for myself, and largely about myself, in 1985 when my elder sister, Sally—a lifetime sibling rival and always a critic of considerable acumen, older and wiser and more practical in so many departments of life through her training in political history, diplomacy and international relations, her practice in law and banking—forced me to pay attention and understand that our mother Helen Millett could actually die and indeed was old and recently ill enough to do so certainly, and perhaps soon.

The first three sections of the book are as much about myself as about my mother: indeed as Sally has often observed, I rarely write about any subject except myself, so that there is a good deal of the egocentricity and ambition of the artist come home to confront her past in her parent and her town. Mother Millett was of course the catalyst but not the main player yet—not until reality takes over in Part Four, halfway through the book. The turning point came when we all discovered what was killing our mother: a benign tumor pressing upon the brain, paralyzing her mobile capacity and, while it had no effect yet upon her intellect and the excellent faculties of her cerebellum, was slowly making speech difficult and writing impossible, even to signing her own name to a bank check. The tumor was in the medulla oblongata and, as it continued to grow, might even asphyxiate her and become the cause of her death.

After this discovery, everything changed. We realized that she had been right all along about her growing infirmity and her regular physician wrong and arrogant—even culpable in dismissing her condition as mere age—and medically irresponsible, in view of her symptoms, in never prescribing a CAT scan. Then came surgery, the great hope of recovery, then that hope dashed by complications and the onset of hypercalcemia, an often fatal condition.

What began as casual personal writing became a narrative we were both now living inside, even a book which my mother lived to read in a new life, restored to her own home and freed from an institution she had seen as a living death, two serene final years with all her daughters and caretakers at her side in support.

Part One

"Now turn that light on." How she fusses, I think, but I get up and turn it on. "There, this is just how I imagined it would be," she says. And it comes over me, that she has planned it. Each element on the table: the placemats, the mahogany, the silver. This is breakfast, but even breakfast was romantic, imagined beforehand. She had actually thought of the lighting, must have practiced it, decided that this table lamp should be on; warmth, backfill. It comes over me, the studied and terrifying love of mothers, like Amina, the Moslem mother in Maguib's *Palace Walk*, the book I have been reading downstairs in the guest room this morning, that patient all-conquering love they have everywhere—Japanese mothers, remember the mother in *Tokyo Story*. If I had not noticed this little phrase about having imagined it, I might never have had to face this love, it comes at me like the fear of speed, like the ferris wheel, like my terror of losing her, like my guilt and unworthiness: I am an imposter accepting this goodness, loved this outrageously by the little being across the table, smaller each time I see her, her strong eyes behind their glasses, the large handsome shape of her skull more pronounced with each visit, those great Irish peasant eyebrows, fierce like her father Patrick Henry's, like my own, her beautiful silver hair, that strange big hooked nose, Indian or Hebraic, unexpected but full of character and her own individual strength, her life-long mixture of timidity and stubbornness, acumen, insight. Her little shoulders tiny: absurdly, childishly tiny in the sporty knit blouse.

She had looked forward and imagined this moment with an open heart. I had met her with dread and now feel sorrow, a special fright. However complicated it is for her, she is still welcoming her child home. I am that mixture of anger and resentment I have always been, the outlaw of the tribe, the artist, the queer, even the crazy, since in certain ill-advised moments, my sisters and even my mother have seen fit to deliver me over to state psychiatry, through which I was made a prisoner and later a shamed and stigmatized being. An episode that darkened my life for over a decade and which I recently described in a book called *The Loony Bin Trip*. The family read it in manuscript and took its publication very well: the wounds are healing, we have come back together as a unit, having ejected the foreign body of psychiatric formula, alien unreason to a group of Irishwomen living out a new kind of independent life on courage, common sense and wit.

My mother is America to me. The America of the Middle West and the Mississippi River, "Amazing Grace," and "Will the Circle be Unbroken?", the homestead at Farmington where she was born and raised until she went to the University, the polite St. Paul existence of her adulthood as a wife and mother, even the short streak of hard times endured with grace after her divorce during the difficult years of her early professional career, itself a regular miracle of hard earned success and distinction, a prominence that even led to prosperity in its later years after I had left home.

Those years she became a fixture and a legend, the big shot at conferences, the role model of a whole generation of women coming into American finance and insurance. Even there she led as the gentle open-minded liberal with acquaintances—even fans—in every quarter, all goodwill, justice and sympathy toward minorities as well as the visionaries she had taught me to admire in childhood and adolescence, the daily reports of Gandhi's marches we followed in the St. Paul Pioneer Press, the great moments of Martin Luther King's oration in Washington when I came home from two years in Japan and we watched him on television, our tears nearly dissolving our tomato sandwiches, weeping and laughing in glory at the grandeur of his phrases. I was on my way back to New York to work for the Congress for Racial Equality. But Mother went on in her quiet way befriending and helping the Jews and Blacks and Asians she reached out to among her clientele, and a host of Twin City women bless her for an independence they were made to foresee and save for carefully and would never have enjoyed without her because the male privilege of a pension had not yet been extended to most jobs for women.

Only the war in Vietnam ever inspired my mother to actually march in the street, of course under my prodding. But Helen Millett has grown all her life and especially in these last years: she even walked for gay rights from the lovely capital building in St. Paul at night along its promenade sweeping to the Cathedral itself. She was a feminist long before the thought occurred to me. In time she became determinedly pro-abortion and nearly heretical in her opposition to the hierarchy. In these last few years she has come a long way from the immigrant Irish piety of her origins. Mostly she has operated quietly for goodness and equity, going by her standard of "what is fair," her favorite virtue.

~

The orange juice had already been poured and was waiting in the icebox, the oatmeal had been made. She had somehow, walker and all, gotten around the little apartment kitchen and done the oatmeal, having planned it, having planned oatmeal days or weeks ago. The orange juice was a brand my younger sister Mallory had taught her when she was here in January, the kind her husband Thomas liked, Tropicana: better than the frozen concentrate that has been good enough since she stopped having a Mixmaster that squeezed real orange juice.

A Mixmaster and a real kitchen, the old house, the old mornings coming back when I would be served fresh orange juice in bed the first mornings home. The morning after the first dinner—all my favorites: her own light chicken fricassee, her own famous and inimitable mashed potatoes; and then the meringues, her meringues, meringues such as even the French never approach though I have tried meringues all over the world and a hundred times in Paris just to see if they ever came anywhere near that crisp ecru shell on the outside, and inside that perfect chewy consistency . . . but the taste. Cream of tartar she said was the secret. That and mixing in the sugar slowly with the slowness of a master to achieve the structure.

But I will never be greeted this way again; she is not up to meringues anymore. I will never even eat one of her meringues again, forgoing them now without yet understanding the loss. These masterpieces were the gift of her love—leaving for New York indulged with a shoe-box of homemade meringues, whatever was left of the ceremonial batch made in honor of my homecoming, often crumbs when I landed but just as delicious.

Home from Tokyo, or just another trip from New York and my studio on the Bowery in the middle of the slum, home from the ends of the earth to her kitchen, mobilized a day before for the entire afternoon it took to concoct them, each batch commented upon, savored, apologized for, compared with a previous batch. I carry the recipe still but no longer even try to match it having failed so many times. Being home was stealing down at night to consume one more perfect meringue, perhaps even another—there will still be a few to pack into a box and bring back with me, shattered remnants of what at this moment is whole and exquisite, the crisp breast of eggshell lying nestled in wax paper in the round tin box.

But I was still unprepared for her remark this morning, the reappearance of that devastating unconditional love, mother love, that could still plan the lighting, could still try to cook something, homemade oatmeal, a good solution and easy, with orange juice from a carton. One is deceived by such details into thinking you are in the real or modern world: the contemporary apartment, the sealed window onto the "view" of other recently constructed apartments for the elderly, faultlessly clean and up to date, tasteful, quiet, the most excellent St. Paul solid quality. This is really a good place for her to be, I think, reassuring myself again that it is probably better than anything in the country. Of course the main thing, the great thing is that she has people to eat with at night—the restaurant downstairs, in addition to her kitchen—that every night there are a hundred friends to dine with, waitresses from my own high school, Derham Hall, even a printed menu. After eating alone for twenty years, a life of society, sociability. Mother went to college with two women on her floor, her first weeks here were like life in a new sorority house, Mother a new pledge, very popular, making a name for herself with little cocktail parties, white wine, wooden bowls of crackers, nuts arranged on the special china dish, the one with filigree work. Even daiquiris at times, Mother's own cousin Glady Gilbert drinking scotch and smoking cigarettes. Glady was across the hall then. Last night Mother told us all that Glady was in the hospital. Later it became clear that Glady has been expelled from the Wellington, this apartment house for the elderly who are still well enough to maintain an apartment. Glady has fallen below that standard now. Her doctor has ordered her into the hospital for a heart condition but she is there only temporarily: she no longer lives at the Wellington, will not be coming back. After the hospital she will be sent to a nursing home. The truth is out.

"There are only two things I'm afraid of," Mother said after we got home from dinner, our first talk alone, usually the best one, "just two things," staring straight ahead, that stony terrible stare of courage or despair I have seen in her plenty of times, always the worst and most essential times (my commitment hearing, for example).

"I'm scared of falling. And of nursing homes." You're safe with me, I think. I've been put away, I'm not likely to do it to anyone else. Maybe I even say it, "I'll never put you into a nursing home." Knowing damn well I don't make these decisions anyway, Sal does, the eldest; though I would fight Sal I would probably lose. And what substitute do I have? "Sally has told me I could go to her, she has room in that new house. She said that she and her friend Ruth both had mothers and they had extra room just because of that." I admire my sister, a better daughter than I.

"But I don't want to be a burden." The word burden more terrible than the word fate and fate itself because Mother is between Scylla and Charybdis and cannot die when she wishes, may have to live longer than she wants to be alive; already she has reached the point of diminishing return. She says it fairly openly now, looking at the ninety-one years her elder sister Mary lived: her eldest sister Margaret is going to be ninety-nine, bright as a dime, sprightly, able-bodied, a great conversationalist. Mother is eighty-eight and there are probably moments when she must feel captive in life with a body that is steadily betraying her yet will not release her either. Does she think of suicide, I wonder. She had that living will business notarized years ago even before it was popular, but suicide would be a matter of means. Would Huxley's Hemlock Society be available to her, to her remaining Catholicism, her St. Paul respectability? Too much to imagine. Yet one sees the predicament, the feeling she must have of being trapped in life. Moreover the two precipices of the nursing home or the burden are just there: one slip and you fall.

At the moment she is in a state of absolute grace; the doctor has just given her a check-up and proclaimed her to be sound as a dollar. "He says I'm just about perfect," she laughs. "He forgets to mention that I can hardly walk even though they can't find anything wrong with my legs. And I can't hear worth a damn, either." She will adjust to neither of these infirmities, hates the walker, was ashamed I should see it, warned me over the phone in a solemn voice that she was really old now, I should not be shocked when I see her. "Good God, how I hate for you to see me in this condition." I reassure her, I beguile her with humor as I have always done, court her with teasing, flirt, exaggerate, bring out the girl in her, coax out that approbation her laughter has always amounted to, that amused surrender of judgment. If I can make her laugh. I can make her accept the wildest ideas. I even know about the Pampers at night: nothing fazes me.

Yesterday I watched her receiving me in her chair. This was the point of having Steven meet my plane even though I offered to rent a car myself at the airport. Of course it's nice to be met, everyone agreed, even Steven's wife Chris going along with the plan though I offered them a way out: surely this is a nuisance for two busy young lawyers like themselves with a new baby, too. No, Steven should meet my plane—all so that she could receive me sitting down. Seated regally in her chair, the door unlocked, we would just walk in and she would stretch out her arms, I would kiss and be kissed, and she would never have to rise or move. Not yet.

And of course Steven would be right on top of the drinks, her perfect grandson, my handsome perfect nephew, our fair-haired man. And there would be laughter and nuts on the china plate with the filigree and a new kind of snack in the wooden bowls, and drinks before dinner. There would be a whole hour at least with just the three of us before Chris arrived to show the baby like a new queen in her white blanket. During all this Mother would never have to rise, the walker would even be out of sight, unthought of until that moment when it was time to get ready to go to Forepaugh's for dinner. And even then she managed it with a grace that also must have been planned: quietly Steven is bidden to produce the walker while we are diverted with other talk—Chris's new firm of women attornies, her colleagues, those fantastic offices of theirs. "Give my regards to that witty Irish senior partner of yours," I say to Chris, barely noticing the walker out of the corner of my eye. It's only when I realize Mother has gotten all the way to the closet and has put on her coat all by herself, that I come to, imagining that we have neglected her, surprised to hear that she'll be going down alone, starting for the elevator ten minutes ahead of us.

Mother's lifelong punctuality—no, it is not punctuality, it is an anxiety not to be late so intense that she is always early—we have laughed at it, opposed it, bullied and decried it forever. Yet this seems extreme. Then I realize she is going ahead because she can go at her own speed, not hold us back, toot along on the walker at whatever tortoise pace she chooses without hanging onto our arms or the railing in ways that Steven and I had grown to hate because she would clutch so tightly, lean so hard, complain so often that we went too fast. Perhaps the walker's an improvement, I think; it's autonomy, it's her independence.

She leaves us to finish our drinks and chat on a few moments, she goes off on her own. Like every member of his peer group, the generational rung just below me (Steven is my nephew, my elder sister Sally's son), Steven refers to Mother as G.M., ostensibly an abbreviation of grandmother, but actually a pun on General Motors which dates back to Ronald Reagan's celebrated gaffe: "What's good for General Motors is good for America." Mother's grandchildren, all of them, delight in this association; General Motors perfectly expresses their collective awe before the determined and autocratic matriarchal side of her. It is both naughty and affectionate. It has gone on so long and lovingly that by now she accepts the term herself. She has an authority both divine and funny for them, an exaggeration of that Mother I know at a daughter's closer range; for them the greater distance of yet another generation makes her something of a "character," harmless and sometimes amusing, never the devastating force she holds for me.

We in my own generation call her Mother Millett, a teasing and ironic play upon Mother McChree, the very cloying Irish sentimentality we belittle, imagine we have transcended. We are Milletts after all, Norman Irish. Mother is of course not a Millett, nor a Norman. She is also not the least bit sentimental. Yet in being the mother of a new trio of Millett women, Helen Feely has somehow appropriated the Millett name finally and transformed it with a new understanding and full matriarchal rank.

After a few moments enjoying our own company I begin to feel slightly neglectful and walk down the hall to find Mother at the elevators, leaving Chris and Steven to take care of the baby and its paraphernalia. The baby is a wonderful new element in this context, plainly the other end of life, the compliment to Mother's frailty, fascinating as well: I watch its head and imagine brush drawings of that simple and miraculous scalp line, the division between the two plates of the skull still visible, my mind squinting to render the monumental head of a baby as two big black brush lines. Might be fun to try it, probably never get it right but such a tantalizing problem; would they like a few sketches, I wonder. Here might be a child to draw for and write to, cherish, a new one of us, the first I have seen. Steve's brother David had a son already, and his sister Lisa will be having a child this August—all of them Sal's offspring, seeding themselves into a next generation, making me a great-aunt and Mother a great-grandmother. Sally is delighted, Mother too; I look at the baby and despite my odd tangential feeling within the tribe, their black sheep, I am pleased to meet this tiny little girl, pink and just starting out.

~

Every other apartment door along the hallway sported yellow ribbons and celebrated the Gulf War victory, except Mother's. We may have Steven to thank for this; Mother was a bit vague about it all. Chris and Steven deplore the carnage with me, the line of slaughter along the road to Basra, the "popcorn" of allied planes strafing the line of teenage conscripts, trying to imagine how many Iraqis have died for nothing when the sanctions would have worked. We talk about it over dinner, Mother opting out, her deafness, her delicious salmon. I order a Sancerre and go on about it being the greatest white wine there is, remembering Delphine Seyrig who taught it to me, mentioning her to them, how we were going to film de Beauvoir together and never got to it; then Simone was dead, now Delphine is. Telling them about the new video camera we are getting at the Farm: "We can do archival stuff there now, make our own history, interview women we want remembered." Telling them how Bookie wrote up the Farm in an essay for her graduate course at Columbia, said we were "a physical base for cultural feminism—don't you love it?", laughing at it and yet flattered too. Then the news of the latest harvest, the art colony's final self-sufficiency.

We don't mention another family reunion at the Farm tonight, not in front of Mother, because we know now that she will say she cannot come, that she cannot travel that far ever again. Until I arrived today I had always imagined Steven bringing Mother, picking her up at the Wellington and taking the plane with her at the Minneapolis airport. I would meet them at La Guardia and drive them up to the Farm because that little commuter airplane up to Poughkeepsie would be frightening. Realizing now it's impossible—she could never climb the plane's steep little stairs again. Watching Mother get out of the car and into the restaurant, the walker, the growing paralysis, the grueling matter of the front entrance—it was an entire production to get in the door here.

Forepaugh's is an elegant restaurant in an historic merchant's house downtown in St. Paul made over into a supposedly public place which still feels like someone's home: grand Victorian furniture and serious French cooking, my favorite place, our rendezvous on my every visit home. I'm delighted Chris and Steve have somehow never been here before. But tonight suddenly everything is difficult, Mother goes so slowly, is so afraid. Because, of course, it is not frailty; those legs are still good, she even uses the stationary bicycle in the Wellington's exercise room. It is fear that motivates her as the aluminum legs and the rubber tipped feet of the walker pause over each change of surface, dreading thresholds, getting caught in rugs. The world itself so fraught with danger, going out to dinner such a challenge, so exhausting and perilous.

It shocks me; there has been real deterioration. Her own pace is maddening. One senses how the waiters must chafe behind her, faultless still with St. Paul courtesy. One loathes it for her as she loathes it. I tell myself, hell, I came here to see her, if it takes her an hour to traverse twelve feet of carpet, I've got all day. It doesn't faze me at all—I didn't come here to see her perform athletic feats, I came here to talk.

Sal had made it clear there wasn't much time left. When she called I'd said sure I'd go, drop off after one of my gigs within the next couple months. "Listen, why can't you just go out there now, forget your gigs, just bother to get there—fast." I was chastened, ashamed, scared. My younger sister Mallory would be visiting Mother in January, therefore February would be a good time for me to show up. We'd keep coming one after another to entertain her. But when I called in January, Mother said March was better than February; February she'd be busy, she was doing her income tax. I remember being amused as well as relieved when I got off the phone, my guilt in remission. Mother was simply too busy to see me for another month, and March would be better for me too: I could stop off in St. Paul on my way home from that conference for gay and lesbian writers in San Francisco.

Of course by now Mother is blasé about things like gay writers, Steven too. We are so liberated and sophisticated that I can explain to them just how Edward Albee offended by receiving the gratitude of the gay literary community in a speech where he admitted to being gay and a writer but not a "gay writer," thereby insulting those who had meant to honor him. In fact he had meant to warn them against being ghettoized in a minority posture he regarded as diminishing. Together we remember *Who's Afraid of Virginia Woolf?* and the American theater of that day and agree that Albee had no option then but to write straight for it. Tennessee too, I say, but Tennessee was not only openly homosexual and put down for it hard, he always gave off signals of difference. Maybe it was being Southern, what do you think? Mother thought it was time to go, interrupting attempts at serious conversation as she always has with an utterly irritating aplomb. Chris grins at me, I grin back, willing to find this moment funny since I've just arrived in Mother's world from my own, only to be reminded again of the fundamental reason why they are such distinctly different places. There has been a lifetime of being interrupted, my important things less important than Mother's ever-present immediate reality. It's only the first day here, I'm easy.

~

At Forepaugh's I had taken one look at the bill and then handed it over to Steven for help, dismissing Mother's little peep about how she intended to take us all to dinner. Not at these prices, I say to myself, at first having intended to splash the whole thing on to my American Express but on seeing the sum, decided it was better to split it. Steven has half of the sum in cash and they will accept my card for the balance.

Back at Mother's apartment, she scolds me. She really had meant to take us out to dinner, she claims. But the real problem seems to be that she had promised this to Steven and Chris, that they would not be under any financial obligation in dining with her and welcoming me home. My cheeks burn a little: would that make the evening more palatable, more acceptable? Surely my nephew is fond of me, I scramble about, embarrassed. "They've just had a baby, they are not that well off." Mother is upset that Steven has been put to an expense he did not expect. "I wish you had told me all this," I protest, no more willing for her to pay than before. It was an extravagant sum, she's in no position to spend that kind of money, no matter what she claims. As always I catechize and interrogate her closely and never quite believe her assurances that she has quite enough money, is entirely comfortable. No one in the world ever seems to have enough money except the rich, and even they claim they are strapped. She shouldn't ever get involved with restaurants who need sums like this. My ears burn: it was I who ordered the wine, fully intending to pay for it, and then decided to let Steve go halves. He and Chris each earn several times what I do.

I'm still living on twelve grand a year, a thousand a month, a strange little life of borderline insecurity in what we used to call voluntary poverty when we were kid artists young enough to imagine we did it by choice. At fifty-six I realize it has nothing voluntary about it; it is simply that, by rationing my life out in small sums, I can survive to live it. By stowing an advance in the bank, I have something for next year, the year after, the year when there is no advance, like the five years I waited for *The Loony Bin Trip* to get published, or the years there are no gigs, like the Republican years between 1980 and 1990, when there was no felt need for radical speeches on campus. There are some gigs this year. The publication of *The Loony Bin Trip* finally has brought me a moment or two of renewed interest.

There was much noise with *Sexual Politics* in 1970 and for a few years after, then a silence. Nowadays, if I can engender a small hum, modest royalty checks, a few gigs each year, just put together my usual twelve thousand, even allowing for inflation, I could get by for quite a while, do my thing, insure my independence, never have to sell my soul to journalism, court book reviewing, whatever. Too ornery for the University to buy me, too radical for them to want to, too old by now even to qualify or be considered, there isn't much to hope for except a nice marginal life. And if you own a farm, even if you give away every cent it earns just by running a colony for women artists there, it can feed you too when you're up there working its fields. Run it right and maybe you'll never starve.

Sell it and you'd have plenty of money you could invest, they all say. Sal, Mallory, even the women at the Farm are aware the land is a resource, worth a fortune and so forth. "Sell it and you have nothing," I always want to shout back. "Sell land and you have sold your Mother," I would rage, but by now I hardly bother. I just point out that it is stupid to sell something that brings in $30,000 a year even if you have to work for it, even though it costs half that just to farm it, the other half just to feed its volunteer labor in lieu of wages. They'd point out that you might make enough by selling it to collect the same amount it earns with neither the trouble nor the expense: investments and interest and so forth. My Mother is a champion woman of business, my elder sister Sal is an attorney with an interest in a bank. I get a lot of good advice.

Mother used to sell life insurance and was a whiz at it, did so well in the few years she worked that, despite all the discrimination she had to battle when she started, she could still feather her nest at retirement and has used her money so well it will last her to the end. Now I begin to worry about lasting to the end myself. I had actually never given it a thought before, imagined I was a genius to have my next five years already saved up and in the bank—not a bad or even an unreasonable thing to do when you have no income in the sense of a job and no expectations of one either. And lately the problem of publication has arisen—*The Loony Bin Trip* took five years to find a publisher, and *A.D.*, written two years later and five years ago by now, still hasn't found its way into print and maybe won't. My wonderful new editor has been fired. The fact that publication has again become quite uncertain for me at this age, even after my resurrection with *The Loony Bin Trip* and my little miracle of getting the rights to *Sexual Politics* back and then reselling them, I am risen from the dead I thought. Only to fall back into limbo, without an editor and with an unpublished manuscript five years old and no prospects. Years back, after my early success with *Sexual Politics*, I guess I thought I'd just keep writing and getting an advance every four years or so. Come to think of it, I imagined I might even sell pictures one day in my old age, from the vast treasury of drawings and silkscreen prints. The fatuity of this begins to come home to me. In Minnesota the general unreality of my world and its values is always disconcertingly apparent.

Forget your situation, check out your mother's. Is she really alright? "I have $780 of social security each month; that, together with the interest on the money I made selling the house, takes care of this place perfectly. Then there are other investments, they take care of everything else." "What do you eat? What feeds you?" "The investments." I want to be very sure there is enough for groceries, entertainment, fun. Maybe I should be sending her some money every month. "Maybe I should be sending *you* some," she teases me. "No, I'm doing swell, I'm way ahead." "Do you still have Aunt Dorothy's legacy?" "You bet. I still have the principle, though I skim off the interest twice a year."

Aunt Dorothy is A.D., a pun my sisters and I made in recognition of her omnipotence and our own adoration. It is the book about my aunt that I haven't yet sold, a text Mother surprises me by not having read. Only Sal has seen it so far, vetted it for the family; if I ever get a publisher, I will have to run the manuscript past Mother.

In fact it has always been my private conviction that, although Mother is a woman of business, I am actually the real financial genius of the tribe: Sal will always earn it, Mallory will always have it, but I alone can perform miracles stretching the stuff. For example, the Farm; I paid only $31,600 for the homestead and $68,000 for the land and here I am, twenty years after the first purchase and thirteen years after the second, pulling thirty grand out of it in Christmas trees at harvest. Someone this smart can afford to give it away and live on twelve grand.

Then I begin to do a little arithmetic: Mom's monthly social security is nearly what I have to live on and she will have it forever whereas I have only about five years saved ahead, no sure prospects after that, and I won't be getting any social security. "Why not?" she asks, unable to believe me. "'Cause I didn't pay any. Remember Mom, ever since I got fired from Barnard I've been self employed; it's twenty years now." "Your accountant should have made you pay," she chides. "I'm afraid he indulged me, and the Farm expenses ate up everything and we're deductible." "Oh dear," Mother says.

Mother who has seen hundreds of women through retirement with annuities and retirement income plans and has this dolt for an offspring. I can't even blame my accountant, it was my own foolishness. I guess I thought social security was for other people; I was famous so I couldn't go entirely broke. But ever since my first book's money ran out I have been in deficit on my publisher's account and on the bottom line of my income tax form. I didn't even need to pay tax since my expenses running the Farm were what I earned—I'd spent every cent I made just keeping the place. So I wasn't obliged to pay into social security. All these years living on nothing and holding on to the Farm by renting out the farmhouse in the off season so we could pay the taxes, all those years waiting for the trees to make a crop (it takes ten years to grow a tree). "Oh dear," she is saying, her little lady-like expression of the tragic.

She's eighty-eight and you're her daughter, you could live to ninety-eight like Aunt Margaret, ninety-one like Aunt Mary. Maybe you ought to start smoking again. What in hell will you do for money all that time? We're talking thirty or forty more years. And you've only got money for five. When you're seventy and they won't publish you, then what will you do? Kill yourself? Get a waitress job? Zora Neale Hurston ended her days as a housemaid. How are you going to make it without social security? Mother's after the bright side: "Lots of people don't have it. They might still give you a little for the quarters you taught school," she muses. "You better get right on it and call."

The prospect of age. It had never really occurred to me that I could be old, infirm, all that she is now. Instead I had leafed through portraits of artists photographed in their studios, the serene faces of aging genius in beautiful settings. All those nice white-haired masters in their great white rooms; Collette with her cats in the Palais Royale. The actual mechanics of aging has never crossed my mind. So in dealing with my mother's infirmity and longevity I see my own and am scared. Combine all these physical handicaps with a destitution brought on out of sheer stupid improvidence—not to qualify for social security, what kind of an idiot can you be? And yet hardly anyone I know—correction, a great many of my friends—do not qualify. No, further correction, now that I think of it; only a few by now are really "out there" still, nearly everyone is out of the wind at last. Even Sherman, the grand dyke mentor of my youth, an invincible of the old school. But I got Sherman on disability after her convertible cracked up and she nearly ruined her painting arm. Of course she resisted: "The arm is nearly healed, it isn't honest." "Bullshit, we're going for it." And we got it.

When I refused crazy pay, the voice on the phone said "Think about it." "I'm not crazy, so it would be stealing. And though I shouldn't tell you this, it so happens I actually have enough to live on anyway, so I don't deserve public funds, wouldn't qualify." "You qualify right now, lady, and if you turn this down you're never gonna get it again; this is my final offer." Three hundred bucks every month for the rest of your life. There were days in the years that came after, the day I was broke as a dog and just out of the bin in Ireland, I could grin and cuss myself for not having taken the bread, even thought of trying for it again. And then for all the right reasons, said hell no. But it does give you pause: if crazy pay were $300 in 1973, it's closer to Mom's $780 by now. It would at least give you a start, some rent for your studio or food money or something. It would be a base. Because long before thirty years from now you may be destitute, dumb enough to screw up what every citizen gets who chips in. You were arrogant enough not to chip in. So eat your heart out, but stop worrying your Mother about it.

Worry about how you're going to make it up to Steven instead. Come to think of it, he and Chris both loved that Sancerre . . . if I could scout for some after picking up the rental car today, I could drop off a couple of bottles at Chris and Steve's and make up for what seems to have been my faux pas last night. Defer destitution in old age, live it up and give presents, this is Scott Fitzgerald's town . . . But the crack in my wall has already started.

I have come to see age and am seeing it in Mother: the possibility of her death too, contemplated from afar in New York, so far away from St. Paul and her real face here that it could also still seem years away in time as in place. Up close things are different. Her death is inevitable here, probably soon.

~

In the morning, her phrase about having "planned it" completes a process of destruction and I begin to be unable to stop crying. Fortunately I happen to have a bad cold so that tears and snuffling not only come easy but seem relatively natural and are no problem to pass off: you must never let her know how this phrase about having planned it, how that devastates you, reminds you of the greatness of her love, the poverty of your own, your small, so selfish heart, your utter unworthiness as a daughter. Even the daughter that got tossed into a madhouse, thrown away, discarded, even that angry daughter, even the queer daughter, the disgrace, the alienated artist daughter, the brat and snob who was always, in her phrase, "making fun" of things sacred and Catholic or patriotic and American or local and Midwestern or wholesome and related by blood, the scores of Mother's relatives, the good things of life, the sanctity of family living.

The meaning of her phrase sweeps over me, its portent heavy as a freight train. My god—she has expected me, planned for me, rehearsed, imagined. While I dreaded, expected quarrels, knew I would disappoint, rebuked myself beforehand for my persistent impatience and temper, my raised voice, my sarcasm, my snide attitude, my imperfect charity, my endless fury and difference—a lifetime of it. And then of course I am not that different. My family even share my politics, at least a portion of them; the rest I am patiently, persistently dragging them toward in books and phone calls, lectures and arguments. And each generation comes closer, looks at me with clear unprejudiced eyes. From that first moment when at thirteen Steven said he figured homosexuals ought to have their rights, I had stumbled out that I was speaking at a rally for gays, then having to explain gay as homosexual. My hope trembled—if the kid doesn't know the word, there's damn little chance. But all by himself he had hit upon justice, maybe without even Sal's help, in the newer world he lived in. This conversation took place at Kennedy Airport as he was about to take a plane and discover Germany all by himself. The nieces and nephews are natural liberals and fair minded: my books, which have grieved Mother and at moments probably chagrined both my sisters, cause the next generation no pain at all; they actually see no harm in how I live, already one more layer away from immigrant Irish Catholicism, immigrant Irish piety and hellfire.

I am different from my tribe, yet one of them: my filial love as fervent as in the Moslem text I'm reading or my years in Japan. The phrase Mother has just spoken opens inside me a whole sea of sorrow and repentance, drowning in the grief of love and age and coming death and loss. For god's sakes, hold on, stifle your tears before the devastation of regret that barrels down with her approaching death. This lover, this Mother who had planned the lighting of our first breakfast.

Before such mastery, such dedication, you who have never even borne a child, not a mother but an aunt, not a mother but a teacher, not a mother but a mere lover—what would you know, how could you even have an opinion before such qualification? I know this visit is going to hurt, fought off till now with dread and disinterest, guilt and aversion. Try to dodge or thrust it from you and you can't, it's here now, in the room, this hurting. The big stuff, death.

All in her phrase. Not just the love. But time itself, that she knows the timing, last night she even named this as possibly the last time, called the shot, predicted, arranged, staged. Jesus—stop it Mom—stop scaring me, stop condemning me to your death, have I not said it aloud in a letter, that I was aware of the time. The letter I sent ahead, about my friend Emily's mother, how the two of them had time in those last weeks, long days together in the hospital to say everything to each other. As Emily put it, "Very few people get that lucky, you know. So often it's sudden and there's no chance to talk. Well, we had all the time we needed."

And I, in envy of that and newly aware, did my cheapskate planning, a mere three days stopping over on the way home to New York from San Francisco. To confront an epiphany at breakfast the first full day we have together, the day we will talk all day and already I see that I see nothing. See it in her superior planning and preparation and expectation, the moral density of her words. Then too, she has taken aim and said it . . . this will probably be the last time I see her. The hell it will, I think. I am never going to get all my talking done in this one day and it is completely unfair to expect it. When I said this about Emily I had years and years of visits in mind, this would simply be the first of a series of particularly conscious visits. And never relinquishing the hope of seeing her again at the Farm, driven mad by the thought that she will never see this paradise of family reunions pictured in a hundred color photos all over her rooms: bathroom, kitchen, hall, bedroom, photograph after photograph of the place itself and the tribe assembled in this valhalla, the figures by the pond from this year or that, Sal and Ruth by the door of the lavender house, Mallory and her Kristen, Thomas, Steven and David, young Katie and Lisa, heroic presences in nature, the pictures of nobles at their pleasure, the ancestral fairy tale we have created there over and over and then despaired of last year. "And I want you to know it had nothing to do with any pique of Sal or Mallory's about your book. No one even mentioned that. We had no reunion last summer because I could not come," Mother announced last night. "I can't ever go again."

~

The thought that she will never see the Farm again, nor her eyes bless this place she so approves of—"the best thing you ever did" she always says about it, with one of those hard looks, the meaningful unblinking eyes of a major pronouncement—that was enough to make me want to run, to beat it down to the guest room I've rented on the second floor of the Wellington and be alone: read, forget, escape, the kind of thing you just have to bury in a book.

But it too is about family: Amina the perfect wife of Al-Sayyid Ahmad the perfectly conceited male chauvinist husband, a portrait done with such wit and sensitivity you congratulate the author, a man himself, congratulate him by turning down pages, reminding yourself to read this to friends. If you ever did a class, this would be priceless. And as I turn on the light and give her the perfect lighting for her breakfast scene I feel as selfish and stupid as this husband looks on every page, a mark, a monster, the enormity of Mother love washing over me like sea water. I cling to the liferaft of the moment, this coffee, this orange juice, and try not to despair, though I know I am damned and my soul will not be saved.

Looking right at the devastation of losing her finally now—it will happen, it's really coming. And I will know every day of the rest of this bereaved life that comes toward me like a speeding car, I will know that I was loved this much. Forget all your queer and disappointing later selves—you were loved this much, a child loved with a mother's love, whatever lapses or misunderstandings, failures or rages or dislocations, it was there, is still there but then it will be gone.

Revealed in a phrase—what if I hadn't heard it, hadn't understood? She'd said it reflectively, almost to herself; what if I'd grumped about being interrupted in what I'd been saying again, made to stand up and fetch one more thing from the kitchen, perform one more maniacal scene-setting detail, she has put me through fourteen services already, get the cream, get a spoon—what if the import of these words had never reached me? It's likely there have been years of their never reaching me. Or perhaps the love that served so long and never even announced itself, so humble, so like this woman in the book I'm reading, a Moslem wife for god's sakes, a model Islamic servant wife—a lifetime of such attentions and I may have never even said thank you on those thousand occasions I was served and spoiled and pampered, nearly worshipped.

Forget it: you were also scolded, corrected, put down and interrupted. Mother can be a tyrant too, we all know it, we all joke about it and agree.

I have known my father's exasperation and rage against the millions (one thinks in these terms) of her fussing, her relentless pursuit of perfection, the bile rising, the fever coming to the forehead, and you would like to shout her into oblivion.

But behind it, all this. And not only this long-planned and almost accidentally revealed scheme of love and devotion, there is the finality, the finite quality of it which she has insisted upon. But just there I have dug in, resisted, refused. No, damn it, if I have to come back again next week, or even just stay on, marooned in Minnesota, I will not permit this to be the last time we see each other. I have just come to my senses, realized that time is short, but I cannot be satisfied with three days and the paltry things we will say to each other this morning, the mere catching up and laying out of present preoccupations: should I live with Jennifer, should we build something new at the Farm or just take back the houses we've been renting . . . it's a tough decision since there isn't quite enough money yet to follow either course even if I could decide on one. "You will," she says, all wisdom, "You'll decide," far too wise to give me advice on love life or business. I apologize for bringing them up, these are the things on my mind now, lesser things though enormous to me, minimal in the long run of our short time. But she allows it; after all that's what people talk about when they get together, whatever's on their minds at the time. But my love for you, that was to be what I'd tell you about, edging toward it, aware I could go on for two pages in a letter, telling her how I treasured her, how I needed to keep her, was not ready to face the desolation of being an orphan, fifty-six or not, I simply needed—wanted, hell, insisted on—still having a mother in the world. Without that, I was bereft, really alone in the world. Simone de Beauvoir's death had left me without a mentor—to be without a mother too, the mind spins, no. No, as one would talk back catastrophe, fight off fatal assault.

All very well in a letter but in person I dare nothing of the kind; Mother has a nice reserve about her that dislikes effusions. And this morning the merest reminiscence reduces me to tears, I am a faucet, a moron, an embarrassment. You cannot sit here in front of her and cry all day. But even the dishes can set you off. If you even told her how you loved her china, had loved it since you were a kid and afraid of breaking it on state occasions when it was used, how carefully and nervously you and Sal would do the washing up nights when it was the good china.

What if you told her about the day you leaned against her china closet, a mahogany breakfront with glass doors, the china on its edge in its special groove leaning against the back wall, the lead crystal from Ireland proudly displayed in front of it, the heavy Irish linens on the bottom, the light Irish table mats, those apple-green ones, for example, I can remember ironing them in summer, each one starched and perfect. And that day I had the hubris to lean back against the cupboard, having a thought—I distinctly remember thinking a big thought, an enjoyable, historical or literary one, the absurd private content of my twelve-year-old mind, prodigiously ambitious, proud to madness of this private world. And I, in the full enjoyment of this thought, all alone in the house, I leaned back, tilting the whole damn thing back against the wall. Only then did I realize what harm I could cause, one of the great realizations of my life, mind and matter coming into their first major conflict. If it tilted back again those few inches—wham. But you must also realize it is not placed solidly against the wall, it has wood trim on the bottom and there is a baseboard between it and the wall, just there above the carpet. The mind sees the painted board and its trim—the inch and a half between the two surfaces—and comprehends momentum itself. One understands also that the damage is already done, the crystal has tilted back an inch and a half by now, so when you release it and it rights itself in the true vertical, each goblet will keep on going forward toward the glass doors, will fall and break. Moreover, the china plates leaning back toward the back wall of the china cabinet—my eyes see all this through the back of my head—the china plates will fall forward upon the crystal glasses when the cabinet is righted, no matter how slowly you let it come forward again. And you cannot turn around to do it more carefully because then it will all just fall helter-skelter. But no matter how calmly and carefully you release this cabinet back from the wall to its vertical, you will not only fail to prevent the china from breaking—bone china (from dish-washing we know it's pretty strong)—still if it goes over, the dishes will smash the glasses for sure, so the crystal's a foregone conclusion, forget it. And you will also probably break the fragile glass in the glass doors too. When you are twelve, glazing windows is something Dad can do but you can't. Any they'll find out, they'll see, even if you had the money and knew how . . . the crystal for sure is lost.

And the miracle was that I was able to exercise such care or strength or energy that only one small goblet broke, the rest held, even the pink venetian water glasses which fell hard against the glass doors still stayed in one piece. And not one, not one piece of china fell. The glass doors were swell. What if I were to tell her this, walk over to the cabinet and make a tale of it, reveal at last how I nearly destroyed her housewifely pride, her china cabinet, material evidence of social aspiration in the wife of an underpaid civil engineer. But even the prospect is impossible, I could never be funny enough to get by with it, not with just the two of us. Alone with her now today, it is impossible to perform. Even to perform normality.

I must keep mum to avoid further tears, must even avoid greeting these pink straw mats from last time, new ones with hardly any personality or memories, without character or threat. And greet the gate-leg table in silence, it was in the old dining room, on a side wall under a mirror. Now it has been elevated to being the dining table itself in this small apartment. My hand caresses the wood, not that fine a mahogany, but the design is lovely. Say hello to her silver—am I supposed to inherit the silver? I can never quite remember because I don't want to know. Even though she tells us all the time because she does want us to know, to face it, to have it straight, to expect, even perhaps to enjoy the prospect. I would insult her if she knew how little I could enjoy her silver in prospect, have already passed on her dining room table, the real dining room table, the one I did my homework on, a beautiful piece of art deco with ivory inlay, passed on to Steven. A table she cherished but I could not imagine either at the Bowery or the Farm and was loath to rent a trailer to drive across country myself or even pay freight on. But Steven had the wit to give it a room right then and there when it needed it because she was selling the house. So it is his.

Across the table from me, Mother is dispensing money now, not silver; I'm already supposed to know about her possessions. But now she is announcing that we will each get money, part of the house I suppose or those investments. Why not live forever and use all the money yourself, I don't need any money from that house. I didn't need the house either, it was in Minnesota. Though we used to talk about holding on to it and renting it to cousins. Fortunately Mother decided to sell the house and live here at the Wellington Apartments, using the house purchase price to pay her rent, an excellent plan. Let's just continue it; with interest it should get her way past a hundred years old.

I don't want this money and I tell her so. I want her alive and as to investments she knows very well I disapprove of stocks and bonds on political grounds, would never invest money in the market, we've all been over this, "So I really won't need this bread, Mom. Spend it yourself, piss it away even, take cruises, buy silly clothes, indulge grandchildren, think of something." "I want you to take it easy once you have this money," she says. Little does she know how desperately I may need it, life without social security, what an asshole I was. But we are not talking sums that would get me through old age, I'll have to think of something else. "Hold on to your money Mom—Sally and Mallory are very well off, me too. We just don't need it."

You must be tactful here since she is enormously proud of having anything to leave; when you start from scratch as an abandoned wife with three kids at forty and little work experience, you've got to be quite a smart cookie to come out ahead after twenty years on the job and twenty more living in retirement. Mallory left a magazine behind on the couch which outlines what one needs for retirement these days—amazing sums, portfolios of this and that, foreign and domestic, all rather mysterious to me. Older people will be poorer in the future and require more money as well, it cautions; a recession lessens all expectations.

~

Life in St. Paul is no more representative now than in Fitzgerald's time, the place is a dream world still. One of the old women down the hall is named Ramalley, a Brahmin name here; Mother mentioned it to cousin Jamie the next night when he came over with his wife Laurie. Laurie is Janey Washburn's cousin. Janey and I have been best friends since college and her cousin married my cousin so we are even related, cousins ourselves as well as friends. Cousin Jamie said that he'd seen an old picture of Ramalley's dance hall—and there's Scott Fitzgerald on the right and Laurie's dad on the left. "Would Janey's mother Harriet Washburn have been there too do you think?" he asks his wife. "Harriet Ingersoll then," she corrects him. Laurie thinks she was too young to have been permitted out. It's a St. Paul-type story, we relish it, though like all St. Paul stories there is another, darker, matching story. I hold back what I remember first about Laurie's dad, for a moment unable even to recall if he was an Alex or an Archie. An Archie, remembering the day of his suicide in a hotel room and Laurie a frightened little girl with a frightened little brother, whom Janey and I, big-shot college girls feeling adult as social workers, swept down on to save, along with their mother, a frightened woman dangerously alone. Archie had squandered everything; his kinfolk didn't even approve of this wife. "Shot himself over a muff," Uncle Walter said to a crony drinking scotch at the intermission of the symphony that night, Janey and I within hearing, student ushers stopping for a free drink with A.D. Her new husband Walter has no idea that Janey was Archie's niece, nor that this was our first suicide, scandal, tragedy. Muff was a word we could only guess at.

I say nothing to Laurie, we're being upbeat; there is just time for one glass of wine before we dine with Mom downstairs. This dinner is a reconciliation: years ago cousins Jamie and Laurie, younger and credulous, went along with Mother's still more credulous faith in a psychiatrist who instructed them to have me locked up in the Mayo wing of the University of Minnesota, a short distance from Northrup Hall where the Minneapolis Symphony played, my own aunt its guarantor and only a few hundred yards from Follwell Hall and the English Department. On my own college campus I'm to be a prisoner at the instigation of a jerk who happened to be chief of psychiatry at the big U that year and with whom Mom has had a lot of ill-advised conversations. He used to play football for Oklahoma and has never heard of me, but Mom says I'm famous and gets a small glimmer of interest out of him. At his urging she persuades cousin Jamie to conclude the fried chicken and strawberry meringue dinner to take me over to the University to meet this guy, who's real busy, can only see us that very night, is going out of town tomorrow, all his four kids with him, fishing and so forth, gotta see me now. "Look, Mom, Sal tried this psychiatry thing on me in California last month," turning to my cousins, "Don't you understand this was a terrible experience?" Listen Jim, these places are indescribable, I mean they forced hideous drugs on me, you've no idea, it's a jail." But Jim and Laura were in on it too.

I found this doctor a real nothing and told him so. I also refused to see him in his office. A month before, Sal had deceived me into a doctor's office in a locked facility so I'd been that route and insisted the big doctor see me on the campus grounds. I mean walking the grass, nice summer night. Still didn't need his services, thanks anyway. Cousin Jim had tried to drive right down into the parking lot under Northrup Hall which is not just for symphony goers, but also connects to the emergency entrance to the hospital and once you're in that you're done for. Knowing all this I just stepped out of the car and said I'd see the guy outside. Which persuaded Jamie and Laura I was behaving weirdly and maybe even was crazy.

It hardly mattered that I had escaped capture that first night. By seven that next morning the doctor had talked Mom into signing the papers that committed me. In those days you could do that in Minnesota. A good samaritan heard the news however, a feminist social worker and she got on the phone. The white coats came for me at eight or nine, polite as St. Thomas Academy boys, no point in arguing. But by ten there were civil rights lawyers to help me, Donald Heffernon of Stuart White, wonderful top of the heap lawyers working pro bono for the Minnesota Indians who took on my case with the understanding that if I could get busted in my home town, imagine what the Indians get. "Think about them up at Anoka full of thorazine," they said. They'd found the right person: I'd worked at St. Peter's Asylum the summer of my freshman year—the bin had been my first cause in life. "Do you suppose we could tape it all for the big U—might be real good for the psych archives," I laughed. "Teaching material, don't you know, research, all that jazz." Heffernon laughed too, then explained that the University itself would be a minor adversary in the hearing he was going to request. We were going to risk a real State commitment hearing we could actually lose. Then what? I was scared. "We are asking you to gamble . . . for principle," he said. I swallowed and said yes. "We've talked to the feminists, they'll be your support in court, even here in the hospital when we can get them in. We can promise that you won't be drugged; we got that stipulated already. That's all we can promise before the hearing. It's a long shot; we can lose just as easily as we can win."

We did win and drank champagne in the judge's chambers. The next year, 1974, the Minnesota legislature changed the law to one of the better state commitment statutes: you have some chance at a hearing and a real defense. It was just a little step, though we thought it was earth-shaking at the time.

It was hard to go on trial for my freedom for possibly the rest of my life. It was hell to sit at a table across the room from my family: Mom, Sal and their lawyers, our chief adversaries, the team trying to put me away each day in court. That first morning their own dandy junior attorney, Mr McGirl, showed up in some Music Man costume, straw boater and ice cream pants, to accompany me to court. I turned him down and drove with my jailor, the Sheriff of Minneapolis. I was a prisoner at the University which is in Minneapolis, but I was being tried for my sanity in St. Paul, my birthplace. And rode in a squad car the short distance over to St. Paul where the two teams, Mom's and mine, debated my competence.

They are not only different towns, they are different counties, different cultures and religions. They even have different rules for what is crazy. The whole thing was played out before a good St. Paul judge who was a year behind me in parochial school; my team of attornies bet on the judge and were themselves better lawyers than their adversaries so they sprung me. I wasn't allowed to open my mouth: one peep out of me and we might have lost. Mother testified against me, her eyes dead as stone, empty as the void. Jim, my favorite cousin then, was on Mother's side. He was also probably bewildered, maybe feeling a little superior and excited, the way people get around this sort of thing. I was his babysitter in childhood; he should have known better. He was in business now and respectable, Mother's main prop at the moment, one of the few men in the tribe. I have not spoken to him for something like eighteen years, Laurie neither. I do however have one sad memory of Laurie coming to visit me in my psych-jail and I told her off; I still see her face collapsing under my indictment. I remember again how I once nearly bought the strip of land right across from theirs on the St. Croix, nearly became their neighbor in Marine, friend of all their friends. I would have been a Minnesotan, part time anyway. We had found a beautiful stretch of the river, had its own island even, directly across from their house, the water running like a street between us to be crossed by canoe. We would buy it altogether, my sisters and I, on the model of Janey Washburn's family compound just a mile north . . . all plans destroyed now. The reunions at the Farm were all that was saved of that dream. Tonight's reconciliation is important. It is actually the second such: Steven and Chris arranged one last year when I was home, drinks at their place. Jamie bragged that he was going to be named a Regent of the University, I was envious and pissed off. I wasn't ready yet.

Tonight I like him and the bond renews, heals itself. Laurie has quit real estate and has rented a studio; at last she's going to paint. It was Mother's advice; "Life doesn't go on forever, money is not that important," Mom lectured her like a bohemian: "Do what you always wanted to with your life," which gave Laurie the courage. The new Mother Millett, the wisewoman. We talk of Janey, of how Mom and I ran into Gena Lewis at the grocery store, Gena is Laurie and Janey's cousin as well, and Gena had told me not only that my pal Janey was sick in Santa Fe and unable to paint—I knew that—what I didn't know was that Janey had been broke as well, down to her last dollar too. Gena said Janey made it through by selling a painting, unfortunately not one of her own, one her folks had left her. Gena couldn't remember the painter's name, early modern, very valuable. Janey persisted and finally found a buyer, made it through her illness, is even able to work a little bit at a job now. I told Gena that I could have helped Janey, I could have sent her money if I'd known, why didn't she tell me? We've been writing and talking on the phone every few months, obviously not often enough. I had no idea: it makes my skin crawl.

Then I also remember that last August, when Janey was at the bottom, was also about the time *The Loony Bin Trip* was published; she too might have taken offence at this book. Janey had been in on Mallory's attempt to get me busted in New York, the second bust, the bust in 1980 which I escaped with the help of a New York City policeman who knew civil liberties law. Only to fall into the clutches of the security police at Shannon airport, where my record made it possible to bust me for my political sympathy for the Irish hunger strikers.

In August my book had just come out, I had money and could have helped Janey. Never mind, everything can still come together. I have just written her and all the members of the old "communist party," to tell them this will be our thirtieth anniversary. I turn to Jamie, "Do you remember the Thanksgiving dinners we used to have?" "True Communism is a party," he says, repeating our slogan. "We even say that now down at the River at our own Thanksgiving dinners." When Jim was doing a master's degree in business administration at Columbia our circle adopted him as our "square"; a kid, someone we could teach and tease and correct. "What do you mean, you've never heard of Marcel Duchamp?" Explaining him to Jamie was an evening's entertainment.

"Those were the best years of their lives," Mother says later, "Those years with you and Janey in New York. They were happy then with a happiness that has had to last them here." Before they left, Jim tried to say he goes on remembering that time: "You guys gave us so much in those years, you and Fumio and Janey and Bill Rivers." It is still in his voice when he says it, in his eyes, Laurie's too.

Mother fidgeted while I talked to Gena at Lund's, this is after all our trip to St. Paul's mile-long gourmet grocery, supposed to be her time, a fairy-tale visit because her new infirmity makes going anywhere so difficult and arduous she hardly risks or bothers with it nowadays. And Lund's is an astonishing store, probably the greatest grocer in the world, a super supermarket, exquisite. Homey too, there's free coffee and a little area with comfortable tables and chairs to sit down and rest from the rigors of spending. Very smart of them, freshen up and you're right back to it. Mother had been enjoying the sight of five men and women, white-collar workers from the neighborhood, "having a picnic" there, as she put it. We ourselves have been picnicking here for hours, the store is so huge and Mother so slow that we managed only one circuit. And that only after a rest from the rigors of the high Minnesota winds in the parking lot. We drank coffee and homemade chicken noodle soup by turns while I made forays alone for toilet paper, Kleenex and furniture polish, returning with two varieties. Mother passed up lemon Pledge for the original lemon oil, her judgment as sound and basic as ever. These are purchases which I am capable of performing alone, but Lund's is so much my mother's dream store—imagine shopping all your life and running a model household and then being imprisoned in an apartment and too frail for trips to a favorite grocer—that she must navigate the entire wonder show at a snail's pace while holding on to a cart.

How Mother has hungered to see Lund's these past weeks, how she has missed it. Mallory took her in January, but it is March now, her eyes consume the fruits and vegetables, the pastry done on the premises, custom butcher and fish counter. She cannot really shop for dinner, since she eats downstairs, "But sometimes I still cook . . .," her voice trails off. I bite my lip and refuse to cry again between the meat and fish counters. The end of cooking is nearly the end of food, which is truly the end of life.

I would buy her lobster, crab, I would dazzle her with days of seafood. If there were enough time. But it is always time that we haven't got. However, we take it slow here at Lund's; I want it to last all afternoon. But too soon she is tired. "We have all day, let's have another coffee break," I say, giddy, reading aloud to her from a book I found in the book section—they even have books—a tremendously funny book about how to speak Minnesotan, Prairie Home Companion stuff. "This guy wrote for the show, Mom; it's not Keeler but one of his henchmen"; I am laughing as I read aloud to her in a voice carrying enough for the nearest checkout man to enjoy as well. We are all laughing when Gena comes by and reminds me we used to know each other thirty years ago at the University.

Actually, I remember being somewhat intimidated by Gena then—Wash's folks were "Old St. Paul" and Wash once referred to my Aunt Dorothy, who had married Louis Hill, heir of the Great Northern, Northern Pacific railroad, as "new money". Being the poor relation of new money did not give me much confidence with Washburn's solid bourgeoisie relatives. And when by senior year I was rumored to be queer as well, I seem to remember that I was not invited, or rather invited and then disinvited, to Gena's wedding. When I saw her next she was already divorced and living at the family land on the St. Croix. I remember it as a wonderful night in a marvelous old house or series of houses, river houses, house-at-the-lake type houses, hand-built, rambling, improvised, works of art, in fact. And the greatest ornament of all was an octagonal room with a highly elaborate octagonal ceiling which the uncles had done one season probably out of an old framing book, one of those antique carpenter's manuals that women from the farm like Sophie and Keats collect, texts very demanding even to read. To follow their instructions would require angelic patience and an utterly unencumbered lazy summer. I loved that visit and remember Gena fondly from that occasion. Though I also remember she was bitterly unhappy that night. Today she seems serene, looks young and healthy, sporty, contented with life. Yet I find myself noting that the backs of her hands are aged a little, check my own and find them younger-seeming and realize I have begun to be obsessed with death and aging. That wedged between an aged mother and a young lover just now, I have permitted this sort of thinking to corrode my consciousness.

Mother is restive, almost rude. I keep explaining that Gena is Washburn's cousin, that Wash has been sick, that Gena has important news I didn't know. Gena stirs, will give me her number; I can call. There won't be any time of course: I come to St. Paul only to see my Mother. It has been this way so long that by now I don't know anyone else here anyway. Any soul who lays eyes on me must be cleared with Mother, she has permitted a nephew and a cousin this time, that's it. Only family. And I only see them on Mother's sufferance; there is so little time and she needs every second of it. Years ago I used to be permitted a night out with whatever college buddies still lived in town, the few with whom I kept in touch, Judy and Tommy Pryor. I nourished a fantasy that Tommy was a cousin too, Uncle Harry's byblow. Harry was close to Tommy's mother who lived on Prior Avenue, that was good enough for me to turn into a story. I stayed away from high school class reunions but there were always nights on the town with younger cousins, the famous 'bumpkin hunts' of yesteryear, explorations into road-house life in little towns, Polish polka parties, ice fishing.

But over the years it all narrowed down: the break with Jamie and Laurie, Tommy and Judy's divorce. Mother grew older and more jealous, more demanding, possessive. Why not? She was the real reason I came back. Were it not for her, St. Paul and Minnesota would become the place where I was born but not a place I ever came back to. I grow afraid now, foreseeing her imminent disappearance: soon I will have no connection at all with the place I came from, the place where I grew up. She is not only my mother, she is my home. My own roots have withered and will die when she dies. In a more dangerous sense, in losing her I dread the loss of family itself, each of them, estranged so many times and on so many grounds, my relations with my sisters becoming strained and difficult or just boring and without sufficient interest. Will I lose everything in losing Mother, my own childhood over forever then, over so categorically then that it would almost seem never to have taken place, not only finished and past but actually vanished into thin air? Writers cannot afford to lose things, they live by memory, so my art is threatened too. Even my nationality, for Mother is my connection to America—were it not for owning land in New England I might have thought of living in France or Ireland years ago. A small protest in exile when the reactionary times set in, say around 1980 with Reagan's election.

Staying has made me make peace around *The Loony Bin Trip* and other kinds of liberation politics, but I have not felt at home in America for a long time. Not since the days when we had to stop hoping and admit we couldn't change it, not since Reagan came in with the 80s and we realized that the place was controlled now, no longer a democracy at all but private property, owned by another element altogether, a cynical money crowd everyday more arrogant, people who really didn't give a damn, were happy to junk bond the place, liquidate its assets and wreck its manufacture, waste its treasure on weaponry to explode as a trade show for armaments in the Gulf

War while its citizens slept in the streets. Owned by a bunch who were content to gamble it all, to risk burning the world and endangering the very planet itself for oil and munitions. All the while sly multinational money pushed an idiot patriotism upon the proles, manipulating them with yellow ribbons while it went on transcending borders. Money itself is a nation now, superior to the nation state: George Bush and the emir of Kuwait, the king of Saudi Arabia and the chief holders of the oil companies belonging to a new order as old as crowned heads. There are only a couple thousand people running the whole world now, it gets smaller and smaller, they will soon all be on speaking terms, a world oligarchy having no culture or even class in the sense of history or responsibility beyond mere wealth, a group who miss nothing that homeland or tradition might offer.

Once you steward land you have to stick around. Even after you've given up on the government. And your Mother still lives there. With her gone there might be less to hold on to in America. For this reason it's pleasant to be with Steven, to find Jim again, and to be comfortable with their politics, to feel the old family solidarity in political, social and moral vision, the sense of shared values and honor, intelligence and skepticism, the habits of readers, of citizens who think. Habits especially pleasant these rigged-election, televised Gulf War days, habits I've missed everywhere else lately except among committed progressives, professional intelligentsia, a tiny hard core. One no longer expects an informed citizenry, coming home to one was really coming home.

But still, everything depends on her. On Mother Millett. Of course she has staged this reunion with Jamie; if the last one didn't take it was probably only because she was not sufficiently in charge. She will give my cousins back to me. If all competition was eliminated on past visits it will be permitted on a carefully rationed basis from now on; she is leaving and so she is handing me on.

But not to Gena, Gena was unplanned. And as Mother later explained in the car, she needed to go to the bathroom, has wet her pants. "Why the hell not say so? Lund's is so good it even has a toilet, something no grocery store in New York would ever condescend to provide no matter how much you spent there." She is silent, I go on, annoyed despite her discomfiture. "Mom, I made use of it just before Gena showed up—why didn't you?" No need to ask: the walker was parked all the way across the store. She had been using the vast grocery cart for mobility and was too tired, too timid, too embarrassed, and too overcome to tell me her need. Again, there was no time. Over and over there is no time, not even to talk to Gena. Mother had insisted, been rude, a pain in the ass: now, hearing her reason I repent.

If it is Janey Washburn who connects me still to this town when I'm in the east among people who are certain that St. Paul and Minneapolis are identical wastelands, the connection comes at me again through Laurie, Janey's cousin too, in her choice to paint. Mother has surrendered one of our three precious evenings to bring me back together with Jim and Laurie over dinner. If I want to cultivate Gena Lewis I can do it on my time, not Mom's. We follow her schedule. I acquiesce, realizing how generous she has been in permitting some local college kids to steal a whole afternoon. In a moment of weakness I had agreed, over the phone from New York, to submit to an interview by their video journalism class.

I woke the next morning in a sweat; there would only be three days in St. Paul and I have been vain and lax enough to promise a whole afternoon of it to strangers. When we discussed arrangements I asked Mother if she would like me to refuse, cancel it, renege. Dying to do so. "Of course not, don't be silly, it's a good idea they're doing it." Finally I thought so too, even asked if they planned to save the tape or throw it away, erase it and move on to the next "celebrity" interview available to Augsberg college students: such a tape would be a primary source and there is nothing on record about me in the place where I come from. I hammer this home to the young writer who asked me.

She is in her element today, graduating senior introducing me to her instructor and a class of twelve, a video crew of two, a little set with water glasses and artificial flowers in imitation of commercial television "talk show" format. I lectured them a bit about all this, the rigidity, the tedium, the unimaginative slavish copying of a bad model, trying to explain how well the Europeans do conversation on television. They were nice about it, put up with my long self-important answers to their questions, never permitting them to get a word in edgewise. Your real swell-headed egoist, I realized too late. This interview is supposed to be to train them in the art of interviewing, they are supposed to be graded on how well they led me along; instead I grabbed the leash like a St. Bernard on an outing.

Their instructor is a delightful woman and very interesting: she's studying Sumerian, wants to read the cuneiform of the very first signed piece of writing in the world, The Exaltation of Inana. "Earlier than Gilgamesh?" I ask. "Sure, but like it in a way, remember Inana is in Gilgamesh too. Both texts are probably much weakened and distorted already by the patriarchal takeover. But remember it's Inana who says at the end of Gilgamesh, 'Of course there were too many people, but did you have to kill everyone?'" We relish this line and I describe the Sumerian reliefs I saw this spring at the Louvre, wonderful things but so coldly monumental, even alien. "This is, too— it's religious art, a sacred text, public after all. The original may be terribly distant in time, already ancient in the oral tradition long before it was written down. The voice of the writer herself may be filtered through the new masculine ascendancy, seriously distorted; there's no way to know." Together we lament the Iraqi sites lost just this winter to Yankee carpet bombing. She promises to send me a translation of this strange poem she's studying.

It turns out she's married to little Louis Branka who went to kindergarten with me; I imagine him as still five years old despite the fact he's about to retire from university administration. She says he calls it university trivialization. For that term alone, we ought to have a drink the next time I'm back. There might be a lot of people to play with out here if I ever came home again.

But of course under the circumstances of the last ten or twenty years there has been Mother and then only Mother. When she is gone what reason would I ever have to return? Would I ever come home again? This little town which I love and hate, create and destroy, glorify and turn into myth only to return and find the real thing shabby, provincial, dull. Praising it in drink in the east, the real America, the lost blah blah. What would Easterners know? They have even forgotten the Mississippi river by now. Nixon did it, Nixon redrew the map and rewrote history, pulled the wool over their eyes entirely, erased the French and Spanish past of the continent itself, boiled the whole place down to the thirteen original colonies whose independence was being celebrated in the bicentennial, the result of a gentleman's agreement, never a war—how inconceivable—with our best friend Margaret Thatcher's Britain.

All of this led the way to the new America where everyone speaks television anchorman's English; there are no accents or dialects, no regional speech, no language of any interest or distinction at all. Wonderbread America. Our history is expunged as the constitution is dismissed, unread, ignored, no longer even recalled. There is less and less of an American past, we are a continuous and meaningless present, without a culture of our own anymore nor immigrant threads into other places: one homogenized ten-minute attention span. We can't remember last week, I joke with the cousins, a joke that makes us sad; our only pleasure within this loneliness consists in the fact that we both notice the loss together, this last shared apprehension.

~

To remember St. Paul would be to take things seriously. Like being an American or a writer or an American writer. Because I am not even American when living in New York. St. Paul makes me that again, makes childhood and place. Ambition and cannon intrude on me here, cry out for connection, a spot, acknowledgment of being part of it all. Usually I just live with that deprivation, the knowledge that I can't—because they won't let me—be an American writer or even a writer in America. France, maybe in your dreams; they have their own ideas about Americans. But in New York, forget it; there you just try to stay alive, just try just to get published, maybe just try to keep writing.

But in St. Paul I remember too much, all the crazy hopes and dreams when growing up, my very love of country, of writing, the sacred calling itself, how I told my aunt in her big car once when trying to tell her I was in love with her, but said instead—it was nearly as dangerous—that I wanted to be a poet. "Like Wordsworth," blushing. All that spring semester I'd been declaiming Wordsworth out the window and down onto the asphalt roof and over toward the Snyders' open dormers. Mother heard me, even the neighbors must have been troubled by these effusions.

Bob Snyder went to live in San Francisco, we all knew he was a "faggot" and the Snyders cursed with an arty queer: now my folks were too. I was not as original as I imagined, yet I wallowed in my condition: solitary, provincial, and isolated. An arty freak, of course, but at home you were not up against the mayhem, the frontal assault, the lethal and massed hatred of New York, the cold of New York publishers, dealers. There at the pinnacle they really hated writing; in New York books became money and only the cruddy ones made money. New York was the murder of all enjoyment and respect, the murder of the subway as your basic beat, the rage of people living badly. Snarling, savage.

When I first lived there I used to get in arguments and was actually ordered out of a store once because I could not endure such rudeness and ill-mannered hostility without suddenly, unexpectedly, resorting to cuss words and incensed behavior. Treatment like theirs resembled nothing I had known since neighborhood alley fights with apples or snowballs. It was inconceivable that one could be so mistreated and insulted just for politely trying to buy a bottle of milk or shopping for a used refrigerator. We had saved the money for an icebox for months, were customers for god's sakes.

My quiet St. Paul manner brought me nothing but contempt, passed over in the line for being polite: these animals step in front of you, talk loud, push. At the corner store they are so unfriendly, cold, hostile, so without charm or humor you never even get a chance to flash your wit, say the fun thing that had made our Irish day in a world so far back now, so long ago. Finally you give it up and forget, learn the lingo, even the humor.

But it hurts to remember, it hurts to be home. Wash and I used to pretend that Connecticut was St. Paul or a reasonable facsimile since people had comfort and manners. So we refused to visit it again. Since once you have given up a way of life it is pointless to make any foray back into it: it is superficial, without focus or conviction. And we had left it behind. Like college, like growing up, like family. St. Paul was resolutely behind us, an indulgence we had known once, a sense of home and goodness, safety—it was over now and we'd live in the wilderness, camp out, wander the desert. We'd made the choice. St. Paul was the place we came from but it was not where we were going, it was a whole series of admirable values, a commendable way of life but it was not where we were heading anymore. We had chosen art and it could only be practiced in that mean and privileged enclave we had derided throughout college as the Mystic East.

New York: to make our choice meant that you left home and all the civility it represented. Maybe we went to death only, would find nothing but the dirt and the cold of downtown and the cruelty of uptown. It could turn out like that, that empty, that much a joke on us. But in our better moments it was the bohemian warmth of whatever handful of exiles we could find to feed in the old Bowery loft, having pooled our money and our booze, our goodwill and loneliness and in no time we were high and sure we had made the right choice. After all, hadn't we recreated community without losing our principles? In searching for the art we'd left home to find we'd furnished the desert with orange crates and made it as much like home as possible in the essential sense and as much unlike it as possible in the dreary respectable St. Paul world of bourgeoisie snobbery and slender vision we had bitched about, chafed at and campaigned against. Self-righteous superior little eggheads and art snobs that we surely were, we really couldn't stay home, and had to get out because we were choking, suffocated.

Of course the New York we went to wasn't New York really but a place we created with other kids on the lam, Midwesterners often but Southerners and Westerners as well, other youngsters who had also disappointed their folks. Middle- and working-class parents don't send you to college to do things that middle-class parents find silly and working-class parents find not just silly but frivolous too.

St. Paul is probably different now. Minneapolis sure is—all sorts of groovy types around: leftists, conscious thinkers, artists, rebels and originals. Then too, maybe, if we'd stayed long enough to look, tried grad school or studied the bars. But we went east the way Americans had gone to Europe in the century before, even in the decades before. All our mentors had already lived in France; we belonged to the first generation of American painters and writers to stay home and watch the art market come to us. Seeing too how it eventually poisoned New York with art buying as an investment, we had also missed out on the better experience our elders had had abroad. The earlier American humility was better for our souls than the new Yankee triumph . . . imagine what the Gulf victory will bring us in bigotry and egotism in the coming years. Empire is ugly after all: an undeserved and corrupting edge over others.

As for the inferiority complex, how well you get to know that state of mind coming out of St. Paul and to the east, to Europe, to any capital. Then add being a woman, a poor relation, whatever . . . keep at it long enough it might even turn from bitterness and envy into a humbled perspective. Perhaps, finally even, contentment.

We approach the point where Mom and I differ and not only in degree. She would have me count my blessings and I do: I dutifully report on the Farm harvest, repeat my little boasts that the trees are like an oil well in the backyard, we're set now, the hard work's over, just got to figure out how to run the thing, find a little more time to write, everything is really good. But after Jim and Laurie left I poured a scotch and started really leaning on the new America, a fury in me, forgetting to talk soft, when will I ever learn?

And fatuous, breathing my ambitions to her like a lecher, whispering of fame, the big stuff, literature, I want to be that, damn it, write stuff that will last. Mother coughs her embarrassed little cough. She's coughed this tiny cough all her life; it is how she copes, how she gently, persistently, moves troublesome things out of her way, things like protest or passion. I come on like a Millett, my father's people. Mother is another breed, a Feely, more patient, far less flamboyant. Passion makes her distinctly uncomfortable, always has. She has no idea what to say: I eliminate possibilities. "Look, this is what my life is about, you listen to the others, Sal and Mallory and Sal's kids, your own cousins here, all eighty-six of them: the lawyers, the businessmen, the parents . . ."

"I know just what you're talking about, dear, but I can't do anything about it." "Who the hell said you could?" Does she think I take her for a publisher, the chairman of the department? "Listen, all you got to do is listen." She stirs, hating to listen. Try this then, I say to myself, whorish to win her over, "Look, don't you think somewhere I'm writing for you, like other daughters of my generation whose mothers went to college but they had kids and didn't write after all." "Yes, I do," she says, "I'm not the only one who thinks so, we all feel it, yes, you are writing for me." "And you hate what I write." "I don't hate it," she clears her throat. "Well, you sure dislike it, most of it, lesbian horror stuff, you know you disapprove," realizing that *The Basement* was inspired by her interest, that she was the book's first reader and editor, that *Sexual Politics* got approval too, once she got past the smutty quotations in the first chapter.

But it's the stuff she hates that I prefer to harp upon, how else do I hang on to my grudges, fearing assimilation? I glance away and remember Doris

Lessing on mothers and writing; Lessing's mother hated her stuff the whole of her life; there was no pleasing her mother. "Mothers die," Lessing said, "but they don't die because of books."

And here is my mother still alive and I want her blessing, because this is my second scotch in fifteen minutes and my ugly writer's way of intimacy while approaching the last important messages in this life and I am crying out to her for air, for the chance to stay alive, which is to say, in print. Pretending even that it's a right, insisting I'm not twenty years old anymore and just trying to get my first effort between covers. "Mom, what will happen if I can't publish, if I can never get the stuff printed?" begging to escape asphyxiation, feeling the throat close. As if she herself were the culture police, the censors, the government, the country itself, the zeitgeist.

She shakes her head and her eyes go blank. It is too much to put up with, she refuses—the habit of a lifetime, really a reflex by now—she refuses to get involved, to look down holes into the pit. Keep it light, lady-like, social. I could shake her, have always sought in vain for fire in her and found common sense instead. But she has every right now. At eighty-eight, frail and tired and having given these ungrateful kids so much already, you really ought to be able to unplug entirely. I acknowledge her absolute right of refusal. But I won't shut up, three slugs of scotch in me now and a rage against the world, the country, the place—everything she would be wise to agree about instead of pretending to identify with and defend. I know she can't change America. I don't even confuse her with it.

"It's a place I don't recognize anymore now either," she shakes her head, glad to be leaving, "But I can't do anything about it, dear." "Christ, do you think I expect you to? I just want you to listen, to hear . . ." "Believe me, I hear every word you say." The trouble is, she hears the way I say it too, which is all wrong. Why do you need scotch to say what you mean, why do you need to get angry, to weep your mixture of head cold and despair. Why can't you, with perfect control, explain lightly and reasonably, perhaps even with wit and charm, your fears as your life narrows toward its close and hers moves finally out of sight? Are these your farewell words? Complaints? Bitching? Craven fear?

"It doesn't matter if they print it," she insists, at the end of her rope. "Sure it does, for god's sakes, if the tree falls in the forest who . . . ?" "No it doesn't matter, just write." A sibyl now, the eyes as old as the world, Ireland is only a moment in time. "But maybe I won't have the heart to, finally." "Sure, you have to, you have to. And forget all about money, you think about money too much." "What a lousy thing to say, I'm giving the Farm away and all it earns, sharing it with other women, living on this little margin I've created to preserve and discipline myself, and you tell me I think too much about money? I'm more insulated from money than anyone; there's a wall eight bricks thick between me and writing anything for money." "You have to erase all that from your mind completely, then you'll be fine. Now I have to go to bed."

I have failed at the final scene, her last blessing is delivered to a fanatic who cannot hear and is not even willing to quit talking. I've been dismissed and am not even leaving. I hang around pretending to help her undress. Then discreetly phoning Steven while she is in the bathroom. He'd like to stop over in the morning; I'd like to have a drink with him now, would rush to his house, the Lexington Bar, anywhere, to have someone to talk to. "Someone my own age," I almost catch myself thinking, looking for youth, for another family member I complain to, bitch to, meaning not quite disloyalty or criticism, just the comfort of comprehension posing as agreement, however frivolous or pretended. "Yeah, G.M.'s something lately, she can get you down for sure; there's a certain inevitable distancing . . ." then he might laugh, searching for the perfect phrase: "It's like a conversation with god."

His mother Sally feels it, he feels it, but tonight he has none of this in mind, is just home from dinner at the grandly renovated St. Paul hotel; it's been a fancy night. He wanted me to take Mom there last night; she wanted to go to a cheap Chinese dive a block away instead. A trivial instance of her ominous oracular phrase that "people make mistakes in life." Steven is content at home, settled in for the evening with his wife, his child. Nobody wants you at their house with your damn out-of-town emotions, literary daughter baggage. They want to go to bed, they must both practice law early tomorrow. Don't push him, this lovely spirit, this almost cinematically beautiful and beautifully serious young man. This elegant and polite nephew of yours is now a princeling here, a camel-hair coat aristocrat. He who stayed home like Tommy did to inherit the town like Tommy did. Unlike Tommy, he will never leave town, won't need to.

Steven doesn't hear or chooses not to hear my need and I haven't announced it in words. Since there may not be time in the morning, we should try to settle something about reunion. What does he think? Reunion without Mother, would there be any point in it? She won't go; we are fairly resigned to that. Perhaps that shouldn't cancel it forever either—we don't say we could resume after her death, since the expression of the thought is obscene and we would forgo reunion forever if it kept her alive. "She thinks we should go ahead and do it without her because it is important for us to keep renewing ourselves as a family," Steven says. "But without her? The matriarch?" "Well, what else?" Steven's logical. The other problems are simply timing and cash for tickets. I interrupt his ruminations here, fatigued with the complexity of coordinating his siblings. He'll do that, he volunteers. Great, I think, I hate calling people and begging them to come to a party. "I'll canvas everybody for when and if," Steven repeats. "After all, Kate, you do all the work just by having us." What if the guests are reluctant, lackluster, without enthusiasm? This is a service I perform for my clan, conscious I have not been treated all that well within it, but willing to treat them better. Of course, this is not his problem, his generation never sent me to the loony bin or condemned my sex life; their only considerations will be finding money for airline tickets and vacation time they would prefer to spend on more exciting things than relatives. And they're having babies right and left now, so spouses and new families will take the place of the old original, if we can't make a myth and live up to it in actuality. On the other hand, if reunion were the best party of all . . .

"Give me some time," Steven says, while I calculate, for in fact I will have to schedule the Farm rentals to begin only after my family has had its three or four happy days and decamped. How to explain all this to the women artists, whose colony it is. Can all these competing interests be accommodated, physically, let alone emotionally, politically, in the real and not the imagined world, especially the world of the imagined slight?

I don't even want this discussion; I want to have a drink with you to mull over a prodigal's fate, my heart beating as if I were making an illicit proposition to a man; what a long time since I've felt anything remotely resembling this rush. When Steven calls back five minutes later I take the call in Mother's bedroom and the dialogue sounds like a movie rendezvous: "If you promise not to keep me up late I'll meet you at the Lex." Of course I could say, "No, that's okay Steven, never mind, Mom's going to sleep now." I should just go down to my room and read for a while till the need passes. Simply swallow my guilt and failure, cross off this trip. That way I would be his aunt, older and distinguished and not this needy adolescent who answers "Sure, see you in twenty minutes."

She knows, I suppose: people going out to drink when they should be in bed, the sort of thing she really hates, the sort of thing Dad stood for, worries over car accidents and booze. Yet she says nothing and pretends she hasn't taken it in. I kiss her goodnight as guilty as an adulterer, as my old man's kid, a Millett after all.

~

Steven's having coffee. I have one scotch and then slow down to coffee too. We only talk an hour: I do not keep him up. But it helps to have him commiserate: "She does it to me, too. G.M.'s like that, she really can't be bothered." "But I feel terrible, Steven, I came on like a nut with my literary claptrap, literary ambitions, can you imagine?" "Yeah, well, why not? But don't imagine it's just you; she really turns off when faced with emotion. My mom has just about given up on her in this direction." I can imagine Sally's frustration; it is Sally who takes care of Mother, under the rubric that she lives close enough, Nebraska. Mallory and I let Sal do much of the work of daughtering. But Mallory stayed three weeks when she was here. The thought overwhelms me; I could never do three weeks. "Not at your rate of intensity," Steven chuckles. "How about some more coffee?"

"Steve, has it ever occurred to you that G.M. has a British feel to her?" "Now that you mention it, yes; she avoids feeling, always has; it's how she is". "Steven, the Irish have a term, they call it West Briton. How else do you explain a woman who fitted up her first born with the name Elizabeth. As a middle name, since Sally's not a Christian name, not good enough for the font, so Mom came up with the name of the Virgin Queen. The Virgin Queen, think about it." "You're wrong, Kate. Sally's named after your grandmother Millett, Elizabeth Esch." Then it's a joke, then it's history and a story about A.D. still remembering Campion's death, then it's philosophy.

Steven's there at the end of the bar, grinning at me over his coffee cup and joking with the waitress. He has humored me and he has also been a friend, something more than a dutiful nephew. I cannot remember ever having asked him a favor outright before and it humiliated me. Aunts should give, not take. Then it doesn't matter, we are family, the five minutes that elapsed before he called back were time to get permission from his wife and decide to settle this at the bar where we have all done our drinking, his mother, his uncles, his friends, the bar where Aunt Dorothy took me to lunch the day we bought the steamer trunk and the Holland American Line tickets to cross the Atlantic Ocean by ship because she was sending me to Oxford. The lunch where I discovered through an inadvertent remark that her adored brother, my father, had not only run off with a woman, but now also had three new children by her. Replacing me, orphaning me. I cried in the ladies room here. And then, as Mother's child, went back and kept face.

We have celebrated every wedding, every bridal dinner, every death and quarrel and reconciliation in this room. I found the place like a homing pigeon. And when we leave, our cars are side by side in the parking lot of the Lexington Bar where Steven's mother, my elder sister Sally, was once robbed at gunpoint in quiet St. Paul. We warm our engines and take off in separate directions across the ice of a new snow.

~

It will be a bad night in the guest room on the second floor of the Wellington, a room so identical to a motel room that I keep thinking I am here on a gig and must make a speech or have just made one. Ah, but you did, you blasted your Mother with your embittered personality. Without even raising your voice or growing blasphemous or any of the usual signs of your alienation all these years, you have brutally disturbed her peace, on the visit when you were to be a lamb every moment.

This is the last night, I leave tomorrow and right up 'til tonight I had behaved myself, repressed myself, put aside my small nature, my whine against fate, my dissatisfactions with life. Pacing the room I find I cannot even think, have lost the ability to talk to myself even in rebuke. Read, shut off the radio of the mind, unplug your growing shame. You will regret this evening the rest of your life. What if this turns out to be the last time you see her? And why does she say things like that? Has she got something up her sleeve, can she will her own death? Is this a deliberate punishment, a device to get my attention or a way to devastate me finally, a last curse? My god, read, shut up and read.

A bad night: I held on to Maguib for dear life, a book about families so I can go on running my tongue against that particular sore tooth till three and then four in the morning. Little experiments with sleep only hurl me up from the pillow; I cannot stop realizing that I've ruined the last interview I might ever have with my mother. She has made it the last, she can even control this. Damn, if I could ever convince her, make it plain and sunlit and obvious that I love her, too, love her as much but not as well as she loves me, my guilty screwed up passion as overwhelming as her superior motherly grandeur, the love that has planned even the lamp light. My own emotion is ill and crippled and crazy, but it's driving me nuts tonight. People make mistakes in life she had said. It was like a sentence. You're going to remember that absurd conversation upstairs the rest of your life, all the years that are to come without her . . . I am devastated. Angry even at her, but mad with rage at myself. Keep reading, try your Minnesota humor book. It's past five now, at six you can go out somewhere for coffee. And pack the car so you'll have more time with her when she wakes.

I had said I'd be upstairs at eight, but yesterday she was already up at seven—would she see me at seven, receive me, what if she refuses to speak to me in the morning? Look—go in there and say it right away, the minute you're in the door—Mom I love you, I couldn't sleep 'cause I hurt your feelings. I came on too strong, I should have either shut up or said this stuff in a letter or something. I should have been light, it's just that I'm so scared. And I can't stop crying; I got carried away this visit.

And then she'll do this last time we'll ever see each other business again and I'll freak out. I almost wanted to shake her last night, frightened by the sheer size of my emotions, like someone out of control, a dangerous person, maniacal, watch it . . . with your rep. My whole life in this family a struggle not to cry (childhood), not to shout (adolescence), not to open my mouth (adulthood) . . . and in all difficult moments, to read and keep on reading.

I read my way through my childhood on Selby Avenue, right through the parental quarrels and the separation and divorce. I became a bookworm and even finally a scholar out of a steady need to block out domestic reality.

Reading is still my only method of finding calm, curing hurt, centering self.

By now I am reduced to finishing the Minnesota language book so I can leave it for Mother to read, a sacrifice since I would love to bring it with me to regale my buddies over Bowery dinners, and I may not find a copy at the airport. Hoping that Mother will pick it up, of course hoping most of all that she will not find it cruel and spiteful, patronizing, the "making fun" which she has feared always and hated most in me. With reason, too, in the past, less reason now.

After all what did happen, was said or done, that was so all-fired terrible anyway? There were other, ostensibly riskier moments; that first night when she asked about lithium: "I haven't had any in three years, Mom." "So it's alright" she said, "You're alright." "Look, I never needed to take it in the first place, I was just so broken up about being put away, no credibility, not even to myself. So I wasted thirteen years taking that dope, Mother." "Well you're alright now." "Sure, sure, but you don't get thirteen years back." "What did it do to you?" "It made me stupid," speak slowly, carefully, don't race, don't raise your voice; "It's a major tranquilizer," my throat sore, the word hard to say, voice going, this damn cold. Crying and saying it was the cold. "You're tranked out, you're not working on all your cylinders, your intelligence is hampered, you have to work twice as hard." "But you wrote books on it." "Yeah, amazing, isn't it; it amazes me to think about it now, to realize, to remember." "But it's all over now." Damn—how easily she dismisses trouble, how patly all those years disappear; thirteen years as a mental patient, a psychotic, etc., waved away—all a lie and I believed it. The way it blighted my life was real enough.

"Mom, it made me broke, don't you see, the word got out, I didn't get any lectures, I was down to $800 when the grant came from Germany to write *The Politics of Cruelty*. Then the political situation turned off all the funds for radicals anyway, no room for them at the big U, ten years of Republican rule." Now we were off on a safe tack: my new book brings gigs, I report happily, offers to lectures here and there. Gloat, perform success for her. The only acceptable news is good news.

I had just come from the Outwright Conference in San Francisco, a different world altogether, the very idea of a conference on gay writers, 2,800 strong, all sitting before me. "You must be readers," I said. "There cannot have been this many gay writers since the creation of the world," remembering for them the first time I'd heard the word lesbian: Sal's beau Ed Regnier saying that word to Mother while I blabbed away to Mary Quin on the phone, madly in love within their hearing. "Your daughter might be a lesbian," the young man said pompously.

I didn't even know that word, had never heard it and yet understood perfectly that it was anathema and it was me. Mary Quin and I were utter innocents who told everyone at Derham Hall we were in love. Not just the seniors, who laughed, but even the nuns, who raised their brows and said nothing. It took Ed Regnier to say the word. An eighteen-year-old boy, but speaking in the voice of full patriarchal authority: the voice of the society, the shrinks, the police.

To give her credit, Mother didn't respond. Just another one of those little coughs, embarrassed, harassed, put upon, ignoring stimuli she doesn't choose to rise for. But he had her; she'd just been letting it go by, a crush. Our world was full of them, a house of women, girls' schools, Catholic romanticism and repression. Now she'd have to take notice; that evening I was reproved. She let me down. Not that hard of course. But after that I was an outlaw, became one with the naming of a name.

During my first years in New York Mother used to make timid inquiries, that girl Zoe that I lived with, were we lesbians? Everyone knew about the scandal my last year in college. That I'd continue this sort of thing off in another town would not be that surprising. In my senior year there had been a serious attempt to cure me: if I didn't stop seeing that woman I wouldn't get to go to Oxford, Aunt Dorothy's deal, her money after all, though the whole family denounced my lover, that "divorcee" as they called her, Mother and Aunt Dorothy both divorced women themselves.

When Mother would ask about Zoe, I figured I knew better now, I just lied. Strangely, Mother had ceased even to appear to disapprove, seemed merely curious. Perhaps the scolding would come with an admission of the truth. But not from me. I was a liar now, and while I lied it was okay, all they wanted was a resemblance of probability. Then I married Fumio: relief all around. Then the movement coming to its crisis in women loving women, doing so again for some of us and for others for the first time . . . and speaking out, telling the truth. Trouble. Big trouble. Phone calls to Sal, could she break the news, *Time* would be on the stands in a few days and Mom would hear from a magazine that her newly celebrated daughter, all honor and excitement turning to ashes, was also publicly queer. And the neighbors would read it; St. Paul would know. Being lesbian was nothing compared to it being known, to saying so, to admitting it.

"That lesbianism, will it have that awful lesbianism in it?" Mother winced, hearing about *Flying*, repudiating the book even before she had read it. "I want to dedicate it to you, Mom." "Don't you dare, it's disgusting." At one point she offered to sue me if I did dedicate the book to her. I dedicated; she neglected to sue.

But my coming out was Mother's ordeal before publicity. She has endured a lot after all, and in the end she has come through brilliantly. She hated *Sita* and asked me not to publicize the book in Minneapolis: I called the publishers and cancelled the tour but told her that was the last time.

Then slowly, wonderfully, a change of heart; it was alright to be queer if I were only happy: a mother's position. Then still more enlightened positions emerged; she read books on being a parent of gay offspring, and gay lib's own progress went along with the family's new liberality. By now Mother surpasses herself in radical sophistication; all her earlier selves would be astonished: Farmington is way behind her. She has even accepted the fact that Jennifer is so many years younger than I am. The idea itself astonishes me as well; it still seems an accident, a strange circumstance suddenly remembered in surprise. Two years later I still wake up to remember there is Jennifer and grin, loving her more all the time. What do you think? I had asked Mother, fearing the worst: "If she's any good she'll get you to quit smoking," Mother's sole comment, tantamount to acceptance. Jennifer has taken it to heart.

I had pneumonia in June and quit, stayed on the wagon for six months and then fell off in January, got a cold as punishment. I have now had three head colds in six weeks and know I should never smoke again; my body can't take it, has given notice. But this moment and even with this cold, I wish to god I had a cigarette. Especially now that I'm packed and ready for the road, the moon silver in a crisp blue ultramarine sky, indigo ten minutes ago, but lightening even as you watch, when it's cobalt there will be coffee. McDonald's is just a block away—would they sell cigarettes? I can't hold out any longer. I have somehow violated my mother and suffered for it all night long but this is only the first sleepless night of the rest of my life. What if she were already dead upstairs? But for god's sake, what was it that hurt her so, why should some hand wringing about publishing create such offence? As her writer out there writing for her, did I scare her that the game was up? Have I dashed her hopes, enlarged her sense of powerlessness with my own news from the front that we might lose altogether, never make it into the record?

Yesterday she said the oddest thing, she began a sentence by saying "When you pray to me . . ." "Are you planning to be canonized, Mother? What on earth do you mean?" "I just mean that when I'm dead you'll be talking to me, surely you are in touch with other people"—she has read my *Elegy for Sita*, can imagine the book to A.D. There is even Dad, all those open phone lines. And she is merely taking her place there. "When you pray to me I want to hear how everything is going." So of course she will be getting reports and things may not go as grimly as I tend to predict. Pessimism is part of my grand design; ambition on my scale deserves caution. What is wrong with confessing one's ambitions? You could do worse than aspiring to literature, you could rob the poor or wage war or bump people off.

So why do I feel I have just about bumped off my mom by the time I've finished a satirical primer on Minnesota English to use up the time till she wakes? We laughed at this book yesterday, memorized and even practiced using the first three necessary phrases: "you bet," "that's that," and "whatever". Expressions we have of course used all our lives though never consciously; using them consciously, as when one learns a language, made it hilarious. Why am I crying merely to remember laughing? Go buy coffee, this room is haunted; how many visiting offspring have slept here at the end of their parents' lives?

What offence do I feel guilty of? Fatuity. No big deal, nothing special here. That you persisted in this egotistic flummery when time was so short, the real issues of life and death so grave that your little self-important press release was especially trivial. She's making it a visit about death when it was only about getting ready for death. This was not to be the last conversation; how dare she pull this pre-emptive strike business and say that it is. Is she trying to get at me through my years of neglect, self-importance? But she couldn't; you were still blathering on about yourself. I already apologized for that. "Nonsense," she said at breakfast, "we both talk about ourselves, that's what people do when they talk: I talk of my health and this apartment, you talk about your loft and the Farm and your work. I talk about the Wellington and tell you about old women who live here who have no interest for you at all except that they are my neighbors and therefore interest me. I could give cocktail parties every night here and show you off but I want to keep you for myself."

And here I am after three days, creeping out of the building to find coffee, maybe even a smoke . . . I feel that vicious. Even McDonald's will not have me, its smirking teenager help will not open the door for ten more minutes. Screw 'em, their sign says no smoking. I head for the airport expecting to find a diner on the way, fail to, nearly stay at the airport—just get on the plane, she is so sick of you she probably doesn't want to see you again this morning anyway. Return this car and call it quits. But of course I don't, instead I turn around and go back to St. Paul and out of Minneapolis, that dumb new world. St. Paul will have a real diner, it's an old-fashioned town. It does, it's called Mickey's. The biggest truck in the world is parking there as I walk toward the entrance. Got a smoking section, even a cigarette machine, I'll wait, rescue is so near at hand.

Then I wager myself, a familiar business, mentality of an alcoholic I think, hearing myself debate the issue in first and second person: if she forgives you this morning, you don't get a smoke. If she doesn't I get to buy a carton 'cause I'm gonna need it. Annoyed by the persistent feeling that I abstain for others, am being controlled, policed by Jennifer and Mother, that I am acting for others and not myself. So I want to smoke just to be ornery, original, headstrong, the independent artist slowly dying of lung cancer. Asinine prospect, but consider Mother locked in her still-healthy body wanting out. Read the paper, cuss the war, George Bush was given a hero's welcome in Congress. Can you balance your irascibility against your admiration for the really good-looking lady Major, a surgeon—real style, front page color photo, this morning's prisoner of war released by an Iraqi guard. Even he appears to admire her. Intend to save the photo, then forget, so eager to arrive before that little door, apartment 503, its *St. Paul Pioneer Press* already taken in. That means she's up. The door's unlocked. I am not yet an orphan.

~

An awful dread, coming in the door, the fear of God. But her eyes are not blank with rejection, only faint, sad, old, so old, the little figure in the Lanz nightgown, the gay little girl look we used to affect as children. I was once a waitress in Sun Valley in pretend Swiss costume à la Lanz: to see the tiny patterns, the long flannel sleeves and floor-length skirt, the lace at collar and cuffs on her tiny wasted body is both charming and pitiful. The walker marches around, but I am early enough to be enlisted as breakfast maker, crisply following orders for instant oatmeal, just this much water in the little cup. When it boils add the oats, then simmer. Obeying instruction like an eager automaton—any way to do penance. I have already delivered my "Mother you've got to know how much I love you, even if I mess up and say it wrong every time" speech. Duly noted. She is bored, tired, sick of me; there will be no backlighting by table lamps this morning. She is not only sick of me she is sick with fatigue, emotional stress, the pressure of involvement. Passion, that was always my sin here. Get with it, be efficient, let her off the hook.

Soon I have a plane to catch, am leaving and there must be no fuss now, no emotionality, not even the margin she might have allowed for at first. You have worn out your welcome, you have worn her out. Now get to it, wait on her, you know this kitchen—march.

I pour the orange juice, the new bottle, the real orange juice I talked her into letting me buy at Lund's yesterday, showing her the machine, the real oranges piled at the top, the good strong glass bottles, hopefully not too heavy for her to manage. This is the real McCoy, Tom's stuff is hardly better than concentrate, letting her have the truth, bragging up my product, pushing my tastes . . . you're gonna love this. She had said orange juice was "tricky" in the morning; let's hope this is not too acidic. I go on to prepare the coffee, instant, another nicety forgone. Real butter is now cholesterol, real coffee is too much trouble, how life winds down: is it age or just the new America? Shut up, don't comment. Doing everything at once, last night's dishes, this morning's breakfast, model of cheerful surface self. Even I can display this shell in an emergency. Which this seems to be, a social occasion marred by a certain awkwardness; I have made a scene or something last night, now I must make a decent exit, everything just lovely, wonderful visit, was real nice to talk.

I look around to see her sagging on her walker, jumping to retrieve her glass of orange juice. Wouldn't you know it has turned her stomach. Why didn't you let well enough alone, she adored Thomas's brand, was proud of it. For a moment my shame and disappointment hide the facts—she is really sick, she is falling. "I'm right here, Mom, everything will be fine." Thank god I was still here, how many times might this have happened with no one around. All alone she would be so afraid. Not only you fall and may lie there helpless, but when they find you they may take everything you have away, the last autonomy, dignity, the apartment. Then maybe the nursing home then. Of course she is scared to death of falling.

I decide I won't turn her in. Deciding it even this early, wiping the orange juice from her mouth with Kleenex, holding her up, asking her to put her feet back under her, lean on the walker, center herself. But she can't, doesn't want to maybe, is letting herself fall, needs to. I consider if this is dramatic behavior—a real possibility—her pique last night got my attention. This does even better, this and all the grim prediction of this being the last time I'll see her. Curses, warnings, turns in the lover's quarrel of our long courtship.

"Mom, stand if you can." "No, I want to be on the floor." And nothing I can do can stop it, her tiny body is the heaviest thing I have ever tried to hold up. I the farmer, stronger than any woman I know. But it is nothing against her strength, weight, dead weight, her determined pull toward the floor. I'm stunned, powerless. Dear god, I'm supposed to be able to help; its a godsend I'm here and so forth and yet I seem to have no effect at all.

Of all of the concerned parties—Sal, Mallory, Steven, Jamie, anyone in this building, the management itself—I am surely the most incompetent, the worst choice, the most inept. Why me when the trouble comes? Rotten luck for both of us; I have no idea what to do, jabbering on like the soul of confidence: just stretch out here, take it easy, no problem. Watching her head, too near the door jamb, the fear of falling gets real: alone she could hurt herself plenty. At least she's not in the bathroom: all hard surfaces. Every room here has buttons and alarms; residents are checked on each morning. If they have failed to display their little "I'm okay" sign by nine o'clock, someone knocks. Mother's sign proclaims she's okay, she displayed it when she took in the newspaper. But now, she's on the floor. So you're here with her, don't panic, pretend it's a little rest. She reclines on her blue shag carpet in her hallway. Nonchalantly I produce more blue Kleenex to wipe away the orange of the juice.

When she is well enough to stand, when the dizziness has passed and she retreats alone and with dignity to the toilet to repair the damage of diarrhea, I wash the orange juice out of the carpet as if my life depended on it, projecting all her urgent disapproval of messes, of damaged material surfaces—Mother, who asks eight times in a row if one's cocktail glass is on a coaster. I know what she cares about and I'm going to get this stain out if it kills me, aware it is my own guilt I wash away so frantically. Meanwhile I'm deliberately leaving her to her own devices, her own independent if difficult privacy, knowing and sympathizing with that to the smallest nuance. Fully aware that a responsible person would already be on the phone to the manager, to Steven, to whomever. I'm not going to, not unless I have to. And I will take it to the very edge to save her all she stands to lose.

Come off it, she could die this morning while you make your airplane, Mother already needling me about the time, shouldn't I be leaving, she doesn't want to make me late, I had planned an extravagant budget of time: an hour to return the car, an hour to deal with the ticket and gate and luggage. I still have an hour and a half before I had planned to leave; she is already cleaned up and able to walk, able to sit down at the table and "keep me company," a convention she insists on.

I go along with it, with everything, anxious to catch the plane since this is one of those unalterable tickets. Never mind, your mother is sick, really sick; you can make them change flights for something like this. But there's a gallery meeting tonight, miss it and you get fined; it's a co-op, you are letting them down. From the beginning this had been the obstacle to staying longer. This damn Thursday night meeting.

Learn measure and reality; your meeting is trivial, your mother may be really ill, if this is a fall it's part of the dreaded falling sickness, this odd discrepancy between her visual judgment of distance and the actual placement of her feet. She has lost some ability in the third dimension that has scared her into near paralysis. It is why she has grown so frightened, why she has degenerated to the walker. There is nothing—they have been saying this for years—nothing wrong with her legs. Except atrophy: damn soon unless she keeps on the exercise bike. "You're right to insist about this," she'd said. "I'll stay off the weed; you keep those legs strong," I'd answered. Our pact. Yesterday.

But today is the terror of having watched her unable to stand; I have also experienced her fear of falling, I have lost my balance or ability to judge distance too, a few times at the Farm, it put a panic in me; will I end up like this too? All the time here the fact of her age and infirmity have been with me, I feel twenty years older than when I came. Even if I'm not sure I share her condition, I certainly believe in it at last. This morning I have even begun to believe she could die. Soon. Not in the abstract, but in the reality of this little apartment. Maybe now, this morning, maybe with me here, maybe only me, the clumsy one. Maybe the moment I'm out the door.

Conversation is a chatter that floats along the top of this real condition of terror, the guilty farewell. If I'm to go, it is nearly time. "Let me put you in bed, Mom." "I think I'll spend the day there." "Sure, why not take the day off and read." There's a television set in her bedroom too, a good reading chair. "Here's the book you were reading when I arrived." There's a Le Carré, and our little manual of Minnesotan, placing them on the chair, hopeful, encouraging—will she ever read it? Reading fails to hold her now, she cannot concentrate; does she think of death and dying, is she scared under it all—or is she as willing as she claims?

"If I died today you should feel happy about this visit," she says from the bed. It stuns me. It strikes like an insult yet was meant to heal, to forgive, to assure. "No way, Mother. And please don't scare me like this," an entreaty, my voice a child's again, as afraid, as lonely, as bereft.

The little figure on the bed is saying she will have to tell her doctor she has been sick four times since her last visit, she says it like confession; four instances of incontinence. "When you say sick do you mean nausea, diarrhea, or the fainting?" "All three," quick as a calculating machine, as objective. What will this mean for the deciders? Does it mean trouble with the bureaucracy, the authoritarians who decide when the elderly can stay in their homes, when they ought to be doped to the max, etc. In the airport I had seen a great poster of an old woman stroking her cat with the caption, "Most women her age belong at home, their own home." Damn right. And if it means keeping my mouth shut, I sure will.

I say goodbye again and again, scared to overstep, to expose her to danger, to protect her privacy too far, even to be a selfish New Yorker in a hurry to catch a plane, rationalizing. "You're sure Mom?" "Of course I'm sure I'm alright, perfectly alright. Now get going or you'll miss your plane." Is her irritability sufficient to assure me? Remember her every tone, a lifetime of judging them—is she really okay? is it martyrdom? is it drama? Mother is not beyond meaningful gestures when dealing with her daughter's meaner needs. Is it good soldiering? If so, too good?

Listen hard and remember this is not just the lifetime of challenge and barter; this really might be the end. This is serious, your mother might be dying while you succeed in catching your plane. How will you live with yourself? Not so well. I get out the door and come back. See that springy member of the management leaving the apartment next door all cheer and bouncy step. Call her, tell her you're just a little bit worried about your Mom, you wouldn't even mention it if you weren't on your way to an airplane, etc. Good God, have you no conscience? But it's just that, I risk exposing her to danger and what she would regard as condescension, unnecessary fuss, the greatest indignity—etc., etc., just to salve my conscience.

Odd, but conscience feels better going along with Mother's gutsy living on the edge, her gallantry and courage. And I trust her judgment; I must finally, I have trusted it all my life. She is the mother, not I, she is still the mother. And you are still the daughter, self-serving, devious, on her way. Then back again: qualms in the elevator. See if indeed she really is okay, the door is still unlocked, steal in and observe. I do.

Of course she knows, hears, feels, intuits probably. I have never managed to fool her in my life. "Really, I am just fine, go get your plane." More "I love you"s, more kisses, more terror and indecision.

At the airport, I succeed in impressing a young Japanese clerk that I might need to bend my unbendable ticket, he accedes, understanding; filial piety is second nature to him, but the new security procedures prevent him from holding my bags, I must drag them around to telephones while I check on her. Go ahead, send them to New York, I don't give a damn: if she doesn't answer the phone I'm out of here and back to the Wellington, even if I have to rent another car. If she doesn't answer the phone, call Steven. But remember, you are not the police, the woman is tired and unwell, there is no reason to pounce on her if she exercises her right to ignore the damn phone. Cross your fingers, here goes.

When I call her from New York there are times it rings on so long, in her deafness it takes forever to establish itself. Then there are times it simply isn't answered because she's at dinner or out with relatives, her social life. Yet every time my heart seizes. Then I would remember she was out of town, at Sal's, a winter trip to Arizona, the old days. No more trips now . . . go on, take your life in your hands, dial . . . over breakfast this morning I finally realized she would never see the Farm again and almost choked on my tears. I cry in airports now, it's like breathing.

She answers on the second ring. Very composed, the voice stronger than it frequently is when it has to travel all the way to New York. This is the last chance to run back . . . it will take good judgment now to decide, it is crucial: you are going to suffer the rest of your life if you make a mistake here. She has had a nice rest and feels much better, she'll take it easy today. She sees the doctor next week. Of course it will be a nuisance to tell him, but Sally will be in town, it's the new baby's christening party. It seems I called it right, she is still there and strong, may last for years.

"Remember me here," she had said, being gloomy. "No, Mom, I'm not going to take any chances on remembering—I'll be back here pretty damn quick, believe me." Call her from New York tonight, and talk to Sal, get an overview, make a plan. It's safe to leave now. You can come back next month in April, May too. "Mom, I have a lot of time now, I can come any time you say," you had told her this in her bedroom, fighting off the last chance business, you are fighting it now. Will you win?

Part Two

I arrive flamboyant in a leather jacket with two bunches of strange off-white tulips, beautifully stippled at the base of the flower with a soft mauve flame which at first you are not quite sure you have seen. Perhaps you have only imagined it. That's it, I said, the perfect thing to bring, feeling like a suitor. I have a fancy car since the plain ones were rented, a luxury of gray Oldsmobile. And in the back, the wheelchair. I fought the rental car clerks for a phone book, I fought the phone book for a St. Paul location, I fought the pay phone for use of a plastic card—seven attempts to get around the fact that I had already spent my last quarter calling her, telling her I was already at the airport and on my way. She was annoyed; I should have called her earlier, I have caused her anxiety. The disparity between her reality and my own illusions.

I had said I'd be there this afternoon, how could she doubt it? Full of doubt as I try to get my hands on the wheelchair. My pal Joe Barnes gave me this idea as we sat in front of his beautiful all white canvases, why not rent a wheelchair? Since it is exhausting for her to walk, get a wheelchair and you can take her anyplace—restaurants, the theater, ball games, even the museums out there. Just the thing, an inspiration. So it had seemed on Greenwich Street: here in an airport phone booth, it seems a bit harder to achieve. I go back for another look at the phone book, heckling the operator that it's an emergency, mumbo jumboing medicalese, handicap politics, genuinely scared I'll never find a listing within my known geographical range and deeply afraid of Minneapolis, which has every service and is modern and up to date. But I only know sad old-fashioned St. Paul and damn little of that anymore. The Hertz brochure even claims that the twin cities are now triplets and a suburb called Bloomington has boomed into a town; I am thirty years out of date.

But then this little place in St. Paul swims into view, Jackson Wheelchair Repair and Rental. Great, they can even fix something still, a rare trait now. Neighborhood place, small, friendly, right in the middle of those little homemade-looking St. Paul houses, blocks of them, wooden frames with small front porches, not your Summit Avenue splendor or even your downtown Victorian, but the real meat and potatoes of shelter here. And just when you are sure no business in the world would locate here and there has to be a mistake; there it is, around the corner. Hardly even a sign. Then a nice guy and an army of wheelchairs and you're set. Except that it's pretty hard to fit in the back seat of the Olds; I lose confidence that I'll be strong enough. He shows me a few tricks. Okay, I'll chance it. Now, just to persuade Mom.

Because of course a wheelchair is a step down. Wheelchairs are an entire grade lower than walkers. She's got a walker. If her neighbors at the Wellington see her in a wheelchair, will they feel that she has slipped a notch? Will she feel this too? Will there be repercussions? Have I overconsulted my own convenience in fact? No more ten-minute walks to an elevator a mere hundred feet from her door, no more endless holding of doors while she creeps through with the walker. All speed now, convenience, cheer, optimism, etc.

Of course the point of the wheelchair is merely mobility; we can go places to which we would never aspire otherwise: museums, the movies, the park; the sky's the limit. Mother will see the world again, take a new interest in everything, the two of us will see the world this way; we'll go to the Walker Museum, to the Minneapolis Institute of Fine Arts. I will show her pictures, I will show her my world. Suddenly, when talking to Joe I wanted to bring her into this place of seeing, this place of ours. Joe's a Midwesterner too, from Michigan, his father just died last February. Joe said they became wonderful friends in the last ten years of his father's life, his father confided in him, told him things he had never told Joe's sisters and brothers. I had to smile at the pride in Joe's voice when he said this. "Maybe it was because I'm an artist and different than the others, maybe that difference made it easier to talk to me in the end," Joe mused, still pleased. His father is dead only three months but there are no tears in his eyes, the memory is entirely pleasant. Of course his father lived to an astonishing age, was actually over a hundred years old. Joe hadn't thought of a wheelchair until it was too late. On the last visits his father would go along to the museum with Joe and then wait for him in the car: "It was simply not worth it for him to go in, he didn't have the strength and he didn't mind sitting in the car. But he wanted the drive and to keep me company."

I'll bring Mother inside, wheel her through the rooms. It would be a cinch to run over to Minneapolis some afternoon by myself while she's taking a nap and zip through the Institute; I've seen the Walker already, don't really need to go again. But to look at pictures together with her and share them . . .

Joe kept saying that it took him decades to reconcile his parents to his art, they'd hated it when he turned out to be a painter. "Funny thing was, when I was finally sure of it myself—you know I was very ambivalent myself, it turned out; I shared a lot of their distrust, their conviction that this was a poor choice, too risky, too hard, too uncertain and unrewarding—but when my own faith in what I do was finally complete, they let me be. Not till then. Only when I was sure."

The room around us is white like Joe's pictures have been for years now, just white, a meditation, a last Zen perfection, his drawings mere lines dissecting pure handmade Japanese paper, spare, masterful, even the pastels they were drawn with were handmade. So spare and lean. An outsider might interpret them as either a final perfection or nothing at all, frauds or masterpieces. Framed as he will frame them they will look extremely handsome over in Germany next month at his show there. They will then be sophisticated, expensive. Today in his studio, they are what they are, the final or at least the latest gesture in a life dedicated to this discipline, its mysterious, winding and elusive goal in the unsteady meaning of marks on paper, oil on canvas, subtle, slippery as a fish, a meaning which is all meaning for a while and then evaporates and is nothing, though it leaves behind this beautiful artifact. Just before I leave we notice one of last year's drawings, framed, handsome, good—but not a favorite anymore, not the newest child, not radiant as the freshest pieces, still unframed, pristine, new minted. We took a walk and sat in front of a café and had lunch out of doors, it was a lovely day. It was lovely to be artists. I walked home full of hope, wanting to draw. Next time he'll come to my studio.

So the wheelchair was to be a link to bring us together; I'd take Mother into my world. And this time I'd be smarter. Not like that time in New York, years ago: we were going through the Met together and Mother remarked innocently before a Flemish picture that illustrators and designers must visit these paintings often for ideas. The notion horrified me, how dare they, inferior self-serving branches. And I was sarcastic, arrogant, judgmental as a narrow-minded kid artist, purist self-importance, the mystique we floated around in when not practicing being tough as nails at the Cedar Bar. The picture was not a holy card for Mom, not sacrosanct, simply a healthy artifact. I had made it as magic as the lives of the saints, as Keats's urn: I had replaced my childhood Catholic superstition with art and was close to a savage in unreasoning reverence for certain names and times and places. I had also fallen in love with certain golden and brilliant colors and this picture glowed for me.

But my snobbery had hurt her feelings, I could see her wince, could feel the sting of tears in her eyes for a humiliated moment: questions of taste became questions of learning and I had made her feel ignorant, foolish. I have remembered that moment a hundred times, a touchstone. Now it can also be expiated, transcended: why not, here at the end, share something as important to me as pictures? Now that I know and I love them better, more wisely. Now that an interior, a Bonnard for example, celebrates and summons a room, its color and intimacy a hymn of reverence for all the domestic experiences which she first gave me, Selby Avenue mornings as she and Celia practiced making a better and still a better pot of coffee, the sun on sofa fabric, the music of cups and saucers, light on flowers, the world of women and the sheer pleasure of talk, of living rooms and coffee and chat and sunlight, the miracle of living, just living, the very beauty of that. How good that a man could have found this out, could have painted such a morning's exhilaration, such an afternoon's quietude. What if the two of us could together enter such rooms, such memories, could share these sensations, so essential and complex, so ripe and ultimate they are the real mysteries of civilization, the last points of knowing what it is to live.

And something as ugly and mundane, as unpleasant and hospital-like, as institutional and boring as a wheelchair could get us there—wow. Wait till I tell her, wait till she hears. Sure I'm a little late, but I need some Bordeaux and a notebook, and then I can show up with my tulips and big ideas.

~

And she goes for it. We are so excited I almost open the Bordeaux before unpacking the car. We're going to have a great time. Of course we both understand she is not wheelchair material—let's hope everyone in the building gets that too. Even with a walker Mom is still on her own pins, no paralyzed legless being fit for a wheelchair, but self-propelled and on her own two feet even if she likes to lean on this walker contraption of tubular aluminum, its little rubber wheels in front, its rubber stoppers behind. If you lean on them they function as a kind of brake, there's a little sling and a pocket for your Kleenex or a key or the mail. Handy, but merely an adjunct to someone who is still out there on her own.

The wheelchair is just for outings and outrageous gadding about, no substitute for walking. She must not only go on doing that, she must keep on riding the stationary bike in the work-out area on the first floor. Or else lose the use of her legs. A real downhill course we are sure to avoid. She has promised to use the bike. Tedious, strenuous, even dangerous-seeming since she worries about everything that has to do with falling, her very infirmity a form of worry, sometimes nearly perceived as an hysteric formation that has come near to invaliding her. Her doctors cannot understand it since her legs themselves are alright. But this is a real enough ailment, some failure of the physical sense of balance, the very equilibrium that gives us all our security when upright. In a strange way this has failed her enough times and with a sufficient sense of surprise and sudden endangerment that all movement now is hazard.

Of course to pop into a wheelchair would be a great way out of all that. Provided of course that one had a personal slave to push it. Mother has me for six days only so I doubt she would become addicted and I must make sure she and all those around her, the management as well as her cronies, are under no illusion that the wheelchair is the path of the future, that she has fallen to this, etc. Let scandal keep a distance: we got this chair on wheels for fun and frivolity, for stepping out, for the world beyond the Wellington. Because, except for safaris to Lund's, two since January, and for a dinner at Steven's or some other relative's house, Mother has stopped going anywhere. The chair on wheels will change all that, will put her back into the world again, the public sphere. That and a fancy car.

It's beating back the tide. It is all beating back the tide. And there's no beating it really. It's rather late to start looking at pictures; you should have thought of that before. Now finally you're here, a bit behind time, and the time has past. She says it, her companions at dinner say it too in their very bearing. No, I insist, it is not too late, while you have a mind no experience is too late. Of course they may simply not want to bother, may prefer to be left alone and in peace in boredom and familiarity. But I am a teacher type, an endless professor and enthusiast, an artist begging my mother to know my world; desperate now, no longer content to be ignored and misunderstood. We have only a little time, we must arrive at a rapprochement in the few remaining days and weeks, years even. No, I will not let you go gently into that good night, even if I have to rage myself. Busy fool. She is at peace, she is with what she knows. Leave it alone. Can't you see her speech slurs at times, that she forgets things; other people would let her be. But I won't, nor will I set much store by her absent-mindedness, have too much of my own.

At dinner there is some dismay about the food from our table-mates Ruth and Jim. Mother too is embarrassed at the Wellington's decline. "First we had Lee's as our caterer, and then it began to fall off, so we complained and they got another company and it's worse. Now we are afraid to complain." I wonder about reprisals. Will they decide you are too sick if you are a nuisance, evict you? "No, they don't want to evict anyone, they have vacancies now, they're trying to fill them, there's an open house this weekend to get more tenants." Ruth is a retired librarian, very savvy and elegant.

But I have made a mistake by using the wheelchair to take Mother down to dinner, have exposed her to loss of status among her friends: the chair was for forays into the world, I have been frivolous, wanting just to try it out, thinking it was fun, a new toy. I have also jumped in with my opinions at dinner: Ruth used to live in New York, went to Columbia. She would not go back again, however. "It was fun then, but now . . ." I try to persuade her that it is rent which has ruined city life, going on to fulminate against

Mayor Koch for giving the city to the landlords and against the growing spread between rich and poor bringing crime because of real needs and justifiable resentment. "And fifty thousand homeless: can you believe that this is the same number as there are warehoused apartments?" "Why would landlords not rent?" "Because they get a tax break and they are waiting to co-op where the big money is, then they can sell and get out of it altogether. It's difficult to pay taxes and provide services, selling out is easier. What is amazing"—they are amazed at the machinations of capitalism and real estate in a place so disordered—"but what is amazing," I say, knowing that I shock, but determined, "what is amazing is that people sleep in the streets and don't break down the doors." "There are squatters," Ruth says; she knows her stuff. "But so few, there's so little protest. Isn't it crazy that people submit?" I would break down a door before I would sleep in the street, I say bravely, stupidly, Ruth just looks on as I flounder; good manners and private property are things we share but in somewhat different proportions. "People's spirits are broken, everybody has taken money as a religion now, whether through success or fear, people stay in line, if you saw Grand Central with all the sleeping bodies . . ." "No I don't want to," she objects sensibly. Of course.

We did Nancy Reagan too. The new book of gossip, Nancy and Frank Sinatra flirting at private luncheons and so forth: smut, tell-tale. Ronald Reagan wrecked my country, I had pointed out to my seat mate as we landed in Minneapolis, having begun our chat by discussing his lap top computer, the man an airline pilot flying as a passenger and doing his letters and business affairs, his accounts and note taking, all on a Tandy something. And so amiable that we started on the new book about Nancy Reagan, just out that day. Of course it's scandal and scandal mongering, who cares if Nancy has Frank, who cares if Ronnie was horny and had six girls on the string as a boy star? It's clear, however, that these folks were hypocrites. Just say no, Nancy told us all; one's even willing to congratulate her for having taken one puff of marijuana in a lifetime, a glimmer of imagination. But they ran the country like bandits, Contra Gate was an impeachable offence, they threw an American election, stole Carter's presidency, made a deal with Iran long before so that the hostages would be released to Reagan at the moment he was inaugurated. And they were. Rafsanjani got his guns in time to smash Iraq. Iraq, which Bush has just smashed again, leaving Saddam in charge to massacre the Kurds. "Everyone knows and doesn't know because it is not said on television, only in print." The pilot was silent. So are my companions at dinner. I have overreached, overdone it, talked too loud or long or hard or not wisely, surely not well. And am tired now, a strange fatigue taking over when we are upstairs again as Steven arrives with Chris and baby Victoria. I am running out of steam, feeling a little old or susceptible. We are quiet. But there is one spark, a reference to Patrick. Mother's father, P. H. Feely, one sees his name in terms of the big letters on the granary down in Farmington, P. H. Feely and Son. Because Patrick's son Tom inherited nearly everything, and the daughters got to go to annual meetings on Sunday afternoons in August, where it always seemed the business wasn't doing well enough to give them more than this little pittance for their shares.

"Do you have a picture of him?" Chris asks. Patrick's stern face was in a stern silver frame next to the phone when mother sold insurance. Urging her on, probably giving her courage, the peasant patriarch who had made his fortune. "Patrick had two moods," she starts to tell us again, remembering his return home from the Minneapolis grain exchange at dusk in the last years, where he had won or lost great sums. "If it was good he hummed; if it was bad he frowned." Frowned and leaned on his stick. Always the rosewood stick, his shillelagh. As I child I saw it in the corner at Aunt Mary's house, like a holy relic, the closest thing to a saint's bone, the remembered phallic remnant, treasured, revered. But Aunt Mary is dead and her duplex is gone, she and her daughter Joannie moved to an apartment, then finally a nice tight new little house, furnished with all the heavy mahogany of Aunt Mary's wedding set, grand old pieces preserved in these unfamiliar new rooms. But the rosewood stick, this strange object? Where is it now, Aunt Mary's relic? Perhaps it's with cousin Joannie, a good daughter who never married but lived with her mother until she died at ninety-one. They still do that out here; at fifty Joannie was left to live her own life.

And Patrick, his face. No longer in view now in Mother's retirement. But she has the picture somewhere. I'd like to show it to Chris, it would say so much. And I'd like to see it myself, suddenly in need of the past in this sealed modern building, with a physical need of some link back to where we came from. I get up to find it, expecting it to be still within reach, maybe the drawer in Mother's desk, it can't have gone far. Mother would rather not be bothered but calls out instructions, first a desk drawer then a box in the closet. But even with Steve at my side now it can't be found.

Just before they leave, taking with them this little baby whom I have held in my arms, feeling her along my arm, feeling her happy and smiling at me, I make one more try at finding Patrick hidden in a box. And find, even before I find him, a strange slightly out of focus landscape, infinitely moving, the pond at the farm in Farmington. The homestead, the oldest place, a stretch of water and a tree on either side, unbelievably lost and sad, the artifact becoming the place, as if even the blur of old photography or the inept use of a long gone camera could evoke more solidity than the walls around us. Could not only summon then, but create it.

Mother takes the landscape in her hands and it is clear she is moved, clear too why she would prefer to let it be. But it has happened to her now, and the emotion of memory has taken hold: "I used to walk just that far," she says. "Just that far, when I was little." This picture used to hang by her desk too; I had mistakenly imagined it was Hastings, my father's home, thought it a view of the Afton, the river near his childhood. "Flow gently sweet Afton," the Milletts would laugh, all their screwy songs and tales of neighbors; "When Hastings was but a pasture and Vermillion Street was but a lane." They'd drink champagne and can-can to stuff like this in their typical hilarity and joie de vivre, the primitive nature of their shared past now another cause for sophisticated humor.

How astonishing that all along this scene was actually the farm, Patrick's farm. I see the picture for the first time, and am stricken by what it must mean to Mother, this lost pond on a lost homestead, the farm sold years ago by her brothers, sold for a building lot. In helpless wrath Mother and her sisters insisted that the homestead be torched to the ground before the sale took place. Burned, not bulldozed. And here is Patrick, grim as ever, steely eyed in his steel rims, just as well these eyes did not live to see his sons dispose of a 14-room farmhouse that was the achievement of his life, his eyes as ancient and foreboding as the Galway poor, although by this time he had succeeded and the original farm turned into many farms and a granary.

Why is there no picture of Patrick in youth; he must have been different once. Loose or handsome or easy. Pioneers, even the faces at Forepaugh's and in the Hill mansion, now a museum, or the book on Jim Hill—every man of them old already, patriarchs by the time they are recorded: beards and black coats and prosperity. Patrick of course has no beard, only a mustache. Not the founder of a city but a town, only a grain merchant who had once farmed and then thrived, and his great grandson Steven is an elegant young lawyer who will take us to lunch at the St. Paul hotel grill on Friday and give us dinner at his house on Thursday evening before he goes to Florida for a vacation.

I am glad to have this much of Steven's time, and Chris's, knowing their busy world, so different from Mother's retirement complex or my tenuous grasp on the motel room downstairs. And we did find Patrick. Just where Mother said he was, though we doubted, thought her forgetful, vague, dared to patronize if only in the inner recesses of our minds, mine anyway. When we are alone I come across a good picture of Sal, a portrait when she was in college: Steven would love it. His mother in her youth and glory, handsome and vital. "I want to keep it," Mother says, firm. But you only keep it in a box, Steven would put it on the wall. You have so many pictures of Sal, and you haven't got any more room on the wall. "I just took it down the other day, I'm not ready to give it up." She knows her mind and I cannot change it.

How I love her determination, how I admire her stubbornness. How it has always infuriated me, all of us; yet everyday I come to respect it more. In her more typical combination of certainty and uncertainty I resemble her. Steadfast and a weakling. One look can knock us off our perches: little women, little hand wringers, little iron women who climb back on again with such difficulty, again and again, destroyed and annihilated and restored with such effort. How I hate our vulnerability, our femininity and frailty, our selfhood so brittle it is a joke to dismantle us, an invitation to sadism and arrogance. That familiar churning recognition in the gut, the tears near the eyes stinging already as we know ourselves undone. And then all that work to put it back together. We do it.

But there is another element, the tide bringing us down. And here it is enormous, here in the motel room. This fatigue and hopelessness I remember as my chief memory, the final knowledge of this town, its erasure of possibility. I used to see it in the bare winter trees out the windows of Selby Avenue, nights Dad didn't come home to dinner and I would wait with her, knowing that by now he wouldn't come. Winter and abandonment, the small cheer of dinner with two children. Sal already away at college, Mallory and I her only company, eating on the second best dishes: we could not waste the china on ourselves. Maybe if I could get her going though, make her tell about the University, the Harvard guy who taught writing and said you didn't know what you meant if you couldn't say it. One sees him as she saw him, red-haired and superior, right enough for expository prose but wrong as well: I have also written to find out what I knew, felt, remembered. Let's get Mom off on *Riders to the Sea*, get out the Synge and get her to read it with us. At least get her to recite Millay. The good nights.

But the trees out the front windows toward the River, where the man picked me up who tried to rape me but I escaped and was somehow guilty still and afraid still. The River and winter and the shrinking evening of any and every opportunity—while life is going on somewhere else. I came down the stairs once from my room and my endless reading there and told Mother I was going to Paris to meet Gertrude Stein: Mother said she was already dead. The Israelis were letting women fight and I couldn't get there either. There was just dinner at the kitchen table. And after dinner nothing. But the Milletts had known Fitzgerald and Aunt Dorothy had danced with the Prince of Wales on shipboard, although that was in the past and when Dad left there wouldn't even be any Milletts. So I went away from here and am back now in this motel room to get through the night. Reading.

Like an addict. Edmund White, good, elegant even, literary, and beautifully realized. All the other worlds, the east and Europe and the gay life, gay men, distant as that, yet in this motel room as close, closer, pulling me away from here. Waking at three in the morning to start again. Like cigarettes or sunflower seeds, like booze to an alcoholic, reading. One book and then another. Still at it in the real morning, the clock moving from six to seven, I should begin to go upstairs and don't, following White through the Midwest and childhood, cornholing in sad sex with another little boy, the secret always there, between him and his father, pursuing him in prep school. It is eight, I should stop. And cannot call a halt till nine. I put down the book, embarrassed that White is better, that he is making literature, is acknowledged and I am failing in this probably mistaken premise of writing about this place, having nothing important to tell of it, finding only my own distance and inability, probable snobbery, artiness, and estrangement. Will I be honest enough to say unkind things about these people, would such observations even be honest? I consider how even chance offhand remarks offend.

And the boredom and despair, or the despair that seems to be boredom because it is too hard to examine so you just close off and read and pretend it is boredom because on examination it could be so much worse. For you, not them. But you are afraid it is them, their emanation, and dare not speak it. And then must keep silent because what you know cannot be said, the reason so many people do not write, wisely and well are silent. Or not wisely and not well.

"Why your relatives?" Jennifer had railed at me, "Why your relatives, why not someone else's?" "Because I know them, I don't know any others." "It's elitist, you can publish your relatives, your family, why not everyone?" "Everyone should write their own damn book: can't you understand this is all I've got." "Why not everyone?" "'Cause they don't want to bother. 'Cause they might offend. 'Cause they're doing something else with their lives. 'Cause not everyone wants to write. Writers do, it's what we do." "But their relatives . . ." "Yeah, get put in books. We have to have somebody's relatives in books, or we won't have anything." "You make yourself so important." "It's not making yourself important, it's just making anything at all." "Bullshit." "Listen, if women can't write about what we are seeing now, we won't know each other." "You can get it published." "Hey, that's what you don't understand; I probably can't. And if I do, I take the chance that any dumb remark, any silly observation, is taken as the whole measure of my soul. One moment's inattention or unkindness becomes who I am, my entirety in the critic's eye. And more people read reviews than read books, so you get to be defined as some little small heart dismissed with a character judgment, maybe forever." "It's all bullshit." "You're damn right, everybody takes writing so seriously, too seriously, it's just a form of talk; we are not judged by what we say over coffee."

But I know it is important, more important than talk but not as important as we make it, since not everyone writes books and we are far too impressed by those who do and by what they say in them. Yet something has to be said, no matter how carefully and conscientiously. If nothing is said, we have nothing and go through life in the dark. Why do you suppose people read biography so voraciously—there's a whole bookstore in the Village, just biography—people read it like food. Why, because they want to know about other people's lives, because they're flying without instruments themselves and have no idea—not that a book would tell you. But a little truth and some exchange of information might help: how to live your life is the most important thing there is. Let's let everything be said and then we can pick and choose and suit our moods—life is a million moods, that's the charm of it.

As various as the moments with Steven, the pleasure in seeing him, watching him hold his daughter and kiss her over and over in rapturous delight and then also see him enthuse when I tell him that Mother and I are going to see *Dances with Wolves*. "It's great," he says, "You're going to love it, you'll cry at the end—I did," the biggest smile on his face. His smile fades when I repeat my pal Naomi's strictures at the dinner table at the Farm last weekend when she pronounced it colonial, patronizing. Then Linda Kavars, who we always call L.K., said, "No way, the guy who made it risked everything, went all over town with that script for two years and no one would touch it. Did you know, he made that epic film for just $18 million?" And someone else said you could build a Lakota university for that money.

But not even having seen it yet, I had actually hurt Steven by repeating this. I could do that while loving him, probably still prepared to agree with Naomi. She has the long view, she's a New Zealander and has watched a native people destroyed and can make out the imperial English shadow as it descends, while we ourselves never notice. Even as we mumble here over the Kurdish rout. Things go by degrees surely, are true and not true.

"Just because it's a superior cowboy movie—John Ford made *Cheyenne Autumn*—you should rent the video, Steve—this is not the first time someone has included the Indian point of view." But already I have wounded his confidence when all I meant was to play with ideas, which at first I didn't even mean to put forward seriously. But in no time I was serious and America is so awful that a movie can hardly solve anything. But talk can hurt, Jennifer has won her point.

So does one say nothing, having nothing to say? Read and forget about writing. Just be here, just live, forget your record keeping, your hidden agenda. Last week at the Farm we had been picking tent caterpillar eggs off the ornamental crab apple trees that Skip and I planted together years ago; pride trees, in blossom soon and they must not be harmed by these bugs. "See how they even spoil the bark," teaching the young artists there, on a walk, pretending to work, but converting it secretly into free time, time to make them love trees. As we started back L.K. ran out and said my mother had called: it was important. Call her right back. I am nervous while the phone rings; I had dared to send her this manuscript, jinx a work in progress. She is old, she is dying, break a rule. She had also sounded pleased that I was writing about her. But what if she hates it, disapproves, is offended. Then it's over.

Miraculously, she liked it. She would hate the rest then, but there won't be any rest of it, quit while you're ahead. There is no subject here, a voice announces in my mind like the rattle of a New York editor: the subject is too small, insufficient for general interest; it is all too ordinary. There are also Jennifer's strictures against the vanity of autobiography. And the chief thing is, there isn't really anything to say. Or if there is it might be unpleasant, boring or wrong. Forget it, read someone else who did get there. I read Edmund White and wonder—is this really White's father? Is his father dead? Were they enemies, cut off from each other, can he say anything he likes now or merely the truth? Which truth? Go upstairs. you are here to see your Mother, do it.

I am here to see her off in a cab: it is the day for the hairdresser. I am not to take her, since I should stay here for cousin Laura who is having lunch with us and might arrive to find no one home. Metromobility will drive Mother; in St. Paul she can go anywhere for a dollar and be picked up with a phone call—shopping, the library, the beauty parlor, even the movies if she were frivolous enough. Unfortunately she isn't, but the hairdresser is still my mother's idea of necessity; her generation, her personal system of importance. And her beautiful white hair which is her public self, utterly important, crucial. The cab driver is a classic trucking dyke who even—here in St. Paul, I am thunderstruck—wears a teeshirt that has "Diesel Girl" proudly stenciled across her very wide back. Mother appears not to notice anything at all. Is she that cool, that out of it, that beyond it? I feel like a third sex, somewhere between the two of them and am further amazed to notice that the cab driver has actually painted her nails despite the presence of her own femme beside her at the wheel. Enough nuance for Henry James, right here at the Wellington. Things have changed a great deal, or else I never knew anything about the place even when I lived here.

Both true. We are in error about the driver however; another elderly lady claims her. We never thought to check names and the driver is in a real big hurry because "the lady in the front is gonna be late for work," the impropriety of using the cab as her personal and family car quite beyond her, she is further piqued at having "wasted her time" installing my mother not all that gently in the back seat. From which she must be removed now to wait for another cab.

"How did you know all that about them?" Mother asks as we sit calmly in the sun waiting for another cab. A black man. At first a reassuring sight; he will be gallant. But on closer inspection I notice that he too is uninterested in his passenger, personality of a drunk. Maybe the dyke was better, a woman with a woman's standards under her brusqueness. Mother's favorite cabby is a guy who reads my books and is trying to quit smoking, using me as a model. A very unwise proposition since I think of cigarettes all the time even a year after quitting, long for one even now, am frantic to drive off for a pack at the least suggestion of tension, have the personality of a drunk myself. My father's child, substituting Marlboros for Canadian Club, the longed for release, companionship, the tiny thread of independence.

At lunch I watch the women at their tables, tuning into other lives, women's lives. The restaurant is Mother's choice and her treat. The much admired Mandarin Lee Ann Chin has a very grand place in the old depot building downtown, beautifully renovated and sophisticated, furnished with Chinese art. Now Lee Ann has just expanded into the fast food lane and this has sparked Mother's curiosity, her sense of adventure. All around us women at their tables, overhearing their talk, other lives, other kinds, other stories: "Her husband died last year"; "My daughter's new baby"; "They moved out to Anoka"; "Her mother's operation." Family, the web of family and job and place and relatives, the whole world of relatives, distant so long, suddenly so close, so all around me. Even with Laurie, for whom painting has gotten mixed up with her cousin Janey somehow, how Janey spent her inheritance and still doesn't paint and Laurie, having relieved herself finally of real estate, letting the last clients slip away, goes to her new studio and wonders if it will work. "Bring a book, sometimes you just have to spend a certain amount of time there, loaf even, just inhabit that space, it will come," I say as if I knew.

Then there is her own mother's family, recently, almost accidentally discovered. Laurie's mother had in fact discovered this family's existence years ago, herself an orphan born at St. Joseph's Home For Wayward Girls. "Imagine the place," Laurie says. "The name itself a bygone age," I smile. "But listen, my mother went there and bullied the nuns, raised such hell, wouldn't leave, an adult now, no putting her off. And she made them tell her what her own mother's real name was. Way out in Montana. My pregnant grandmother had been sent to St. Paul—the customary trip out of town until it was over with, don't you know. But they still had the records." Laurie flew to Montana with my cousin Jamie. They had already gotten the phone book of this little town, and the second call they made to someone with this surname acknowledged it all. Laurie's own mother and grandmother were both dead by then, but there was an uncle: "My great uncle. Jim and I just met him this year. We spent three days out there. I suddenly acquired a family. Montana people, country people, real nice, warm, friendly."

I think of Gena and Janey and the river compound, not as warm as Montana perhaps, more complicated, off-putting. And haunted after Archie's suicide. Driving home after lunch Mother said she thought Laurie's own mother, Helen, had been a suicide too. This devastated and unsteady woman with two small children whom Janey and I imagined we were "rescuing" during the week after Archie's death. I can hardly remember our sophomoric failure. Did it all end in Helen's eventual suicide? How it keeps going on, the report from Archie's gun still echoing thirty years later. Put to rest for a while by some strangers out west who were friendly to Laurie and gave her comfort. "Not just that, I could feel that they were blood," Laurie insists; Mother joins her in the belief in genes, common faith out here. "The twin studies," Laurie says. "Right here at the University, they've been studying twins for years." "One's schizo, so is the other," I say skeptically.

They ignore me and go on. Around us the talk of babies and marriages and relatives, none of it relative to my life, which is therefore perhaps less real except to me. The artist thing, the queer thing. Can Laurie paint as a businessman's wife with ski trips and visits to Germany and Russia where he does something I don't understand, her grown children now in college? There is no real reason not to, if it's an identity she can live with in this new empty room of hers. I am there and not there, home and not home. So long gone, so foreign; moreover the rules have changed now. So more is possible.

Walking up the seven flights to Skip's loft on Bleecker Street last week it had all been so clear. Why we left, why we had to, what we had to get out of, what we had to come to in order to create this slender little religion. "Just look what I've done to this place over the years; I even got two new windows out of the landlord just this year." The immaculate big white room, painted and painted again, peaceful, perfect for her. "While you got two new windows, the other kids in the class put several children through college," I laugh. They did, and we know it. "And the kids who were born in Manhattan have their own ad agencies," she laughs. "My boyfriend in the eighth grade has been a judge in St. Paul for something like fifteen years now," I tell her. "Yeah, but I'm from a little reservation town in South Dakota. Back there it's the unhappy white people at war with the unhappy Indians. I didn't grow up in St. Paul; little towns in Dakota are real different."

We left all that behind and we got this. And a nice wine and Chinese take-out and a candle and her good glasses and with a little dope we are high on our choice and proceed to think up a book we'll call "Naked In The City". Her pal Shelly will pose, Skip will photograph, I'll write an essay. They have done the first shoot already and the prints are lovely. Here is a great nude before the cityscape, the whole alien concrete landscape defied by her beautiful flesh and somehow as strong in the surprise of the contrast. The nude, which before had only seemed safe in nature in her previous book, *Rising Goddess*, secure only in a world without men and machines, amazons pictured at their ease in a world of their own. Then it came to her: what if one photographed the nude in the city? Say, very early in the morning, before people were out, the city still empty. The idea of woman together with buildings, flesh and brick, cars, trucks, city streets. We never see people, still less women, naked under these circumstances. And for good reason; we asked Jennifer to pose but she thought it was screwball, dangerous. We'll have a car and a raincoat, we'll get by with it, we'll be careful. At our last dinner we thought it up as a show, but why not make a book? It would be a delight to do, who cares if they'll publish it, maybe later sometime; you do it to do it. When Jennifer refused, Skip asked Shelly, who was all for it. Shelly's even got a car. And passersby were not threatening, there is even a shot of Shelly in conversation with some gay guys on the piers. It will be a joint project, we three will be partners. What a pleasure to be alive and living in New York and thinking this stuff up; we'll all have dinner next week and plan it out. "The best time is five in the morning. We'll just have coffee and go." "Five, can you really do five?" Skip asks. And I answer that I really love five, that this hour, especially now with spring coming on, is my happiest time, and I can wake easily, want to get up and do things then, that it is no problem at all. Remembering the early years as an artist here when getting up at all was hard, so hard to keep on believing and doing it.

Thinking of all this in the motel room on the second floor of Mother's building, wanting out, wanting away, wanting back into my loft and my life. Marooned here in Minnesota, an exile at home in nowhere, the place outside this alien room, the Wellington's correctitude, more alien than a foreign country. The wheelchair place today was a little peculiar too. I've taken Mother there, as if it were a gay bar or something equally outrageous from my secret life and we discovered a new contraption called a scooter. Small machinery is making big headway in our world, first ski mobiles and golf carts and then three-wheelers to run over the landscape—dirt bikes and motorcycles were once the wild life, now they have invented scooters for the aged and infirm, shooting right past motorized wheelchairs as complex as computers, as sudden and subtle in the control panel.

But the scooter is something else; we could be just mad and buy one or we could go shopping and pretend we want to buy one and, after learning how they work, rent one for Mother if she could be talked into coming to the Farm for reunion. She could scooter down to the pond, why not, we'd be right there with her? Be responsible. What if she tipped over? Today she's a real sport and lets this guy Dale put her on a scooter whose motor is powered by rechargeable batteries and she's up and down the cracked pavement before the humble offices of Jackson Wheelchair. All the way to the little alley and back, navigating in and out the door, dodging a thousand obstacles in his crowded shop. "You're driving again," I say, remembering how her life stopped when they took her license away after a fender bender where the other party blamed it on Mother's age. The police demanded she take the road test again and she refused because she was afraid. So she sold her car and lost her mobility.

There was also the day she totaled Patrick Henry's beautiful Buick in Farmington, the same day her mother died. Not all that accidentally one suspects, an unconscious protest for the unlived life of Ellen Murray, whose last name is my middle name and whose portrait hangs over my dresser, the Galway farmwife who had eight children, six of whom lived. Ellen Murray didn't seem to get much more out of life than this maternity, I found, when I taped Aunt Mary, Aunt Margaret and mother herself. All of them testify to a shadowy existence caring for children under the great tree of Patrick. As Patrick rose to wealth and prominence, his wife dwindled and was diminished even in the eyes of her children. But her daughters looked back upon her with a certain guilty recall, coming to identify with her as they grew older and saw their own insecure place in the world. Growing up, it had been Patrick's glory they had partaken of in the little town of Farmington.

Does Mother incline toward Patrick Henry or Ellen Murray at this point or both, or has she created herself by now: will she ride a scooter? Should we buy one? She is game and then not game. New, they are $1,400, used $750; worth it if there is somewhere to go. But where would she go at the Wellington? For the Wellington is off in a space by itself. There are no stores, only a bank and a McDonald's nearby, otherwise only miles of private housing. All services are provided by bus, you can go to the Guthrie Theater, the symphony or chamber orchestra, movies, anything so long as you are mobile enough to climb on the bus. But Mother can't anymore and there is nowhere else to go except to Lund's which is too far for the scooter.

Always there is reality. If the scooter were for the Farm we could rent one in Poughkeepsie. So why are we doing this? Why consider it when there is no place to store it, her apartment could not house the thing. Perhaps because two pleasant lesbians have stopped in the store and one of them told how her dad's got one, he's crazy about it, he's all over the trailer park now, it's changed his life. They've come to pay cash for it and pick up the credit card they left while trying it out. Jackson's terms seem pretty friendly.

But Mom doesn't live in a trailer park, a way of life whose advantages I never noticed, stumbling over the limitations of the Wellington at the same moment: the lady-like character of mother's life, its wonderful bourgeois comforts are a kind of obstacle. If she lived in a village, for example, where everything was on one plane and very little traffic—one imagines other configurations and possibilities and then remembers the isolated location of her newly built complex. It is the suburban trap I used to see in my elder sister Sally's early married life, alone with the kids in a tract house while her husband drove the car over to the base to park it and operate an airplane all day, loaded with the atom bomb ready to drop it on Russia for the Strategic Air Command. The husband was mobile and powerful though under orders and discipline and three-hour instrument checks before his ship could leave the ground. But his wife couldn't go out for cigarettes or get a Tootsie Roll on the corner since the nearest store or public place was miles too far to walk and she could not leave her children.

What do you do? You look at the scooter and tell the guy you're going to think about it. And giggle together in the car at the fantasy and then have kind of a hangover at dinner, both of us a little glum and disappointed by all the mobility nearly within reach. In my desperation to bring her back am I forcing her, leading her down impossible paths, playing the adult while really an unreliable child: I can only count on her final judgment since my own seems clouded. We go out to dinner, commanding entrance through the legislated wheelchair accessible entrance which turns out never to be used and has three tables of diners to rearrange in front of the door before it can be opened. The real door is up a steep flight of stairs. They're nice about it.

She's tired. Me too. We don't talk much, we watch the others, a table of women office workers celebrating something, a baby, a resignation, a promotion. Gradual happiness and presents as the wine takes hold and they stop feeling they are in the office. At the other table are the St. Paul intelligentsia; this is Tulips, a new place in the old part of town, gentrified with little black kids passing the windows, children who live uneasily in the houses across the street and could never afford to eat here. One hears the word "book" at the next table, laughing references to Hemingway or a new play; they read, they would be fun to know maybe. Mother seems to think so too, but we don't know them. We only know each other and our relatives. I will try to introduce her to a Vouvray, bragging it up, just the right amount of sweetness, not smoky. The waiter is kind. Another table fills, upscale folk where the office workers were, now talking publishing or something improbable here, big airs of intrigue; by comparison we are locals, awash in provinciality. Behind us a young couple actually talk French and I try not to absent myself by listening to relive the café talk I heard in Paris last January. Mother is beat, can hardly wait for the check. I'm paying but they won't take American Express. How silly; she will have to pay for this only so that I can repay her at home with a check. We are hemmed in here, I feel stasis taking hold of me, feel I am losing.

~

Alone, I go over in my mind, what little I know of her life the years I was away. Mother at Selby Avenue: a life of order and harmony, my first visual impression is of a book or a sweater left on the bottom stair so that it can be brought upstairs by the next person who goes to the second floor. The neatness of that house, its perfection of arrangement, comfort and aesthetic; nothing was broken or out of order. Mother's bedroom and her kitchen, her sitting room, the screened-in porch, the French doors to the balcony, a small house but beautiful in proportion and construction. Inside it her life is conducted with conviction and aplomb. My throat tightens considering it: is it a life of inconceivable emptiness or the greatest serenity and meaning? Absurd questions, questions from my life, not hers. She has raised three children and made a good living selling insurance, starting from nowhere, beginning as a housewife afraid of driving, afraid of the telephone. She has acquired courage and poise and is everywhere admired, actually serves those to whom she sells insurance, is a good agent and an agent for good, a force in her clients' lives ready with advice and connections to whatever they need—a house, a car, friends— her clients many of them women like herself, the first generation into a world that chills and would exclude them. Mother's role is to see that, badly paid as they are, these women will still be provided with an adequate retirement. And in this milieu she is of real use, a person of worth, puttering in her kitchen and coming up with an idea to execute over the phone, as happy putting together A with B as I ever was as an organizer or a friend. This side of her I know, have perhaps inherited through observation.

Not the social life through relatives, however. But what after all are my friends? The bonds of old love affairs have replaced cousins. Cousins are hard to come by far from home, there was only Washburn. So I hold on to lovers. And I made the Farm, circle and after circle, not even lovers now, joined only by an idea and a place. We are supposed to be a contradiction of Mother's world of blood relations and consanguinity. But we are also only a variation, a substitution, an extension by other means. Thought to be an improvement since association is chosen not fated, but in fact often a disappointment since affection is temporary or insufficient and the connection withers and does not last. How will the friends measure up at the end: Mother's kin are still loyal. Steven and cousin Joannie are here every week. The closest friends of her life, cousins Harold and Rosellen, a niece and her husband, seem to see her less now, are themselves getting on and not getting out.

This intimacy of kinship confounds me, the width and breadth of it, the absolute commitment of it, the no holds barred, no secret kept in it, their humor, their loyalty, their pecking order by birth and marriage, their lifelong convictions and attachments, the primacy of this connection over all others, even offspring. The auto trips in summer, the Saturday night movies in winter, the habitual Sunday dinners, the stopping by midweek that fed her life. Was her sustenance and entertainment, her support and consolation. Not her children, certainly not this one, a smart-aleck young artist misbehaving in Manhattan hardly remembering home town or kindred, a harried graduate student trying to get out of Columbia and discovering only how to get fired, then a rabble rouser, finally a nut, the connection with home established again in utter shame: incarceration at my own University's psycho ward and then the sanity trial.

Then someone forgetting, forgetting them all and that any of it ever happened. Not entirely of course, too much like them underneath, too fond, too loyal, aware this was the only family I had and I'd be the loser if I let them go, even as I substituted madly on my own through the Farm, creating families all my life. Even in Japan I organized a circle which was and still is my essential experience of the place. As if this management of support were not only creation but necessity in a life that seemed so hazardous it needed every available safeguard to be survived.

It is the very absence of danger that tightens my throat when I remember Mother's Selby Avenue. Today, when she asked, knowing of course the answer, but curious, checking how I would respond this time: would I ever consider living here, St. Paul? I grin at her and say I need New York. "To charge my battery, Mom." I tried California for a while but after a month or two I felt drained and out of juice, I could feel my motivation leaking out. In New York it's the presence of all the other freaks that keeps you going, it fills the air. There's a charge, a spark, you don't feel silly or pointless like you do everywhere else. This is wrong, of course, elitist, limiting: civilization would be doing art in any place, big or little. But we have narrowed it so and the new America seems to have so little interest or respect beyond its recent habit of turning pictures into investments. Or maybe I am a generation already passing; perhaps they have already solved it out here and go on now doing their work without reference to the big machine that whirls away in my head, the publishers in the capitol, images that enter my dreams and darken my hopes, always at war with success but I am compromised by having given them this much space in my mind. I found I had an editor invading my dream when I woke this morning. Resolving to separate myself further, to write what I liked and to hell with publication. But even this, you see . . . And having left home we are poisoned. Yet had I stayed I might never have flowered. How do they fare now, the natives?

Somehow the image of the house on Selby enters even here, the sense of coming from somewhere, the memory often like a wound, but even that is lost now, torn from me since the place was sold. That sadness and entrapment which the house represented during the years my parents' marriage was coming apart, then the self-sufficiency of the years it was ours alone, the women. Finally it was simply her house and we came home to it welcomed, waited for, longed for while so far away, negligent, distant in our wanderings. When it was to be sold I had a bad summer up at the Farm, even tried to write advertisements for companions to share the house with her. Mother knew better, she knew it was over.

Selby Avenue was there on our drive today and I said to Mother, shall we go past the house? Testing us both. She was wiser: "Not today, not this time." We saw it in the distance, but did not let ourselves see it, this entire segment of our lives, the one we shared. There being a number of Mother's lives—her childhood in Farmington, her married life before Selby, Selby married and unmarried, with and without children, her life alone there. Then the Wellington, this last stage, the house sold and cleaned out—what an achievement that must have been, to dispose of everything even before death. The Wellington must have been, at least at first, a life beyond death, a resurrection, an existence so pared and refined as to be saintly, divine somehow. Mother lived on Selby Avenue for nearly fifty years, from the time I was five until I was fifty something; from the time she was thirty-seven until she was eighty-six years old. In her early eighties, she "redecorated" again with a certain sense of adventure, even humor.

But giving up Selby threatened me, not only my childhood gone and the place to go home to, my room that was no longer there, the lady-like comfort of her bathroom and her real kitchen after decades of lofts and peeling paint, homemade plumbing, the scruff I had chosen, preferred but could always abandon for a while to spend a few days in a real house; there was one real house still. Deeper, it threatened the Farm: would I have to give up the Farm as she was now giving up a tight little house in perfect working order—simply because it was too much work? How much work would that great ramshackle Farm be when I was old, already far too much to care for, barns and houses, and the whole thing only getting bigger, expanding into more houses and studios, the plan. Alone with all that to care for, of course I would fail, and here was Mother's life warning me. Not that I was living her life—always the opposite, my life a deliberate contradiction, a diametrical opposition—but when it came to the end, then . . .

So that in all my estimates and plans I had completely failed to take death and age into account: the end of Selby took on the character of prediction for me. Taken to heart. Solved temporarily with L.K. to manage while I get to write in New York, solved by going further along the appointed road of an art colony, relinquishing it, sharing it more, making it by degrees less and less mine, more and more ours, already artists in residence ten months a year now to run the Farm and do its work. And I sit here in midstream and wonder will it work, can we make it? "Prime of life," Mother says to me, "You are now in the prime of your life." Does she even remember now her own uncertainties then, remembering only her strengths?

The great thing is that she no longer cares for her life that is past, she lives in the present. A thing I have never done exclusively, living in the past and the future just as much as in my latest enthusiasm or love affair. And I seem to have improved upon her ability to worry and to be anxious. Or perhaps she has grown out of those very habits I am convinced I have learned from her, the source of our humor around her, all that we rejected and maintained nevertheless.

That great timidity before life, learned at her side as she went into the world, a frightened woman with three children and now without a husband—she had told him to leave, she would take no more. Her choked and humiliated voice now begging "prospects" for appointments on the phone, while I listened over my school books as the voice faltered and went on, grew strong and even confident, wheedled, sold, succeeded, grew dignified, crowed at times over its "Man of the Year" award. She confided in and made cause with the other women underwriters, planned trips, conferences, delighted in the comradeship and the respect of the men in her line of work, flirted but refused courtship, even rejected marriage offers—there was another one she told me of in the car today, someone who lived only a couple blocks away—she treasured her independence and self-sufficiency too much.

We are different women after all, very different. I have been a slave to love affairs all my life, am in one now of a thoroughly improbable nature. Whereas you, Mother, were vulnerable only once, and then your own woman for a lifetime, relishing your solitude. I used to imagine my life a repetition of your own with merely a change of gender, you were abandoned by my father, and I lived out what I imagined was your fate in being abandoned by one woman after another. Then when I was forty-five you pointed out to me that Dad had not left you, you had ordered him to leave. It made some difference; not enough. Probably it came too late, this revelation, probably I had already established my pattern, my rut in life. Yet perhaps that information coming together with my exhaustion after Sophie will save me after all, may slow down my capacity for repetition; already I find myself forewarned. But I will never achieve your splendid isolation, your reign of competence and self-containment, those decades alone on Selby Avenue.

Twenty years of eating dinner alone, we used to say about A.D., rich and lonely in the big house on the lake, her butler and maid for company, as if it were the fate of money and pride. Then when you came to the

Wellington and had companions at dinner I began to realize you too might have dined alone that long. Seeing you now in company, the cocktail parties all along the hall, the little glasses of white wine and the crackers in wooden bowls, I trembled for what those years may have held. But then I remember that solitude was not your style; there were the relatives and the friends, the clients and the colleagues . . . Yet "when you are eighty not so many people come by," you had said. So you moved in time. You managed loneliness when it became that.

Yet there is still this business of waiting for one's children. You hear it everywhere at the Wellington. My daughter is coming, my son, my niece, my grandson. The words cannot convey the importance, the precious freight of endearment and ego boosting, passed from one to the other, this news of lovers—there is no other word. Like the prestige of a date on Saturday night in a sorority house. And I grind my teeth at the effusion, the fatuity: lives dependent on another's whim, another as careless as I. Of course not, these are dutiful offspring, they have remembered for years, all the intervening years they have come often and stayed long, they have planned trips and vacations.

We went once to Ireland. The years you were able to travel, going out west for a few weeks every winter. Sally went, Joannie went, I never did. Now it is too late to bring you as far as the Farm. Of course I came back to St. Paul every year, but to live a year waiting for some diffident tramp like me to show up—I look at the happy aged faces beaming in anticipation on the elevator, beaming that Sue is coming from Seattle or Donald from Wisconsin and I think of the tyranny of this love, its hideous inequity, to have given so much to get this pittance back, maybe. When they feel like it, when their budget allows them a ticket, when they can bother to find the time from work, when their own children can spare them, when it occurs to them, when the one who loves them so slavishly is really ill or old. Then maybe they condescend as I have, when scared enough. How unfair is life, what a rip off it is to parent, how foolishly one-sided, this single disinterested and unselfish, this unique case of altruism in love. They have given their all, and get only this news of some messianic arrival in return.

There are moments in the elevator when I wonder—and hope—that it's all a put-on; imagining that they are only raving over a visit to someone like Mother who has a visitor when really they are doing swell without us; we just break up the routine, we are merely amusement or diversion to their own superior social life. Hoping they only pretend such pleasure out of piety to the reigning religion of family, contented agnostics every one of them. Terrified of the evident truth. Having myself escaped this trap. Or so I imagine, that in having had no children I have got off scot-free. No such thing of course; I have simply gone my own way into the emptiness of life, a teacher's way, not a parent's—there being two, and I have chosen the lesser one. Less sacrifice, less reward. The Farm has been peopled with generations of women who don't come home, don't come back, never show up again or rarely, and are waited for with a similarly unrequited love, fatuous affection. Another dead end, only more obviously so. The new order has created less hypocrisy and therefore smaller demonstrations, lesser rewards, more tenuous bonds, shorter associations. What was intended to be more sincere is only less obliged. The void extends before me.

~

It was in the museum too. Looking at pictures with an old woman in a wheelchair is looking at them in an entirely different light. They did not hold up well. Right off I remember Picasso's jester, a sculpture, not even a painting but so pictorial it might be either sentimental or an ultimate humanism, you try to explain it to yourself while trying to explain it to her. Or the Bonnard which is surely rich, but perhaps too sensuous, too French in its interior light, its flesh—how forgotten now as she sees it, how never known perhaps. But coming into their room once I was electrified by the sexuality of my parents, or rather her passion for him, she had been on his lap. That was fifty years ago.

Try color, try Feininger trying color and it becomes a blur. A few things hold up, but I nearly wept looking around the room at the Walker's permanent collection. At all that was suddenly incomprehensible, still resolved that this mystery must end. Mother so herself obliquely: "Victoria should see these things when she is still young," thinking of her great grandchild who has just been born. Mother had brought me up on books, pictures were a foreign world to her. It is a kind of illiteracy and she feels it is too late to begin. "But just look," I say, looking with her but seeing very little. Pretensions, secrets, paintings about painting, prettiness, trifling, skill at portrayal, or evasion of it. The pleasure which pictures are to me, the sheer pleasure of seeing, that I cannot communicate because I don't know how to convey it, foreign and too illusive to translate in such a short time. Explanations and thumb-nail history cannot give the experience of sensuality, the delight I had meant to share. The richness of color and light drunk through the eyes. I look around and the paintings are drained and I feel an enormous despair.

The avant-garde exhibition was predictably absurd and yet less so than I might have imagined, the things there closed and mysterious but interesting at the same time, the ingenuity of them, the effrontery, the curiosity of experiment, walls of rocks, enormous Jim Dine hammers welded together whimsically. Some woman who attached a number of canvases down the length of a high wall and permitted a machine to spatter paint at them; for once I was as amused as Mother, both of us puzzled as well.

One expects the masters to work however, and it was there that I felt the greatest shock of incomprehension. These pictures, old friends since college, the work of her own time, her life has coincided with their coming into being, but they were never part of her experience. I felt a great discouragement as if I had invented their value and importance and now saw it questioned, heard a language I imagined everyone spoke, but then discovered it could be incoherent. All along they were out there, *Life* or *Newsweek* bringing the news to Minnesota, usually in the form of fashion or fraud or auction prices, the Walker and the Art Institute gathering their examples. Aunt Dorothy's collection went to them.

Mother loved books, paintings belonged to rich people. Near us a fur-coated lady who's really "up on it all" is telling another that Robert Indiana did not fulfill his early promise and that her favorite Roy Lichtenstein is the piece that's out in front of the building rather than this one. For the thousandth time I want to explain to my mother through tears and with passion that art is not this snobbery, not even her sister-in-law's world of wealth and connoisseurship, that it is something utterly different to artists, that pictures are like ice cream to us, or fresh air, that they are living souls, that we visit them to feed the spirit. We are not civic-minded climbers, we don't give a damn about keeping up; the pretentious temple aspect of these places makes us furious.

The Walker's featured exhibition this month is a great glossy fellow from Italy, hot from Los Angeles and Amsterdam filling two floors with curatorial fad. We head for the permanent collection but even the standard twentieth-century stuff is something Mother has never looked at. She marvels that I know the painter and the picture without checking the labels. I marvel myself and check anyway. I have met a number of abstract expressionists, can I interest her by saying I know them; will she like Noguchi's piece if I tell her a story about a dinner party? Wincing to notice that the date of his death has already been recorded, suddenly grateful he came to my shows, remorseful I never had the courage or the wit to go out to Long Island City to see him in his old age. But still the Maillot, the Mondrian, the Picasso, the cubists, the dadaists, the surrealists—the meat and potatoes—that remain strange to her, unfamiliar, inexplicable. For me it is a cathedral aisle through history, undertaken like a prayer. To her it may be mumbo jumbo, artifice, trumpery, icons without a creed. It is a great sorrowful space between us I am trying to fill as the devout never cease to proselytize.

Yet she sees everything fresh in her way, and is surprisingly open to the present, just as she tolerated the far out stuff on the top floor, she seems to transcend any need for background and to jump right into the present in certain cases. George Segal's diner sculpture worked for both of us and we spent a long time in its aura. Mark Di Suvero's collection of beautiful junk worked because I told her the story of his accident, how he had so filled the freight elevator in his loft building with his pieces when bringing them joyfully to his first exhibition that he decided to ride down on top of the elevator box. Then someone pressed the wrong button, the up button, and crushed him, destroying his legs for two years while he went among us like a saint or hero, fighting to recover their use until he had succeeded and went on. I will her to understand his gallantry and whimsy in a playground piece that moves, that insists it be enjoyed. She is fascinated by Hopper's painting of a businessman and his secretary working in the office after hours. Things take her fancy for themselves, out of context, without expectations, without the faith itself; it is to visit Christianity with a Moslem, it is strange.

The last time I visited the Walker I went with Janey Winter, a painter from the Farm. We romped in the place, pious or familiar or sardonic. It was within a shared system, enjoying the sun in the cafeteria as much as our conversation with the pictures and each other. But today we have only energy for the pictures themselves, asking a guard to ride with Mother to the one wheelchair inaccessible floor, while I walked the staircase. Then I just gave up, knowing I had tired her and she had nothing left for tea-time chatter. On the way back to the car we stopped to see the greenhouse, a sculpture of gardenias where a fashion shoot was going on at the command of a lady in an electric wheelchair, complex instruments at her fingertips; I could feel Mother deciding it was too complicated.

At breakfast the next morning she delivered her ultimatum: the wheelchair must go. Were she to use it regularly she would lose what use of her legs she still has left. I agree entirely in principle, have already come to the same conclusion. But I want to hold on to it for outings, for museums, deliberately refusing to understand that she is telling me that museums are not that interesting. I almost surrender, but not quite. Trying again the next day after lunch downtown at the St. Paul hotel with Steven, pushing her literally toward a small and familiar collection—drawings, nudes, the intimate—there is hardly even a guard, just a young girl who follows us at a distance, visitors are fairly rare.

There are also oriental things, an exhibition of Chinese and Japanese things. I show her how they are done, how the brush with only a stroke or two creates a mountain, the lone tree, the great distances and heights of these imagined realms of spirit, urging a color or a nuance, costume or mood. Getting somewhere. And then a great picture surprises us as we leave, my own uncle Jerome Hill, they have a very good one and large, a splendid scene with a heroic striped dress commanding the picture. It is ours, it is one of us. But no, it is not hers, it is the world of her sister-in-law, A.D., the Hills, the other side of the family, not her side. And she will not take credit. We go home.

~

I wake remembering cancer. She had cancer, breast cancer, a double mastectomy, but that was years ago. How many? Is it still a threat? Is it lurking somewhere still about to strike somewhere else? How susceptible am I to cancer, how hereditary is the predisposition? For months and even years now I have been living in the shadow of death by AIDS. Reading about it in novels, seeing it in films, hearing it in conversation. If you are gay you think of it and dread it, it is destroying your generation, decimating your community. Yet everywhere women today are saying that breast cancer kills more people than AIDS, that it's the leading killer of women in America. My own friends are getting cancer, being mutilated by surgeons in the hope of saving their lives. Sally lectured me into a mammogram last fall, because we are, as Mother's daughters, at a higher risk through her cancer than is normal for our age or nationality. I tested negative and was relieved; Sally now says we must do it every year.

But with Mother's first cancer scare we thought we were well out of the woods; her surgeon, a friend and client of hers, actually ran out of his operating room and into the waiting room, still clothed in his little green surgery suit and vinyl gloves to tell me the instant he was sure that this biopsy had only produced benign tissue. It was ten years more until the double mastectomy, perhaps another ten years ago by now.

She was scared. Both times. Deeply scared, not just the worry-wart habit, the hand-wringing anxiety of a lifetime. This was fear for life itself, fear of death. Distant again after the first brush, Mother's biopsy; following it a great sense of confidence came over us all. So that the final verdict, that the cancer had recurred, resurfaced and was now, though still operable, aimed right for her life, came at us hard. She was brave about the surgery, sensible, but she cringed at the loss of her breasts. I remember standing in her immaculate room, its French doors open to early summer, her geraniums perfectly in place on her balcony, the room overlooking a playing field and a fine prospect of distance and summer breezes, warm and tight in winter, curtained and draped and snug. We stood in the center of the room, between her easy chair and the chaste single bed which had replaced what the Italians call a marriage bed, the double bed of her sexual life (the cradle of mine; I had lost my lesbian virginity there to a classmate at convent school while mother was away at a conference; her business trips were the highlights of my adolescence).

Mother stood naked from her bath, a habit of hers, being frank about her body with her daughters, always bringing us in to chat during her baths, carrying on conversations from our rooms to hers while she dressed, or bringing us into her room at such moments, and this was one of them. It was a small old woman's body, the skin smooth and very fair, slender and well preserved, without fat or slack still—it still is—just a little hint of a belly, tiny, attractive. But her breasts are small, always have been. She has always pointed out to us that we nursed at them, that we left her somewhat depleted and with enlarged nipples, but that she enjoyed the experience. Nevertheless, her breasts were probably her least effective feature, and she has always supplemented them with what we have casually (being ourselves, two of the three of us, well endowed) referred to as Mom's falsies, her dainty slightly padded brassieres. The bullying secular humor of a younger generation. Looking first at her breasts, then looking me straight in the eye, "They're not beautiful, but they are mine."

For the biopsy I swallowed hard tears and kept up her spirits, took her out to dinner at the Lex before delivering her to the hospital and the knife. For the final surgery, we were all there and we were very serious. When it was over, she of course worked it into a story because this is required among us though only I ever write them down. We are all of us engaged in an ongoing contest, but the others all talk faster, better and louder than I, so that friends of mine who know me as a writer, seeing us together conclude that I am talked over and shabbily treated by my kin. What they fail to understand is that on a level playing field against this kind of competition, I am merely the "dumbest one in the smart group," an inversion of my first categorization at our parochial grade school from whence I returned to inform my mothers and sisters that I was the smartest one in the dumb group, a statement they have never permitted me to forget.

Stories are how we deal with things, the four of us, how we conquer our experience for ourselves, for each other and for everyone who will listen to us, so Mother concluded her account of her ordeal with the brag that she now had fewer cancer cells than anyone else she knows, that she was, "in the cancer department," as "clean as a whistle."

A brave little figure making another pronouncement with her characteristic folk authority, the sort of statement which her daughters and other relatives and friends repeat or parody, admiration behind our amusement at her dicta: "If you can't pay cash, you can't afford it," "Handy as a pocket on a shirt," "Old as when God was a tree"—Mother Millettisms, coined or maybe even repeated through generations of Galway oral tradition, words echoed from the mists of time, race memory for all we know. We think they are funny because the succinct delights us in and of and for itself and represents wit to us. Wit being a thing we adore as fervently as any eighteenth-century savant, persons whose values, enjoyment and point of view are still fresh and immediate, homely and familiar to us, an affinity which sets us apart from the here and now. Which it is our chief amusement to deplore.

It is impossible to think of Mother apart from her stature, the determined diminutive body, the erect back, the balanced head and shoulders, the willed courage and dignity of this small nearly child-sized mass. She is less than five feet tall. My father was over six feet. The contrast was always before us. At eighty-eight she is smaller still, shrunken a bit, the posture finally slightly imperfect, particularly when she stands and walks, leaning on the walker, this new and grotesque but so necessary and so essential part of her life.

Much of Helen Feely Millett's life has been a triumph over her size and type: to command respect despite it, weight and authority in contradiction to it. And in contrast to her type as well, for among women she is unmistakably, irrevocably feminine, even lady-like; a "little woman," it must have been hell for her to establish credibility for herself as a business woman. But there was her invincible sincerity—she actually believed she was assisting people to plan, to save, to survive—herself a woman thrown upon her own resources in a hard world for a woman of forty, with three daughters to support, refusing help from her husband's wealthy relatives, ruling out the possibility of it altogether once she had asked them for referrals, the names of friends who might consider buying insurance, and had been snubbed. After that she didn't want a dime, no matter how frequently or fervently money was offered, money which my Aunt Dorothy, in particular, really didn't mind parting with in the least. She had millions and these kids were her nieces, but her friends were also her friends and she did not want them harassed by a sister-in-law she had always imagined beneath her who might now embarrass her by importuning her aristocratic chums.

Family wars are so often class wars. My father was a true democrat, son of a railroad timekeeper, fatherless in his childhood and orphaned by his mother's death. It was decided among the surviving band of youngsters that the elder brother Harry was to have the insurance money to go to law school. Harry never quite carried through with this, at least not as far as the bar exam; in a number of pleasant St. Paul restaurants and gentlemanly bars Harry dispensed a good deal of free legal advice, an undetermined amount of support for Irish Republican radicalism and literature, vast amounts of charm and a prodigious ability as a raconteur. But even later in life, sponsored by his younger sister Dorothy in a second attempt at the examinations, he found he really lacked the interest and so lived a genteel life at her expense with occasional forays into commercial representation of a quite undemanding nature. Harry talked, that was enough; his talk was an art form and recognized as such. Mother, who found him pompous at times, raffish at others, revered him as an artist always; she'd taught drama and respected a master. She saw to it that none of us moved a muscle during his after-dinner performances. Whether comic or political, they were always vaguely scandalous, secular and possibly dangerously sexual as well as seditious and heretical, but you suspended judgment before greatness.

Observing the results of Harry's use of masculine privilege, my father, always his three sisters' favorite, and with reason, took a tough and menial job with the highway department; from this base he then sent these women to college. They never forgot it. He found he learned well on his own and through the apprentice system, rising from road worker to draftsman and finally, with no formal education beyond Hastings high school, he sat for the examination in civil engineering and passed it. His sisters were clever women and great beauties, he was their favorite companion, they all went dancing and showed off together. I cannot imagine it possible that the Milletts ever had more fun with other people, if as much, as they had with each other. Their happiness together, their capacity for the celebration of life as a party, has set a standard for me, an ideal I have only matched a few times; all too often I have watched life wasted. A waste of joy, the potential joy people throw away so casually, stupidly, irresponsibly.

At the Farm I have tried to recapture their bliss, even succeeded at times. Their parties were remarkable and hilarious events that went on for days at a time and varied between long serious discussions and debates to evenings when everyone drank and danced and, at peak moments, performed comic fantasy while dressed up in curtains and lamp shades, the family like a club or circle of friends who were only enriched by the eventual addition of the sisters' husbands, my wonderful uncles. Harry never married. The Millett sisters married spectacularly: Dorothy married the Hill fortune in marrying Louis Junior, the grandson of the "empire builder" Jim Hill the railroad baron of the Great Northern and Northern Pacific, the very road her father had served till his death. Later, Louis had the bad manners to divorce her, whereby she became a divorcee, then a new and risky career, but she entered upon it with a $1 million settlement, which over time she carefully and cleverly expanded to become the $11 million she bestowed upon local cultural institutions in her will: the Guthrie, the Minnesota Symphony and the Minneapolis Institute of Fine Arts. I myself inherited $25,000, the same sum she left her maid and butler who were probably far more satisfactory than I was. I have saved every cent of my legacy, at least of its principal, in the hope of buying my studio as part of a mutual housing cooperative deal with the city engaged in by my entire neighborhood in Cooper Square over a 25-year period of negotiation.

My aunt the patron, who collected art but never quite approved of artists, and never wanted one for a niece, might be nailing down a piece of the rock that guarantees I can be a New York artist forever: I hope she has reconsidered her position. I, on the other hand, have had over thirty years to repent of lying to her that I went alone to Oxford for two years of study abroad which she financed for me after my graduation from college; I went instead with a lesbian lover. My adored Aunt, who was also my first love, detested this lover with a special ardor which seems to have transcended predictable St. Paul respectability and the terrible anathema of lesbianism. Aunt Dorothy, who dominated us all through our infatuation with her beauty and cleverness, her charm and sophistication, her sense of fun, naughtiness and humor, her temperament and her affection, will o' the wisp and absent-minded as it was in one so romantically rich and highly placed, and finally through all that she knew, for she was a private scholar with a large library and access to certain miracles such as the fine arts and music, things unknown at home where the only value was books and talk . . . my Aunt Dorothy, whom I worshipped, had one lunch with my lesbian lover and declared, "That woman dominates you."

She wasn't far from the mark; "that woman" deceived and betrayed me a few years later, carrying on behind my back while I went off to teach college English at my first job in order to support her and her "friend" while one wrote a book and the other painted pictures. At the moment I was being dumped by my lesbian lover, my Aunt, whom I had loved far longer and with even greater conviction, discovered my deception in not having broken with the lover three years before when she, unfairly but with great clarity, made my giving up this lover a condition for the chance at Oxford she had offered me, at first without conditions. Deceived and lied to myself, I was caught in my own lie, losing one I had loved well and faithfully, sacrificed my own family for, forsworn my childhood's idol for—lost my Aunt Dorothy. All in the same season. Dorothy never forgave me, she died without forgiving me. All these years later I wonder why I didn't just tell her that the lover turned out to be an error and that she was right all along—but that would have been too easy. I had been caught in a lie, in dishonor. A Millett myself, I imagined I knew how they felt about honor.

Now I like to imagine that she would be pleased to have given me a roof over my head in my old age, even if I make art under it. In fact I reinvented her in a book after her death and she turned young again, beautiful—no, she was always beautiful—but she was democratic now too, funny without being snide, her anger and disappointment were gone as well, she was a beauty being brought yellow tulips by her gardener, but I was there as well, had never failed her, was her favorite again. These fantasies had an erotic tinge, admittedly, but their real achievement was resolution, good humored friendship between grown women: at last. In real life my aunt's love for me was chaste, however jealous. Mine, on the other hand, was never anything but a passion, however ignorant, a passion that ruled much of my life from age five, which is as far back as I can remember. I came to consciousness in love with her, and it never went away, its summit a deep kiss the Christmas Eve when I was eleven, my first experience of going under to the drug of eros. I knew nothing and felt everything and I was not afraid. Only discreet, aware I could not follow this further: did she mean anything by it, had she only had too much champagne, did I imagine it all? But I was sure, complicit and protective, that no one should see. Not Uncle Harry, not Uncle Walter, her second husband—no one should know what I knew. And for this I must shield her, be more circumspect than she, guard her honor. All this folderol from someone eleven, instantly savvy, a cavalier and conspirator of love. When I got to college courtly love was as familiar to me as an old sweater, my bones and marrow and culture and heritage; the convent and the court of a great lady had raised me in that road.

Of course there was Mother, my other teacher and far greater influence; juggling the two lesson-givers was confusing at times; I have been torn all my life between two families, clans and classes, even two different peoples.

So I live in a derelict building and have Persian rugs I was smart enough to get cheap. Sitting up on the roof of my loft the other night, looking over my slum along the lovely curved, even tree-lined (who would believe it? but it's true) boulevard of the Bowery and across the low tenement buildings of the lower east side, the last hold-out of affordable housing, the last buildings low enough to let in sunlight so you can write books and paint pictures or just raise kids and pay the rent, I figured my Aunt had got her money's worth by investing $7,000 to send me to Oxford.

I'm giving her value, far better than those nitwit curators and administrative personnel at the cultural foundations where she dropped her cash; they've eaten it all up in salaries by now. Rich kids who majored in art history and keep the market up for their class who buy art as if pictures were stocks and bonds. Even if a few bucks might have slipped through the bureaucrats' fingers and landed on the plate of some society composer, you can be sure no real painter or sculptor ever got a cent of her money. So I run an art colony and distribute support on a shoestring, because I hate to see money wasted and I earn mine harder than she did. That being the case I am sorry if she were to be displeased to land me a studio at last; I'll be sixty when it happens. I expect she wouldn't mind at all to see her legacy pay off this way. I'll be home at last, a studio I cannot be evicted from under the thirty-day lease I have held for fifteen years, afraid each day's mail would order me to leave. So if the dream comes true, I expect she'd see it as a "real deal" as we say at home, imitating our own dialect. Under this arrangement, so long in coming, the several hundred families who survive in ruined city tenements in Cooper Square and the maybe twenty artists living in derelict lofts will, in a few years, if there isn't a hitch or a new administration etc., get the place fixed up and deeded to a co-operative they have spent all these years working to form, fighting city hall, demonstrating, holding the line against rich developers and other sleaze, holding the roof up with blood, sweat and tears and saving precious building stock.

The city gets a real deal too: it gets rid of its ruined buildings received in lieu of taxes years ago by bad landlords. And then these buildings will be back on the tax rolls again. Perhaps best of all, it gets to brag that it is supporting low-income housing, since it was too stingy and is now too "poor" to create very much of that itself. Mayor Koch handed the town over to the speculators and under Denkins New York was broke. I belonged to my neighborhood association twenty-five years and have been an officer (vice-chair of the artists' committee) for five of them, sacrificing what seems a million Wednesday evenings to our long torturous meetings; they are good folk and great fighters and we beat city hall time after time. Maybe we'll win in the end.

Whether we do or not, I'm to be the loser: our building alone in the neighborhood is the one structure that cannot be saved though it is in terrific shape and is five full floors of studio space that will never be replaced. The idiocy of the market, in which my comrades concur, dictates that it be destroyed, it is valuable frontage on a big avenue, surrounded by empty lots, combine it all and you can build big and house many. Soon I and my neighbors at 295 Bowery are supposed to be relocated, moved down the street to another derelict building they say is to be rehabilitated for us—at least to be given a staircase and a roof: A.D.'s legacy might establish me in the co-op since I am a title-vested tenant who has lived here for fifteen years with a city lease. So I'm being bullied to move, leave the home I built. When I got this place it didn't have heat or even windows, just tin nailed to the openings. Of course, no kitchen, no bath. I gave it plumbing, rewired it, painted it, sanded the floor, built bookcases and put in fireplaces. I guess I'll never get the greenhouse on the balcony. The idea of moving all those thousands of books, floor to ceiling bookcases, makes me dizzy. Moving will consume an entire season in town. It will be a year without writing. I'm promised a mover but it's tough to lose a year's income. And the home I made with my own hands has to go.

Logistics and real estate values require we be a sacrifice for the majority;

the tenements will be repaired with what the city makes selling the land under this house to builders. My neighbors in this building and I fought like hell for years to save it, we still hope something will intervene and preserve this structure. I have defended it at a hundred meetings already, trembling but swearing I would not leave and let a good studio building be razed. When I look down the boulevard—I will of course still live on the Bowery, it will be my third studio on this sacred street of misery and sorrow, I would never live anywhere else in the world—I try to imagine the studio where I will die.

Of course I will never own it, the whole thing is a socialist co-operative, one of the first American experiments, we are New York's pilot project. I will own neither the building nor my loft or the land under it. But I can stay there till I die and do not need to live in terror of eviction. Though I will be supervised a hell of a lot more than I like, harassed about my improvements and the code and so forth, and will probably still be dragged to endless meetings, the usual price of self-government.

So you see, Aunt Dorothy, it is not your kind of thing, this is not a millionaire's solution to anything. No more than the Farm. More Mother's kind of thing, though very far from Patrick Henry's hard earned success in Farmington, it is probably better than the Sunday afternoon meetings where the sisters learned from their brothers that there was no dividend again. It's a new order; plenty of times it sickens the anarchist individual in me who is plenty scared our socialism is really a polite fascism with committees to spy on everybody and everything and in the end we form just one more bloody bureaucracy where outsiders get salaries for bossing us around and providing us with shabby maintenance. I can't sell my loft—they're paranoid on this issue—but of course I wouldn't want to. The rent will be cheap so I'd have to be crazy to sell since I could never make it in the real world of market rents, would have to give up New York and live at the Farm. My whole desire is to have shelter and be left alone in it. When I die, unless they permit me an heir, who would have to be another artist, the studio goes back to the co-operative who will award it to an artist. Good enough, these are precious things, studio lofts, and must be preserved for the uses of art.

The building they have in mind for us has no view like mine, less light, is crammed between others, claustrophobic, no grand prospect as from this roof, no sense of being high and alone as this building has, this commanding view so rare in New York, 360 degrees above the city. Sit here and watch the lights come on in New York and drink a martini and you think you own the town. I will be hemmed in, but never mind, I will make a garden on the roof and cultivate it, grow old in some security and possible safety, no more thirty-day lease, no more imminent eviction. If they keep their word. Meanwhile your dough is in the bank. They mailed me a statement today that says we have $1,600 in interest—we always cream off the interest remember, and leave the principle. So dear patron, shall we fix the convertible or the tractor, or go to Europe in the fall? We can mull it over in perfect serenity all summer, the certificate of deposit won't roll over till the end of July and by that time we will have contemplated it for many happy hours and perhaps even a few cigarettes. Here's looking at you, schlante.

~

Upstairs, in Mother's apartment, washing glasses this morning, I thought of cocktail parties, summertime, the happiness of alcohol and chat, all the varieties of persons and moods. Other ways to live and feel: there are so many. Longing for them, feeling trapped by the place, the reason that I read when I am here, escaping from it. And then stand in the kitchen, nearly desperate with emptiness, some absence of curiosity, delight, variety, straining after another way to live, my Millett side hungry for the relish of life. I conveyed this to Sally over the phone as I watch the late April snow fall still; we are planning how her next visit will overlap with mine. Much as we want to stretch out our occasions with Mother so that one of us is always on relay, we have not seen each other for a long time and miss each other, could use one overlapping day of respite and support.

Back at the sink I remember St. Paul, living here: there was always here and there, my own there, the ones I made or found everywhere else but here. And came back to proselytize for nuance, for the pleasure of life. Mainlining it downstairs through reading about other places since the crack of dawn. Then Mother does something unusual: she asks me what I am thinking. Mother, whose attention always seems focused on avoiding feeling or introspection or intimate communication of any kind, obsessed with the details of the table, ordering me to get the sugar or the cream or the orange juice. Eager then to have the table cleared even before breakfast is over, inviting me at once into the oblivion of the newspaper and fragmentary comments on the slaughter of the Kurds. To my astonishment Mother looks up and asks after my thought, as if reaching into my heart.

I take her up on it, saying we should do something special. We decide on a private feast and an expedition to Lund's to buy the fixings, then I will make her a great lobster dinner and we will watch the Twins' opening ball game on television together: we will have a party.

The wonderful thing is that it worked. We stand by the lobster tank choosing; the sky's the limit, give us the biggest you've got, feeling her excitement beside me, aware of how rare the occasion must be in her life, she who adores lobster and has lived her whole life in a place where you can't get it—not till Lund's. We have shopped like madwomen, astute in the baking goods, ravenous in the fresh produce sections, circumspect through miles of canned goods and snacks, explosive in dairy. I am painfully aware of how rare and precious real shopping is now, real cooking at home, real gourmet indulgence. This is to be a night away from the catered spaghetti, the planned menu which is repeated week after week, the "mixed vegetables" out of a can which everyone at her table heartily detests. We will do fresh asparagus, a real salad, not the chopped iceberg lettuce of the Wellington, only the loveliest things in the store will be ours. I will serenade her with food.

I look around the kitchen as I begin, almost in stage fright—does she really have anything big enough to do these lobsters, the right thing for asparagus—good, an old iron frying pan. The old skillet from Selby has come with her here, even its lid, the best thing of all: lay them down in boiling water, give them the least possible time. Have I overdone it by buying this shrimp for an hors d'oeuvre? Much as she adores good food, she can't eat very much. I tell her that de Beauvoir couldn't either in her old age, but insisted on ordering things she loved, even if she only tasted one bite. We laugh and are serene and full of expectations. Mother is in the living room, resting, I am totally in charge in the kitchen fondly bringing water to boil in the one huge pot and in the old skillet as well. How many times it gave me Mother's exquisite fricassee of chicken, tender, flaky, gravied. This old iron skillet cooked every piece of bacon I ever ate the first twenty-two years of my life: Dad caught me doing up an entire half pound of it once, alone. I explained I had never had enough bacon in my life and was on a splurge. He approved the idea and encouraged me.

Tonight we are almost that reckless, or rather Mother has let go somewhere; me too. Because our depression is a mutual event, our distemper too, a despair we enter into together and now have escaped from temporarily. Tomorrow I will say something wrong downstairs at dinner, she will want to listen to the radio and I will want to watch a documentary on black history on the television or a foreign film and try to get her to enjoy some footage of Paris and she will resist. And even though I will find a way to make the radio work and even teach her how to operate it, "saving the day" as she puts it, we will be disgruntled again or at odds. But not tonight, tonight is magic, the lobster is perfect, she loves her party.

I even love the game. I used to go out to opening day when the team was the St. Paul Saints, had my first experience of claustrophobia in an opening game crowd emerging from the stadium, but that didn't stop me.

I had little jobs and pocket money and took myself out to the ball game often in early adolescence, even on school days. Baseball and Hollywood spectaculars and Biblical epics with advertised sex appeal were an alternative to parochial school and later to my convent high school: you forge an excuse from home if one is required. For several years I never missed a game on the radio, studied to the sound of Bill Sterne's voice announcing the game and advertising Gillette razor blades, knew averages and figures, made a fetish of them. Then one day it simply wore off.

Mother found baseball tedious and silly then. But in the last ten years she has become a fan, which is curious; my Aunt Dorothy became one too, still more curious in such a scholarly lady, such a snob. The owner's wife was her best friend, which might account for an interest. Mother has no such excuse, but her enthusiasm is amazing and genuine. She knows every player, all the averages, has pets, is madly in love with a plump black man named Kirby Puckett whom she has followed for years. Kirby plays a large part in Mother's life during the season; he has done himself proud tonight. So has a fellow named Hreblok, another of her darlings and a pitcher named Kevin Tepani who now has a shut-out to his credit. It's a great opening game, we are thoroughly satisfied, just enough excitement, no real anxiety. The Twins won handily and can look forward to a good season.

I have found her weakness and begin to fantasize about taking her out to the ball game. "Oh, I'm not up to that, I'm afraid," she demurs. "All wheelchair accessible, I'll bet, Mom." "Do you really think so?" "It's the law now, Mom." "Well, maybe . . ." There's a lift in her voice—how wonderful to feel her yearning towards life and experience instead of shrinking back and shutting it off. Museums may not be worth the loss of reputation involved in wheelchair use; they have offered no real temptation to just sit back and ride while being escorted into the grander world, but baseball is something else. Last time, Dale mentioned that he had a lightweight model; I'll pin it down for my next visit. The Twins are away for the rest of my week here, I pray they play at home on my next visit.

I'll surprise her with tickets, I'll arrive with a lightweight chair, I'll be irresistible.

Our evening together was perfect, she was really happy, so was I. And tomorrow we get out of the apartment and go to the St. Croix to Laurie and Jim's wonderful house at Marine; I haven't seen it for nearly twenty years: once I was going to buy the land opposite and be their neighbor . . . before the rupture. Going there tomorrow will heal everything.

~

But in the morning Jim calls to say that Laurie's new relative, the uncle in Montana whom they had just met out there, the man who had befriended them and given her this strange new gift of family, had died during the night. Laurie is flying to Helena for the funeral. She won't be there, he'd be happy if we came out but it is a grim day, they expect more snow, rain anyway. It's raining now. I realize Jim is leaving for Germany again tomorrow; his son Tod, on his way west to graduate school, is home only one day. He has too much to do to entertain us alone. We agree on the next time.

And then I panic, a whole day before us with nothing to do. A rainy Sunday in St. Paul, penned up in this apartment. I leave tomorrow morning, today's my last day here, I must come up with something. I scramble for ideas. Como Park gardens? Not on a day like this. A drive to Stillwater? Forget it. How about Cousin Joannie? No. Joannie the stalwart doesn't answer for an hour (church, I figure) but when she does, she is adamant; today's her day to get her chores done. Mother is composed, she loves to stay home, prefers it. I realize I am the caged animal, the out-of-towner to be entertained, frantic with the tedium before me.

But you came to see her—why the hell don't you do it? You came to talk to her, talk then. If she won't talk, just "be" with her, "visit" with her, to use her term, a process whereby one reads the paper or a book or watches television, and makes occasional statements as the thought occurs, such as "I wonder how Cousin Jean Ann is, Mig said she had to go into the hospital for a few days for her heart," or "I'm so glad you figured out how the radio works," or "Steven is just insane about that new baby." This kind of low-key absent-minded talk, an evasion of conversation is Mother's style now; it suits her withdrawal into old age. Perhaps it was always what she preferred; these days it may be what she requires. To push her further into operatics of emotion before the approach of death, to deal in this-may-be-the-last-time-we-see-each-other, soul-baring, confrontations with the past, or the real dope about Dad, or any expressed acknowledgment that time is short or will ever end, beyond her own measured references to heirlooms, seems in the context of a day spent "visiting" to be oppressive, intrusive, even "crazy."

We manage to have some real conversation anyway, Mother in her armchair, I at her feet or in front of her on a hassock, close enough so that she can hear—since the deafness militates against the effort of serious expression because one has to repeat everything. Yet even before this deafness she used to make me repeat everything, claiming I mumbled; even then it was a strategy to maintain distance and prevent the intimacy I might ask for or defuse the sort of thing I might say. Even then emotion and enthusiasm was deflated and eventually evaporated in the process.

I talk to her about AIDS and White's short story, "The Darker Proof," which I was reading this morning, the world she reads about in the papers now. One of the ladies at the next table, who had lived in Provincetown till recently, actually mentioned it the night before at dinner, a world far away from the Wellington, where death has another face altogether. We venture near death, but it is Mother who consoles me for her death, the death coming which is hers, not mine. Mine are the tears, hers the stoicism, even the kindness. She is simply glad I am there, I don't need to do anything; she is merely comforted by my presence, "just being here," she says, wiser than I, carrying on that impression of normality she has made a lifetime's accomplishment, that serene surface of sofas and magazines and seemingly random remarks that punctuate making tea or "putting things away," a life where if you are going out for dinner at six you begin to get ready at five, having discussed your bath and what you'll wear since 4.30 or so.

It is as if in being the center it were her role to be the hostess with perfect manners keeping a sense of face among her three tempestuous daughters, women she had raised with a great sense of self, conveying to us, out of the emergency of her divorce and the desperation that followed, a time wherein she created a new woman's life with great difficulty and success in business, that we should study hard and "be somebody." She then found that we had nearly overdone it, so there was a "calm down" and "be lady-like" message that was somewhat at odds with the first and which we generally chose to ignore. We have so galloped away with life that when we come home, too full of urgency, it is her place still to try to keep us within bounds, thwart our passions, soothe us into the right sort of small talk, only rarely giving us a glimpse of the deeper issues of life, work or survival.

Finally, we seem to have gotten into tune with each other this afternoon, doing little things, "visiting" over small services: I cut her fingernails, since her hands have trouble with scissors now. There is something irrevocably tender about this, my hands awkward too, because I have trouble seeing through my tears. Concentrating finally, getting better, getting them nicely rounded, the two of us working away with emery boards, the intimacy of femininity and fussiness, utterly content with our industry. We "work on things," how she might try to be less peremptory, ask rather than command. Her wistful little "perhaps that's why I have trouble with friends," seems to take too serious a view of this; her social manner is impeccable, only with me is she bossy; I would like to be treated more as a friend. We come to terms over the wheelchair and the stationary bicycle as well, vows are made about exercise, I even try to push for an aerobics class, realizing even as I puff up the idea, that this is forcing things. But if she'll do the bike everyday, ten minutes. She pledges fifteen and in return insists I stay off cigarettes, laughing at the bargain.

We go down to look over the exercise room and begin our regime, Mother on the small exercycle, I on a formidable bigger one that runs you by electricity, only to find ourselves on display: there is an open house to recruit new tenants and fill a few vacancies today. We stay for coffee and to satisfy our curiosity. Mother has been exempted from "hostessing" or helping to sell the place to the prospective "seniors" and their families. Ruth was pressed into service but in view of her views on the food, has arrived late and is limiting herself to pouring coffee; she will not show rooms or contribute to the testimony that sells a shopper. Those who do so with success are given a percentage if someone on their tour ends up becoming a resident. The chatty lady whose daughter went to school with me and whose grandson has returned from Desert Shield, to her great pride and satisfaction, has "sold" someone an apartment and is getting a $500 reward.

There is entertainment and we stay to see it. A chorus of athletic older ladies who began years ago as an aerobics class and have done so well that they travel the oldster circuit now, a quite remarkable group, average age sixty-nine. They dance bravely on a home-made stage, eight pieces of plywood laid on a carpet in the middle of the large Chinese rug in the Wellington's very formal sitting-room lobby. I prepare to be embarrassed, remembering my visit to Sammy's Bowery Follies just before it closed, aged alcoholic vaudevillians, women dancing on their last legs. Not these gals. They are doing the Charleston, my dance, Mother's once—she taught me, instructing me to practice while leaning on the bathroom sink. It's a killer dance, you're aloft all the time, it's fast, it takes a lot out of the heart. But it doesn't phase these women. In fact they are a regular miracle, great figures, great legs, boundless energy in step. Real hoofers. We'll stay.

While they change costume for another number we are treated to an elderly woman impersonating Jimmy Durante; not that well, but the sight of a perfectly respectable 70-year-old woman in male drag is still something interesting. Even the "corny" guy who acts as impresario to the ladies' chorus and plays harmonica: "Let me call you sweetheart," the song that ended certain dance parties in my prom days. It probably resonates even deeper in the hearts of the old men and women around me, a big crowd, the residents, the new prospects. He launches into "I've been working on the railroad," then "The Red River Valley," my eyes search the ceiling, I am moved and appalled and then just let go.

The chorus reappear, they are called "The Satin Dolls," they are now in showgirl drag, net stockings, high heels, short skirts, jackets and top hats. They go at it, adding canes in the next number, pure schmaltz ascending to the particular American craziness of "New York, New York," an idea of Sinatra's and not really a place. One feels like an ethnographer, if my French friends could see this, I muse. Or the women at the Farm.

The choristers are pure admonition, absolute wish fulfillment coming true after thousands of hours of hard work and abstinence, exercise and practice. They top it off with pure tap-dancing. One is impressed, and then ashamed, watching them, many years their junior, I don't even bother to consider the notion of "being in that kind of shape at that age," I am not in that kind of shape now and never will be, I've never had long wonderful legs, I never could tap dance, and I feel like aged lard merely looking on: with each number they persuade further, triumph more grandly, represent a greater miracle of discipline. We're glad we stayed.

We even scored a cocktail party: Mother's friend Maim down the hall doesn't feel up to dining with us at Forepaugh's since she fell and hurt her hip, it's still a little hard to walk. But she has asked us in for a drink before we go out. When I get there I realize it's a set-up; she's invited her particular friends and Mother's as well, this is a real Wellington cocktail. I feel part of the place, sitting with them, performing the tree farmer as they interview me, flattered by the attention, charmed by their sweetness, the hospitality and feminine kindness: "This year was our third harvest and now the trees can support the place and even make it a free art colony," I hear myself doing my little spiel, entertaining them, being spoiled by the good manners of their admiration, realizing I have penetrated the veil as it were, been accepted into Wellington society, become one of them these few moments. Of course, Mother knows when it is time to go, but I had a lovely time.

We had a lilting, almost romantic dinner at Forepaugh's, just the two of us. I order the works and an even better bottle of Vouvray and lay it all on American Express. She is pleased with me tonight and goes along with the big date atmosphere, an elegiac note to our last evening. The local pike is divine, something to dream of in any corner of the world. We adore it all, we're mellow, we're buddies. I am a bit too much myself railing at the archbishop on the way home, a benighted spineless man named Roach, who first supported the mayor's liberal measure to ensure gay rights for St. Paul citizens, and then when the protestant fundamentalists and Anita Bryant bigots set up a hue and cry against it, withdrew his support and that of the Church, still so powerful here. The Cathedral itself looming at the top of Summit crest next to the Hill mansions as they all still lord it over the old town while we head home. Poor Roach was arrested for drunken driving a few years later so he too has eaten some crow and learned what it is to be condemned. It's that which Mother's greater tolerance sees. But I'm still delighted with her exasperation at Cardinal O'Connell of New York whose reactionary positions drove her once to swear she could strangle him with her "bare hands." Not bad for an 88-year-old lady. It's been a good evening.

Part Three

At the end of another visit, thinking of the beginning, saying goodbye and wondering if it were for the last time, the summer ahead and the Farm. It may be fall before I can come again. Winter? Next fall I'll be in Europe for a month; how can I manage to get here again, and when? Having said I would, I will somehow. "If you need me, just call. I'll come right away. And every Sunday I'll telephone." Sunday is her hard day. She's said that many times.

Otherwise, she doesn't say much, insisted that she is never lonely: "I'm never lonesome." "Everyone is lonesome sometime," I argued, "I'm often lonely even with people around." At the Farm there is an occasional terrible loneliness living in a group, friendly with everyone, intimate with no one. "No, I am never lonesome." I am convinced, then unconvinced, repeating this. But I believe her, her incredible stoicism; finally incredible. Beside her I am all need, just as I am all tears.

"There is only one thing, I don't want to die alone; I want the three of you with me." "Tell me then, tell me when to come, tell me early enough, don't fake it, don't postpone. Listen for your own signs. We'll be there;

we were all there for the breast surgery. We can get here in no time, but don't wait till it's late, tell us soon enough to have some real time together."

It was the one thing she would say on this subject. No, come to think of it, it was not, it was the second such thing but not the last—no, the last was her farewell: "Remain a family, stay together, I'm asking you that." She knows as I know, how imperfect are the bonds between us sisters, how she herself is the bond, and when she is gone, the connection between us sisters may fail, may loosen and fall away. Also how evanescent is the friendship of the next generation, who did not grow up with us, as we did with each other; Sal's kids, who have their own siblings and are now having their own babies. Aunts are not so proximate; I am only an aunt and they owe me nothing, not the mountain of guilt and affection, anger and passion I have with my sisters. But with Mother gone, that tree which holds the soil in place, how possible that we would erode over the years into mere phone calls; visits too time consuming, expensive. It could go that way with the reunion too, the next generation would melt into other plans, obligations, responsibilities. I see it all, so does she. Like the Farm, the continual worry of how it may survive my death, an institution and a purpose, trustees and a place, property and a colony for artists.

A feminist mourning the death of the family? The extended, not the nuclear. The nuclear will do just fine; Steven and Chris and the baby; David and his baby; Lisa and hers: wives, husbands, children—each little unit will hold on. Small, smaller, with each generation we lose, as we lose Farmington, Ireland, even Minnesota, each off in a different corner of the country. I keep thinking of the St. Croix, how I nearly had sparked an interest in Sal again, what if I called Laurie and asked? Of course that land opposite was sold long ago, but there might be something else, the dream of a compound for the next generation, is it crazy? If we had only bought then, $10,000 for a thousand feet of river frontage and the land went way back, no structure on it, tiny taxes. We could have bought it and waited.

What was $10,000 between the three of us, even then; for three grand we could afford to make a mistake I said to Sal. She nodded.

Laurie's in Europe, I must wait to call, she still does some real estate, would know what's around. Of course it's not cheap anymore. Mallory and Thomas nearly rented a cottage on the river this summer from Laurie's brother Bruce. The cottage is just down the street, how nice it might have been. So often it all comes to nothing. How possibility seems to wilt here, how one gives up finally. It gets to you. It got to me this time, I surrendered a bit, didn't buy the wheelchair. I had propagandized Steven and even Joannie, but Mother put the kibosh on the whole project: it would be a nuisance for Joannie to load and unload into a car, too heavy, another imposition and burden. She will not be a burden, she will not inconvenience these two younger people who are her lifeline here, who do her favors, visit her at the Wellington, take her out sometimes. They must not be stretched further.

I sat in the Day by Day Café with Steven and Chris, my foolish tears visible to Chris sitting opposite me in the booth. I am ashamed to be pushing, because of course I was pushing, thanking them for all they did for Mother, but pushing my damn chair idea. It would be a convenience to them as well, whenever they went to get her they would not have to stand by for twenty minutes while she went down the long corridors of the Wellington with her walker, that torturous long exit from the building. And there would be a whole range of places they take her to now. "Well, with the new baby . . .," Chris begins, protecting what she must protect; they are both busy attorneys, there is already so little time. Chris has three living grandparents, she tells me. There are her own parents too, I think, not yet old, but aging.

Beside me Steven plans sensibly; he'll canvass the family. He'll make some calls, get some contributions. The chair costs about twice what we thought. Four hundred's a lot. I get desperate: "Say I just bought the thing myself; would it be any use to you and Joannie? Or simply a nuisance?"

Steve feels he can lift it in and out of a car easily; the next thing is to talk to Joannie. But the problem remains: is it really useful, would they take advantage of the greater range of places to go that it offers? Their connection with Mother is to "drop by" sometimes. Occasionally invite her to dinner. The steps to their own houses cannot be negotiated with the chair. It would offer no real benefits unless they took her out into the world. "Mother hasn't seen the city streets for ages," I say. "She seemed to get a notion of the town again this time, she saw the blossoms, even went to a ball game."

I am begging, I am shameless and ashamed, the tears are an affront, poor Chris. This is my mother, I should be staying to do this job, not foisting it off. Steven has been a good grandson. "Maybe not just ball games, there might be some other ideas that came to you," I trail off. "Let's get the Joannie factor," Steve says.

Joannie thought it might be good for trips to Excelsior if she took Mother out to see her sister Margaret. She seemed sympathetic. Over the telephone, I try to explain how the foot-rests come on and off. "There's this little gadget, you press it down, 'cause when they're off, the whole thing's even lighter." Then I show Mother how the "companion chair" actually fits in the closet—the real wheelchair did not. This fits, I demonstrate to Mother. "No, it goes back to the store, that's final."

And it was. When it was returned there was still time to go back for one last hug. I took the River Road and listened to sentimental crap on the radio, country songs, local advertising. Even stopped to examine one of our beautiful wrought iron lamps along the River Road, pulled up in a rest stop, a place where I once necked in the backs of cars with high school boys. Pulling up near a woman alone in her car, probably undergoing some life crisis; I have interrupted her thoughts on a riverbank just to count the panes in this lamp.

Every time I ever drove the River Road, my eyes loved each lamp—they go on for miles, are emblematic of this town. When I see lamps like these in other places I nearly weep for St. Paul: the traces of French origin, a certain genteel sensibility, an anachronistic tidiness. Like these wrought iron lamps out of the thirties, each one a sculpture full of emotion. I have always meant to count the panes. I cannot drive a car and count them too, so I just stopped, it was the final fond idiocy. Parked and got out while this woman watched in puzzled irritation, I counted, walked around and counted. Did it three times and still wasn't sure if there were nine or ten sides to the beautiful frosted panes under the canopy. Remembering how we used to break them with stones "for fun" and to show off: barbarism. The barbarism of life, repented now. So much repented now, between youth and old age, the one lost, the other feared.

And fearing still, I made the wrong turn as if by fate at the Fort road. So instead of the airport and Minneapolis I was headed again up Seventh Street to the Wellington. Which is just what I wanted to do, my wrong turn only facilitated my wish. I was supposed to have left, returned the wheelchair and turned toward the airport, but now all over again, I found myself turning back to St. Paul. The first time was for just one last hug, now a second time out of sheer madness. The fact is, I went back not once but twice. Because after our "work-out," each perched on our absurd bicycle, Mother on the little one, I on the big one which is even electrical, Mother had seen me to the door. I was leaving now, this was it. She would take the elevator back to her apartment on the fifth floor, I would get into my car and drive to the airport.

But then I couldn't leave and came back again, frantic, missing the road to the airport. I parked recklessly, blocking the driveway of the Wellington and ran back to the lobby. Locked. Dell was on duty and recognized me. Edith the manageress who is "all business" as the old ladies say, she is there as well. Both notice my tears and my embarrassed little excuse that I just wanted to say goodbye one more time. But Mother has already taken the elevator; slow as she is, she beat me. The car is parked illegally, I can't follow. Dell remarks helpfully that she didn't actually see Mother take the elevator, she might be on the ground floor still. I investigate the exercise room, the party room, the library, even the ladies' room. No, she's gone upstairs, don't make an ass of yourself. Get in your car and go, it shouldn't be parked here by the door. Once you've given back the damn wheelchair in St. Paul, head right over to Minneapolis, return the rental car, catch the plane. This is it.

In defeat I returned the chair, giving it over to one of the clerks in a yellow crew cut, maroon teeshirt—the kind of guy who rolls his pack of cigarettes into the sleeve over his muscle, the look of a tough in any other town but here he's a homeboy, gentle and sweet, and worried the price put us off. Sure it did, it's overpriced. We both know it. "Trouble is, she wouldn't let it stay in the house. Not this time, maybe next time . . ."

But even then, there was time for one last goodbye. I headed back, Summit to the River Road. On the Mississippi River Boulevard, which we call the River Road, I was nearly raped coming home from school in a blizzard one afternoon when I was thirteen. I got away, ran for it and escaped. It always comes back to me. Oddly, I never begrudged the Road and love it still. The forest banks on the Minneapolis side, miles of lovely old houses on the St. Paul side, this favorite stretch of easy winding asphalt, always missing the actual corner of my misadventure. Even when I try to remember I forget to look carefully enough, loving the River instead, my own River, my Mississippi. Other memories overwhelm the evil one: all the peanut butter sandwich exploration parties of Saturday afternoons in childhood, all the courting boys of adolescence, the war monument and the Lookout for "parking" and drinking beer.

Here, where the road curves inland, by St. Thomas, is the exact spot you enter holding the paper sack of peanut butter sandwiches and the coke Mother and Celia have cheerfully packed for you at home; you will be "out from underfoot," busy for a whole day. An entire Saturday to explore the banks and avoid bums and end up doing the stations of the cross at the seminary in casual arcadian piety, having practiced swearing, practiced being an Indian and a cavalry officer, a pioneer, a murderer, a survivor of gang wars and massacres and the wilderness itself. Reading books over the years, I have placed a thousand texts in these woods, so small now when realized in adulthood. A mere six blocks of forested bank by this inlet, but every book about the west, French America or New England or the Wild West, every wilderness or jungle I have ever visualized while reading, ultimately owes its landscape to this one. Not even to movies—but to this poor stretch of sandstone bluff and treed steepness, its hobo and kid hiker trails are all the pathways in the world to me, its rivulets running down to the great water are a kind of ur-nature.

Just as the houses in St. Paul, its modest little wooden and stucco cottages or the grand stone mansions of Summit and Crocus Hill are, when I track them down, the dim original settings for all literary moments to come: Isabel Archer's discovery of betrayal took place in Una Brewster's house which I saw one champagne night with my Aunt Dorothy after the symphony. The cellar in my own *Basement* is a salad of the basements I played in near home when growing up on Selby. But I will not drive by the old house today either; I don't need to. I carry the place in me like a pregnancy.

Returning to the Wellington I park carefully and correctly—I have an extra twenty minutes. Taking the elevator and chatting with the ladies of the Wellington: one elevator is being repaired and we discuss it. Having knocked and heard the surprise in her voice, I disguise my passion a little, use the bathroom, eat two forkfuls of cottage cheese, wait while she walkers herself to her armchair, her throne. From here she will dispense her last word, her last hug. But here I am back again. A pest, a nut, obsessive.

The geranium I brought when I first arrived for this visit days ago is still thriving: "It will be your company all summer. It will sit right in front of the window: just imagine that it's me." I am back before her, embarrassing us both, unable to help either of us. Incapable of preventing this second return. She understands and is kind. "Stay a family," she says, saying everything, her all. It is time to leave at last. There is the last wrenching kiss goodbye. "I'm glad you came back," she says, seeing probably how sorry I am to be leaving, how helpless, how unable to stay longer, how foolish and impotent.

On that first day she had been in her chair and had just come out and said it, "Of course I'm dying. Stop crying. I'm ready for it, it's time." I had placed the geranium on the table, had been satisfied with it there, would try it in three other places, but would return to that spot, the enormous blossoms before the window and with the pure white wall to its right, you see it when you enter the room, grand and monumental, the background for her wonderful head as she sits in the chair, her chair. "I don't mind dying at all, I welcome it."

She is sitting there now, six days later, the same geranium setting her off, the same determination and courage. I, who have come and am about to leave again, with the same useless tears. It is as if I had not been there. But I was and she said she was glad I had come, even that I had come back, this one last foolish time.

~

Arriving in St. Paul for this visit a few days ago and noticing the nursery, of course I had to stop, seeing geraniums at that little stand, lost, or detoured on my way from picking up the wheelchair. As for that mangy little chrysanthemum I got at the airport in Minneapolis, knowing it was not the right thing, yet I must bring something and this can be a stopgap in case I don't pass a florist. And I might forget. Seeing geraniums I remember. Everything.

The balcony of her bedroom and each year's ritual spring planting of the window box, dreaded finally as the house became too much for her. An increasingly significant moment, you now had to fly home to help her do this, to get her geraniums in. How many years I had ordered them for her by phone from Holm and Olson for Mother's Day. One clerk even read my books, they understood the shade she wanted—salmon-pink, always her term, precise, a very definite shade, not just any old geranium, but a dozen true salmon pinks. They set off the color of the house, a lovely slate blue. It's a special and distinguished house on a street of undistinguished houses, with a bold sloping roof in a style Mother has always described as English Cottage. With a balcony full of just the right shade of geraniums. For so many years this house was her self, not only her shelter and her wealth but her identity.

It is Spring in St. Paul today, it is the day you would put them in if there were still a house on Selby Avenue. You have to stop, it is ordained you find this wonderful little nursery on a back lane that looks like the country, a relaxed old-fashioned greenhouse for bedding plants. Old women work here, one of them patiently looks at every shade with me, dismisses hanging baskets, they won't work, maroon geraniums are swell but not the thing. The trailing kind won't do either. And if there are no true salmon pink, there is this utterly gorgeous really big tub of coral ones, off-red, maybe just the thing.

The balcony is gone; this breed are heartier and will last all summer. But so big, so heavy, will it be a bother for her? We decide not, with a plate under them; once they are placed they will need nothing but watering all summer. Mother will pick off the dead heads and withered leaves, she's like that. Me too, I clean geraniums while I talk on the phone. I'm already cleaning up the pot, even before paying for it. Then paying extra because we've decided that plant food, once a week, might be worth the investment. These flowers must last all summer, must be her summer itself, because I may not be able to come again to take her out into the town or by the River. The Farm is ahead of me, fourteen people to direct, a big place to run. So this big living plant, actually four or five plants potted together, must stand in for me. Extreme of course, I can hear her remonstrate already, the size, the expense, the ostentation and lavishness, but I have made up my mind.

Yet at the end of the day, I realize I spent far too much time fiddling over these flowers, deciding where they looked best, while telling my news, presenting my new bunch of pages, "Mother Millett, Part Two." Which she will read when she gets around to it, when she's alone, when I'm gone, when I'm not there to watch her reading. And Sal—I realize I thought more about Sal, whose arrival from Europe an hour after mine from New York stole our thunder—preoccupied us. I focused on Sal then, we both did. We had only a little time together before Sal's arrival and I wasted it, lost the moment when Mother might say whatever was in her heart, when it was fresh and I had just come. "Let's not talk about your writing," she said, because I had also brought the first two chapters of the book against torture which finally has a title. I'm printing it up on my printer to send to the Hamburg Institute which has sponsored all these years it's taken me: "I have eight chapters but here are the first two; you can read them while I'm here"—feeling like a salesman with samples.

"Let's not talk about that now," she says, "I am hungry to talk to you." Great, I think, now at last. "So, do it, I've come all this way to hear you." "It doesn't happen just like that," her gesture impatient, like a woman bullied into intimacy. Of course, I say, knowing her shyness, her hatred of the histrionic. She had at first placed me at the dining table, wanting me to eat strawberries. I'll pass them up for talk; now we will talk. I sit her in her armchair, she will deliver herself. "I am not afraid to die, I'd welcome it."

"Mom . . ." "Stop crying—I have succeeded. You are my success, all three of you. And you have succeeded. Now . . ." I sit on the hassock before her chair. The phone rings, it's Sally calling, improbably, not from Holland or even the airport, but a cab. Cabs have phones? "Listen we've been waiting at the International section for hours, getting through customs, this was the only cab, can you let me in when I get there?" "Sure." "Have you rented a car?" "Yeah, I've got one right here. Do you want me to pick you up somewhere?" "No, but when I'm dropped off I'll give the cab to Mary Norman who's been traveling with me." Now they're rocketing towards us in a cab with a phone. So it was over, the revelations. The great exchange of life and death gave way before life. It was that way from then on.

Later in my room, I realized I had been diverted by Sal, our reunion, her adventures in Europe. After dinner I drove Sally over to Chris and Steven's, where she will stay tonight while I take the Wellington's guest room. I stayed on to have a drink and chat with Chris when she arrived, then to play with the baby, who can turn over now . . . but I forgot Mother. The baby will crawl soon, I think, remembering the patterning I did in England on a brain damaged child, Winnie, how we put its arms and legs through the motions because a doctor in Philadelphia had discovered that without the pattern of crawling, a child could never get beyond to any other learning. So we patterned and I went around London to meetings to get volunteers, ended with an army of gay men trying to save this little boy. And we nearly did, the patterning actually worked, telling Chris about it, lazing on the floor, watching little Victoria, trying to imagine what her consciousness must be like.

But the next morning Mother told me she had waited up for me, thought I would be coming back to talk more. I had disappointed her, without even guessing it. "I thought you'd be asleep, it was late, you were tired, it was past the hour when you go to bed." "It doesn't matter at all," she said briskly. It was like that all the time, near misses. The great hour comes, everything is arranged and the dishes are done and put away and then you will talk. And you never do. The great thing is never said. I come all this way for the moment of communication and it never takes place. It is prepared for endlessly but it never happens. But it is also that I never understand that moment until it has passed, realize everything too late, live in a state of stupid remorse. "It is just being here," she says, "just your being here." "Visiting"—her term for intimacy. This time I accepted her terms.

There seems to be an ongoing tussle between immanence, mere being—her way of communicating—and mine, which is speaking, putting things in words. If we merely sit together, she in her armchair, I on the hassock, close enough so she hears me and that I do not need to shout, since shouting inhibits me, then that simple proximity is sufficient to her. Piddling around the apartment is also nearly sufficient, the air of domestic tidying, taking note of what is needed at the store, taking out the garbage and recycling the newspapers, little references to items in this morning's *Pioneer Press*, humor over President Bush's coming visit to St. Paul as part of his "Education Strategy." Or merely, watching the evening news together on television, the fate of the Kurds or Guatemala, or small observances on the lives of relatives or her neighbors at the Wellington, all the old women I am getting to know, greet in the hall. Mother's milieu, an odd combination of world politics and domesticity.

I am reading to her every morning now. Bits of Susan Sontag's *Illness as Metaphor*, which she loves, nodding away over tuberculosis and cancer, yes, every observation strikes her as just, she is right with me, for a time. Then she dozes off and I stop for a while. I pinched a likely bunch of paperbacks from Skippy's shelves the other day, actually her former lover's books left behind years ago, but still there will be hell to pay if they aren't returned. Mother and I puzzle through Barbara Walker's *The Crone*, absorbing the fall of patriarchy a little at a time, the dishonor and disregard brought thereby to older women and their wisdom, Mother absorbing the text as I read aloud, both of us trying to eliminate religious competition, the goddess and the sky gods, and come into the heart of the matter, the cult of war, the chaos of violence, the present threat to the planet.

Wondering, between the armchair and the hassock, where it all began, the rise of the city states, the property in persons, the population explosion following on the discovery of paternity—I try out theories and we look them over. Mother's interest and comprehension are extraordinary, her insight and perception, once invited, are remarkable. This despite the shortness of her attention span, the sudden way she is tired. She is all there, I think, so much more than she ever was: she knows so much by now.

My own new book is more than she would like to know, however. *The Politics of Cruelty*, the torture of political prisoners, is a world she has only suspected. I see it anew as I read to her, not only Volodin's capture which I retell from Solzhenitsyn's *First Circle*—this fascinates her, she still hopes he will escape. But the great steel circle of Stalin's system, this saddens her immensely. And following its later extension into the "National Security State," the files and fingerprints, the photographs and computer controls, the capacity of the modern state to overwhelm the individual. She grows more and more dejected. The state's appropriation of total control through the addition of torture overwhelms her. Should she confront such possibilities before she dies, I wonder? It is the world just beyond the edge of the television set, what the CIA is probably really about, what actually happens in Kuwait or Iraq or South America—but you don't have to see it, you don't have to look. You almost know but you don't have to know for sure.

We go back and forth from the present terror to the ancient matriarchal past, trying to find some comfort in a world to come from the one we see before us, the one presently in place and getting worse: state power, militarism, the desecration of the earth. We try to imagine it will get better, that it has to, the grandchildren and great grandchildren much on her mind now, there are two of them already, a third will be born in August. "I can't really die yet," she laughs. "I have to see how your book will end and how Victoria will turn out." We go in and out of a terrible seriousness and back to the quotidian, taking in catastrophe and poverty and cholera in Peru and South America, the growing famine in the Sudan, so angry at the televised General responsible for it we nearly choke with fury. And then do the dishes again.

We are women looking at the world we cannot change and over which we feel we have no control and little contact beyond concern and information, which we know is controlled and often deliberately inaccurate. We feel helpless and unconsulted, we experience being women. Her age and mine and our perceptions are equally disregarded. The black children of the Sudan will die, almost as they are photographed. Cholera in Peru is spreading; there is plague.

I remind her that cholera is what the Irish died from, not the famine. Queen Victoria's one act of mercy was to send us a boatload of wheat from India; whether she was aware of it or not, the wheat was mildewed, rotten, its arrival was said to begin the spread of cholera. Uncle Harry taught me as a child to hate the famine queen. "Why would Steven name his child after her?" "Chris named her," Mother assures me. "She's never given Queen Victoria a thought; she simply liked the name." We seem to forget a lot here in America.

Mother transcends the Irish past and concentrates on the present. She says things like, "I want you to feel you are an American, that this is your country, that you come from here and belong here." "Mom, these people have cholera because they have to spend every cent paying America back for some damn development loan, so there's no money for a sewer system. Our banks get rich off the poor of the earth. And they also keep a bunch of crooks in power in such places who don't give a hoot about water and sanitation." "Of course," she says. Mother has understood sanitation all along. But her optimism continues to imagine the South Americans will arrive at a point where they won't put up with it. "But Mom, it's gone on all through this century; that's what those colonels are there for. If it gets hot Bush will call it a drug war and invade."

She doesn't like that; she gives her little cough of annoyance, a sure sign she feels contradicted. It is so obvious to her by now, so frustrating to watch fools in power, spoiling things, killing children, poisoning water and soil. They are poisoning her America too now, desecrating her beliefs, her loyalties and affections. The place has grown unfamiliar to her now as well and she says so. Her church too, unrecognizable in its foolish strictures against birth control, its collusion with money and government, armies and dictators. All painfully recognized at last. "What faith do you still have?" I ask, looking up from a text on the goddess. "I have something still; my own."

I found a rosary in her room, by the bedside, it seemed a relic of an earlier self. I expect she would want extreme unction and the last rites of the church, out of habit, for comfort. But her break with the hierarchy seems fairly complete. Whatever dogma may be left intrigues me—there are moments I wonder as we coast along in our pagan text, guessing that she will stop me at some outrageous reference to the unsexing of the Virgin. But no, we go on smoothly to Eve and the apple and agree on the absurdity of it all. Then we have a little lunch.

I have brought one book with me which worries me a little: a series of essays on death and dying. I'm not sure about it, but after all, this is what she faces, why not use a text to explore, maybe examine and decrease her fear. Or is it mine? It has a preface, all too short alas, by Elizabeth Kubler-Ross. I once spent an evening listening to her on tape and I liked her. There was a common sense and a kindness about her, a directness in dealing with death as a fact of life, in seeing terminal illness as something to confront reasonably, and when accepted as inevitable, there is a wisdom or comfort in the letting go. The essays themselves are psychological studies, mostly of psychedelic states and their resemblance to the experience of dying as reported by people who nearly died, saw their lives in review, experienced a certain bright light, knew the sensation of leaving their bodies and being poised above them.

I read to her from a wonderful description of this by Carl Jung of a vision he had when near death from a stroke, a sensation of rising above the earth and seeing its curvature, his image the globe rather than the photograph of the earth from outer space which haunts us now since the visit to the moon. And Jung's blue-green earth, Ceylon below him and the Indian subcontinent, is very like our own new picture, the picture a number of friends of mine paint now. My good friend Janey Winter has just given an exhibition of such paintings where the motif of the earth shot is combined with archetypal boats and whales, ancient Egyptian and goddess motifs, the whole imperiled experience of life on this planet, re-examined in the new light of now having seen it whole because from a great distance, from outside it and above it as we had never seen it before, seeing it also afresh because its fragility is clear, its permanent ability to support life unclear, its future itself in the balance. Janey's show was a triumph; last week she was back at the Farm and showed us forty slides of these paintings. Janey's also a friend of my mother's, used to visit her on Selby Avenue years ago when Janey was living in Minneapolis. Mother has seen Janey's announcement, we've discussed this image and delight together in Jung's verbal description, which is highly colored and full of emotion.

I take Mother's calm before death as a sign she has come to terms with everything except the possible solitary accident, helplessness in an empty apartment. There is an alarm in every room, but what if she could not reach to pull the little string? There is the ever vigilant staff, the "I'm okay" sign Mother displays each morning around nine. There are still the hours in between, the fear of falling, the possibility of ill luck and no rescue.

~

Then one day in midsummer, a call from Steven in St. Paul to the Farm that explained all about the fear of falling: Mother has a brain tumor. Never discovered by her own doctor who dismissed her symptoms year after year as her imagination, nature's course, the failures of an aging automobile—there was nothing wrong with her legs. He never looked at her brain. Out of frustration with all this, but almost by accident, Steven had persuaded a doctor friend there might be more to it. And this young man knew a specialist. Mother was persuaded to submit to an MRI and then to x-rays: the evidence was very clearly there.

Mother sat in the surgeon's office and looked at the pictures of her enemy, discovered at last. What to do about it is another thing. Surgery is dangerous. But it could help: it could arrest, possibly even reverse a growing paralysis in speech and hearing, even walking. What if Mother could really walk again? We must come together and give her support for whatever she decides. If she agrees to surgery, I must stay till its outcome is clear. Mallory will stay on and nurse Mother through recovery, then Sally will take over.

There are a few days to read up on the subject, to try to understand this area of the brain, motor activity, the tumor's effect and the surgical procedure, to talk to surgeons and nurses, to interview and understand. There is also time over long distance for all of us to rail against the doctor Mother trusted and consulted for ten years, a man who stole a decade of our Mother's life through his arrogance and ignorance. Vivid language to berate his callousness, to swear revenge and malpractice, to hang him from lamp posts and then just let go. To focus on the future and contemplate the decision ahead.

It is all so soon and sudden, so irreversible. This vindicating eventual discovery of a truth we had suspected somewhere all these years: "There has to be some reason why it is harder and harder to walk. There has to be some reason I am afraid I'll lose my balance." Conscious that Mother did not invent her fright, but, unable to diagnose it ourselves, we veered between a worldly skepticism and a baffled sympathy. And now we know, the knowing a clarifying asset and a fatal deficit—a sentence as well as a possible reprieve. From now on it is all risk.

Part Four

I stop the car. This is it, I'm in for it now; this is the place. A raw brick building from the fifties, blank, without personality. The street too, only a few blocks up from the beautiful River Road—my own cousin Rosellen lives in a grand new apartment house on the corner below, but up here on Norfolk Street, check it, yes this really is the street, we are at the very edge of the city—up here it's still frontier: plain little houses, a street without curbstones, ugly mud on either side of the roadway. On the opposite corner a Catholic church, on a further corner its parking lot, the odor of righteous Catholicism everywhere in the instructions about where to park and what days not to. I had imagined something old and easy, something vine-covered and graceful, something that had been here a long time and had comfort in it, not this mean cost-conscious box, neither new nor old: cold, pointless. My God, we have put her here. St. Anne's home.

Of course it would be the nuns and the Church, I knew that already. But I invented a cordial humanity for it all, voluntary poverty and humility, down-to-earth humor and old-fashioned values. In all the raging tearful conversations over long distance with Sal, this place was supposed to be the very best. Somebody who knew these places gave it the highest marks; so much more human than the newer or the more expensive ones. Hadn't Father Lawler recommended it, and of course he visits them all. St. Anne's was the one for kindness and gentle care. He'd know.

But instead it's this. This nondescript building is where Mother is to die. After having first died as a citizen, a person with a home and means and an identity, an autonomous being. Here she is to wait for death. I'm just supposed to drop in and visit, two hours in the morning, say, then another two in the afternoon. Otherwise I'm free and on my own. Sal says I can get a drink at five from Rosellen, another from Joannie at six. There are people in St. Paul I ought to look up—there would be time for making contacts, finding friends at the University, meeting some artists; there's a woman I met at the Michigan festival who lives in St. Paul and sculpts, she'll know others.

I'm to stay in Mother's apartment which has not yet been surrendered. Her apartment will still be there awhile and because Mother is here, I will stay in her home because she no longer has one. Instead of renting the Wellington guest room at $35 a day, I will have an apartment all to myself. I'd find it really pleasant, Sal had promised, the Wellington's a great place to live, beautifully managed.

Of course there is something desperately wrong with this plan. This is Mother's apartment, not mine. I don't want it, I want her back there, I want her well and independent, queenly and serene in her own world, I want her world returned to her. But that's impossible, it's over, I remind myself behind the wheel, gathering strength. It's all over, her life is over, she can never live alone or independently again. She needs 24-hour care, her separate existence is destroyed, she is an invalid now. Sal had said it over and over on the phone when I called from Karen Katzel's that last morning in Provincetown. Sal wept, I wept. "The doctors say she will never get better, will be this way the rest of her life. And it may be years before she dies. Twenty-four-hour care in her own home would be seven to ten thousand a month—there's no way. It would take three shifts of nurses, we're lucky to get her into St. Anne's."

This extraordinary luck is emphasized over and over, a gift of fate, an accident; these places have long waiting lists. But because Mother was coming there from a hospital, it would be possible to jump right to the head of the list and enter her as an emergency. The University hospital demands she leave; she's "stabilized" now, they must have her bed. And there was simply no place for her to go. The Wellington wouldn't have her, you have to be in good shape to live there, it's in the contract that you have to be able to live alone and take care of yourself. So she couldn't go home. She could never go home again. There is nothing else but a nursing home at this point; the time has arrived. Sally feels we might have been remiss in waiting this long: we should remember that even before her surgery Mother was already getting outside help: Carol, aids from the Good Neighbor Agency nursing facility at the Wellington. Mother already couldn't cope. I argue that the tumor was beginning to put pressure on her brain then, the surgery was supposed to relieve that, bring her back. "Well it didn't work I'm afraid," Sal sighs. We both conceded then: tears, sobs. Futile silences. Cuss words.

But I wouldn't concede without an argument. We still had no way of knowing that the surgery was a failure. Mother had been returned twice to the University hospital, the second time in an ambulance and near death: vital signs in great danger, electrolytes drained. On the second trip, her condition was eventually diagnosed as hypercalcemia: a surge, almost an assault of calcium upon the body. Once understood the condition could be dealt with, after a week or so she was stabilized. "Maybe it's just the hypercalcemia," I urge, after all that was a complication; it may have had nothing to do with the surgery. And even if we don't know what caused it; surely taking a few calcium pills and some Vitamin D which retains calcium won't throw you into a nearly fatal condition. But can we be sure the surgery itself was a failure? The wrong thing to have done?

After all, we had gambled, and Mother had gambled the most, had the courage to submit to the knife and to brave death and the chances of never coming through it, never waking up alive. But she did. And from the moment she woke she was so much better, she heard and understood us so quickly it was almost as if the deafness had relented, for we believed the tumor in her brain had destroyed all the hearing in one ear and nearly all of it in the other. But now she heard us easily. She was continent again. The surgeon felt there was a good chance she would be able to walk on her own.

The tumor is on the left side of the brain; since all the nerves cross over, it affects the right hand, the right leg, the right ear. The shunt bypass surgery made such good sense because it relieved that pressure on the brain which the tumor had recently and indirectly created, its growth lately had begun to block the circulation of the spinal cerebral fluid around the cavity of the skull. This build-up of fluid created even greater, more dangerous pressure: Mother was losing the ability to walk, to speak clearly, to use her right hand. The tumor itself is inoperable, too closely knit to the brain to cut away. One can only relieve the pressure indirectly now, by dealing with the fluid. So the shunt, this crazy little plastic tube inserted under her skin behind her ear and down her chest and into her stomach, will relieve this debilitating build-up of fluid on the brain, drain it off down the tube and recycle it back into the body. A clever piece of plumbing. The bypass would produce enormous relief for the brain cells. And faculties lost recently to the fluid's pressure would be recovered again: motor faculties like walking and talking. Since the tumor is in the medulla oblongata, the old brain, Mother's intelligence and understanding have never been affected.

This was corrective surgery, they've been doing it twenty years. I have drawn this idea in my mind and considered it for weeks, read about it, meditated on it. It is a divine little piece of ingenuity, I decided finally; it would give us our Mother again. It would give her back her life, the ability to walk and sign her name and have a place of her own, her own life and independence, everything she represented and stood for to us. The very essence of her personality is self-determination. This is generally a very successful operation. We had every right to hope.

But now there is no hope. Sal says that the University doctors tell her that Mother will never get better. "Wait—isn't she just weak, still sick, just recovering from the hypercalcemia? What does the surgeon say?" I resist, I hold out; I was there for the surgery, thought this man Heros was so good, invested him with god-like powers. "Heros is gone, surgeons just operate and leave; her doctors now are the resident internists at the University and they say there's no hope. They all say she's completely incapable of living on her own: 24-hour care and that's it, a nursing home." "Did you talk to Heros?" "He says she could live another five years." "But it's not a life, Sal." "It sure isn't."

Has Doctor Heros—this handsome and perfect surgeon, this man from central casting, this superb artist whose name is the name of heroism itself—has he casually performed a routine procedure on an aging woman, only to condemn her to a life of dependence and invalidism, merely to prolong her state for five years? To linger and become a vegetable? While paying something like $36,000 dollars a year for the shelter of St. Anne's Nursing Home? And then at last, in this desert of useless and empty days, to run out of money and "spend down" as Sal defined the term with bitter irony—"Which means when she can't pay, the state of Minnesota will have to." "Will they?" "Yeah, but not for a room of her own; something darker and smaller." "Sal—it can't be, it can't be we did this for nothing." "Looks that way," her voice strangled, hopeless. Sal can hardly talk, has such a bad cold it has become bronchitis and may even be pneumonia by now: she is so ill, so tired, so full of despair.

No, we didn't get screwed this way, I refuse to believe it. Before the surgery Mother had already found her life unendurable and was working her way toward ending it in sheer refusal, sheer willpower. Then we discovered the tumor; then there was a way.

The tumor once found, growing all these years, perhaps ten, since her cancer surgery (a double mastectomy back at the beginning of the eighties), yet still benign and making only slow headway against her brain. Stopping the flow of cerebral spinal fluid first, affecting her ability to hear or to walk. Left alone it might do worse, affect her reason eventually. "We had to do it, we had no choice. Don't you see, Sal?"

Sal sees it hasn't worked, has only extended Mother's suffering, has with terrible cruelty only stretched out her sentence of living death. Would someone do this to another being? I feel a rush of blood rage: "What did that guy charge? What does it cost to be put under this sentence, what does an 88-year-old woman pay for this expertise?" "About two thousand for the surgery, lots more for the hospital, tests, anesthesiologist—you know how it goes." An hour's work, $2,000: maybe not that much, given the knowledge this activity requires. This man is not in private practice, he is chief of neurosurgery at the University, a professor, he probably doesn't even get the full fee. He doesn't perform this merely for his fee, he doesn't recommend unnecessary surgery. Heros had refused to try to remove the tumor itself, it would take six hours and she would not survive it, they could never get it all anyway since the tumor's tissue is now inextricably entwined with that of the brain. He did this instead and he must have done it in good faith, certain it would help. Now we must face the fact that it has not; it has only prolonged Mother's agony and humiliation. It has put her in a nursing home. We gambled and lost.

Now you will have to open the door of this rented car and see her there, barely alive in a life that is not her own but the triumph of medicine. Mother who signed a living will forbidding any extraordinary means of keeping her alive, signed it with such determination and so long ago she must have been one of the first to do so: Minnesota state law recently acknowledged such living wills but with the cruel stipulation that the doctor must also concur. Perhaps the hospital staff as well, I wonder. Once more bureaucracy, the state, law and insurance, frustrating even the most basic of human rights. St. Anne's Catholicism would probably make sure you didn't starve yourself or die out of your own little woman's indomitable willpower, I think to myself. You're in a trap Mom, they've got you. Here in this boring building, imprisoned in the body, forced to live on in a life which is not a life. This is capture.

~

And the figure on the bed is like a small injured animal wrapped in white. Like a corpse and my heart leaps imagining the soul already flown, the spirit departed just an instant before. A bundle of dejection, still breathing, yes, but just fabric, white fabric. I glimpse her through the door and am destroyed with shame—this is my own mother abandoned, dying of abandonment, parked here to die like the mothers of strangers parked to die at St. Peter's Asylum when I worked there as a college kid and could not believe people would do this to their kin. Not my Mother, I swore; my Mother would never see the inside of one of these hell-holes, these places of despair and dejection. My Mother would never know that betrayal.

And now she must know it, it is all she knows. This prone lifeless figure, its face turned away, does it even still breathe? I know it by its shape, its very smallness. She is so little now, inches below five feet. Will she recognize me, can she speak, lift her head? There is a moment of sinking uncertainty as I approach the tiny white shape on the bed . . . "Mother?" But she still knows me. "At last, you're here," she says. There is a face, there are her terrible eyes, every atom of her still living energy is in them. They are all I recognize. But for these eyes I would never have known her. So small, so frail, the bones of a bird. And no hair. They have taken her hair away. I was warned but I forgot.

Actually, I like it—gone is that stupid permanent, that silly arrangement of curls. She looks like a very skinny Gertrude Stein, no, like Mary Martin playing Peter Pan. It is a short almost mannish little cut, but finally you see the shape of her head, its beauty and dignity; the old hairdo always made her seem lightweight, foolishly middle-aged and middle class, intellectually discountable. Not now. Now she looks like Georgia O'Keefe or a professor emeritus: if the old hairdo was feminine in a diminishing way, the new is butch in a peculiarly dignifying way, her great age giving her finally a grace beyond gender. She is another person.

Still somehow my mother. Another mother, a new mother, a basic essential mother without her old fussiness, her disapproving airs, her conventional dress and detail. Shorn, pared down, transcendent. In fact there is now more character here to connect with. Serious, awesome for all her frailty, her new being's almost diaphanous texture; so little of the flesh, so much of the spirit. I am overcome with respect as well as tenderness.

I love her like a force of nature now, without reserve, the reservations of years of disagreement and alienation. There is so little left of her now and yet it is so strong. Finally, for this is her last self-creation, her last embodiment. That one so helpless and pure of heart should be left alone in this place of abnegation and depression . . . this awful room, these paltry few feet of space to inhabit, even share with someone else, this meager corner to be penned into for life. One can hardly move around the bed to where her chair is placed, nightstand, the little television from her own bedroom at home at the Wellington. Mother's large color television can be brought over later, when she gets a room of her own, maybe only a few months from now Sal said: if she's lucky. I look at the tired bureau she shares with someone else, the few inches along the bar of a closet, the narrow space leading toward a toilet. That is to be everything, this is what you get for thirty-six grand.

At my birthday party at the Farm a few days ago, my friends were astounded that she would have to pay so much: for thirty grand you could live on Sutton Place, they laughed. But it's the 24-hour care, you see, it's being helpless, I explained. At the moment there is no sign of a caretaker about though one assumes they come when you call. Going past the nursing station there was a roar of bells and no one about at first, later a young woman full of demands on her time tried to speak to me through the din, eventually she just pointed in the direction of Mother's room.

Mother's eyes see me: "At last you're here." A hand has found mine and we merely look at each other, closer than we had ever been the whole course of my grown life. "You're here." Something was established in her immediate grasp of me. Something she has waited for, something I was to do. I am here for a reason, her reason. I do not want to live alone in her apartment and at the end of a week walk off leaving her here. I already know that. If I were any good I would get her out of here. If I were any good I would have been here before, prevented this from happening.

She lifts her head, struggles to rise, I help her to sit up. "I'm here." "Yes, finally." Then she kisses my hand. It astonishes me with its import. I have often kissed her hand that first moment of meeting: she has never kissed mine, never needed to. It was always my role as supplicant, the one who gave homage, acknowledged her greater station. She has taken the back of my hand put it to her lips, quickly I reply by kissing her hand too, the white flesh, its liver spots, its frailty, its wasted fingers. Dead white. There is just this, I think, wrenched with feeling and dread, this is the self which remains. All our fervor is in these two kisses, these hands joined before me, every commitment in the world is in this flesh; I already feel it.

Strange ancient gesture, I know it for a plea, I know it through history and imagination and even memory. It is so old and Irish, so universal, yet so particular to here and now, so unique and unlike her and her clan, unfamiliar, an amazement. One might have expected such a greeting in a Millett: their baronial manner, their theatre of gesture. Seeing it in her, one knows it is genuine, a mark of utter need and surrender. And the greatest endearment. I am overcome, my fraud falls away, any and all defenses gone.

"Now that you're here, we can leave." Her eyes are on me, compelling, absolute. Already she says what I dreaded, was warned against, knew I could not resist, even while hearing the warning. "Now we can go home to the Wellington." I know I cannot refuse, yet I cannot comply either. That was not my assignment. That is the route to madness, instinct, all I would love to do, not what I was supposed to do, not at all.

"I'm here," I say, my heart sinking already: guessing already. I was supposed to visit and leave, I was supposed to spend a week living in her apartment, putting in a little while each day at the nursing home, my only assignment to go over a few of her professional papers which I might wish to keep as souvenirs of the life she had once and to buy her some cotton stockings and underwear which Sal hadn't had time to get. Then I was to pick up the sterling silver I was always to inherit, because of course Mother would never use it again, and carrying it as hand luggage, I was to bring it home on the plane and save the nuisance of shipping. There are hundreds of other things to ship—there's the bone-china to Mallory, furniture, imagine it all. But I was always to inherit Mother's monogrammed silver service, it's been on her list for years, the laundry list we call it, laughing, thinking it would never happen anyway, we humored her in listening. But now, almost a thief, I was to make off with my heritage while Mother was still alive: I was simply to collect the box of flatware at the apartment, and just go back to New York. I was to have drinks with relatives and amuse myself with colleagues and get back on a plane carrying a wooden box of knives, forks and spoons.

My only other responsibility was to see that Mother visited her new internist, young Dr. Conroy, "cute as a bug," such a great find that he was Steven's doctor now too. Conroy is Steven's age and the friend of one of Steven's friends. Another of Steven's friends found the doctor who found the tumor. For all Conroy's reported charm I deeply resent his responding to Mallory's reports by prescribing anti-depressants for Mother when she was discouraged after surgery, gloomy over how slowly she was mending, how weak she was. I even suspect some drug of bringing on the hypercalcemia. Surely drugs weakened her further both in mind and body and made her dopey. Thomas reported as much: Mother became vague, unable to think at the end of a day. Surely psychiatric drugs are dangerous to someone recovering from brain surgery, someone who needs every atom of consciousness and cerebral energy—how mistaken to cloud that intelligence with toxins. Even her grief had meaning, was her own, made sense, was part of the mind's response: its way of coping, even healing.

Fortunately the University hospital's own procedure took her off all drugs when she arrived in an ambulance, and no further psychiatric medicine has been prescribed here so far. I even had hopes, given the Catholic attitude toward drugs and remembering how they wouldn't even give her a painkiller at St. Joseph's hospital that night she broke her wrist, coldly, stupidly denying the necessary relief—that she would be safe from all the noxious and dangerous things that are now routinely served up for the aged to zonk them out in nursing homes, helping to kill them in fact, bringing on incapacity and death earlier in order to insure the respectable quietude and calm so pleasant for their attendants. I have already made an appointment with this young doctor by long distance. I have expressed myself on psychiatric drugs; he will not be advising them again. This Wednesday will merely be a routine check-up. I was to have it easy.

I was to be a cad: when Mother asked to go back to the Wellington I was instructed to lie and say that she wasn't well enough yet. "But she's not going back, Sal, you will be giving up her apartment." "Not yet, but that may be how it's got to go." Sally's voice was hardly better now that she was back in Nebraska and I was back from Provincetown and at the Farm. The absolute necessity of 24-hour care is explained again and I assume that the placement at St. Anne's could be forever. Permanent placement. There is hope that Mother would accept it and adjust.

When Sal was in Minnesota deciding all this and I was at the Cape, what Mother herself wanted hardly seemed an issue: Mother was too sick to want anything. "Do you ask her?" "She just lies there in her hospital bed and looks at me and Steve and says 'you decide for me.' She can't cope at all. We've had to run around the rest of the day and ask people, visit these places, find the best one, get her in—somehow, anyhow. The hospital is screaming to have its bed back, they want to discharge her, she's being hard to care for, she's ornery as hell and rude to the staff." "She hates hospitals," I say almost to myself, trying to excuse. "Well, she's got to get out of this one. She's old and sick and can't decide; we have to." And so it came to this. By the time I was back at the Farm, Mother had already been put in St. Anne's; it was a done deed.

And I was supposed to stonewall. "But if she doesn't want to be there?" "She hardly knows anything. In the hospital there were days she was only intermittently lucid: hypercalcemia does that." "I've heard that too, it's part of the condition. But now that she's stabilized and they've fixed it . . ." "Look, this is the only place she can be." "But if she says she wants to be at the Wellington?" "She still talks about it. So just get through it, if she does." "How can I lie to her?" "You have to, we have no other alternative, she has to stay there. That's how it is."

But instead this is what I find: this small, old, frail, ineffably dear being who expects me to save her, who has waited for my arrival, conscious or unconscious that I was really coming—I only spoke with her once in this whole month I have been away—one moment on the phone. There were always other people answering the telephone, telling me how she was, Mallory or Thomas, Steven or Sally. Even paid caretakers like Carol or voices without even names at the Good Neighbor Suite when I would call, aware that at last Mallory was gone and Sally hadn't yet arrived. If I could ever talk to Mother by myself and see how she was—but one time the voice that answered told me that my mother had just that moment been rushed by private ambulance to the University of Minnesota Hospital. Mother never answered her bedside phone at the hospital, she was too ill, the nurses were probably too busy. If they were there Sal or her son Steven answered, otherwise I heard about Mother when I called Steven's home or caught Sal at Mother's apartment. Mother's own voice had disappeared. Along with her selfhood and any ability to make her own decisions.

Only once did Sal put Mother on the phone from her hospital room. An odd hoarse voice, exhausted, hardly recognizable, but very urgent: "I love you. Come soon." I have been following that command ever since I heard it. I could have gotten here a day or two earlier, I remind myself, if I'd paid for a full fare ticket instead of just the extra hundred dollars penalty. She's been here nearly a week; I was slow indeed if she's been waiting for rescue.

What rescue? Where could I take her? The best offer so far has been from Mallory who talked of bringing Mother to her place in California; I concurred with Sal in bypassing it, still nervous about the psychiatric medication and afraid there might be more. California was so far away, Mother would be cut from all her roots and relatives here, and I naively imagined until I saw the place that she might enjoy a greater independence here because of paying her own way. At Mallory's I foresaw dependence and a sense of being isolated and hemmed in, living Mallory's life in an apartment next to Mallory's. When arrangements could be made, Mother could be installed next door with private nurses. But Mother could feel beholden there, I thought, at the mercy of whatever private nurse Mallory would employ and govern. Here, I imagined, Mother would still be in charge; there would be a whole team of caregivers, some would surely be kind: one could maneuver. And there is Rosellen on the corner, a great point, Steven is also nearby, all her connections and past are here, it might be risky to transplant her all the way to California, where her only resource would be Mallory and Thomas. Really I wanted her always at the Wellington, in her own home.

But then came the catastrophe. Having nursed Mother in her own apartment for a good number of weeks after surgery, Mallory and Thomas had to go home a day or two before Sal would arrive and in that interval the hypercalcemia struck. Sally arrived to find Mother dying in a hospital. Sally reported with authority that the Wellington is now utterly impossible. Mother's apartment will be relinquished, her life there gone, cancelled. In the St. Anne's Home I had conjured up, I tried to assure myself Mother would still have her own world, or a semblance. That was before I entered this building and absorbed its despair, the control of the nursing staff, the gloom of the corridors, the slack figures of the residents, the negative ugliness and repression of the air here, even the dejection in the statue of St. Anthony just outside the door.

There is no exit. No solution. Still, I cannot refuse this creature who is still my Mother, helpless, the little figure already gathering herself for rescue, escape, salvation. At least I can free her of the bed itself, which is really a cage. There is a double railing which prevents her from getting up and out and leaving. Even to the toilet. How could she ever get to the toilet on her own I wonder, surely it is hard enough using a walker and her insufficient strength, the precarious balance that is the tumor's most insidious effect, so that she is always afraid of falling and often in danger.

"She falls all the time; there has to be 24-hour care." I hear it over and over in my mind, merciless, hopeless. She is in this thing because otherwise she might fall. Because she might get sick and tired of ringing for help and try it on her own. The bells at the nursing station ring all the time, often into emptiness. So, lest she take matters into her own hands they have made her helpless. How frustrating to her precious new continence.

As the incontinence came on with the tumor, Mother's life became unbearable for her and she turned toward death. I glimpsed an early moment in this living hell several summers ago when she was in Philadelphia for her granddaughter Lisa's wedding and had to leave the table suddenly and mysteriously during a lavish restaurant lunch. That moment the entire occasion turned to horror and mortification for her. This had been growing, this uncontrollable thoroughly unacceptable condition: there were plastic panty things in her apartment last spring, the whole unthinkably embarrassing question hidden, unmentioned. She went to the toilet alone and disposed of these things herself. As long as she could.

The perfect lady, she was not merely inconvenienced but suffering beyond endurance, wishing to die if life were to be lived under these conditions. And she was making some headway in this direction until we discovered the tumor and turned her around. She risked death by surgery for continence. But still lost everything. Now, in this place, she could surrender. And appeared, the first moment I caught sight of her, to have done so.

But then she saw me, an occasion. In the Wellington is the life that used to be. Going there she would be home, her own will, her own way. Hopeless of course, but she hopes, is deluded, insists. How to refuse? I can't. Neither can I cooperate in some nutty kidnap or elopement. Though every part of my being cries out to.

Have I myself not escaped the loony bin, not just the one Sal had me busted into in California, but the very Mayo wing of the University of Minnesota Hospital Mother herself had so unwisely and naively signed me into at the urgent behest of its chief psychiatrist. All those years ago. Hating psychiatry, no wonder I put my hopes in Heros the chief of neurosurgery, when by an ugly fate Mother herself was discovered to have a real and not imaginary pathology of the brain, this tumor which has been my enemy for months. It has won now, we are to believe, and therefore we should give up hope and leave Mother here, clearly against her will.

What other choice? Don't choose—prevaricate, hold back your helpless and dishonest tears and think of a treat, an immediate solution, anywhere else, any temporary place of refuge. Like a restaurant—would they let you take her out to dinner? Could she get that far? Away from here, for whatever nugatory relief, momentary respite—let's get outside fast. I am beginning to strangle here, overcome with claustrophobia and revulsion with this room. I can't stay here another second, becoming as desperate to leave as she. Watching her put her small legs over the edge of the bed, fetching her shoes on command; her voice, originally hardly a whisper, getting stronger now. She is on her way, her eyes assembling her purse and her walker and her wheelchair. She already wears a coat.

A small white wool jacket—dirty, I see with horror. Stained with food. Is she aware of this, does she dribble, does she feed herself, is this how she is to be the rest of her life, in soiled clothes, unkempt? She is making her getaway and completely unconcerned with these things, hardly interested in stopping to go to the bathroom, a precious opportunity forgone, a privilege she must lie in wait and beg for, ring and pray for, call out uselessly and dream of. That wonderful renewed power of continence that she had bought so dearly in blood and bone and steel and pain and proximity to death, withheld again and again, made useless if one cannot endure long enough. And how do the staff, when they finally get there, view the nuisance of bed wetting and the labor of changing sheets?

I watch her, realizing what she has in mind is one thing—this departure—I know it for another. I would therefore dissuade her from packing her photographs, the icons of her grandchildren, great grandchildren, new infants in frames, myself and my sisters in every moment of our lives: weddings, family reunions, graduations, babes in arms. The most sacred series of all, her three daughters in their childhood perfection in linked gold frames, old black and whites skillfully colored by a friend and client of hers—"This one, we must take this one," she says, urgent. Imperious. The old indecisiveness is gone from her voice, the polite little cough that prefaced every statement, self-deprecating, the old tags of "I think" and "It seems to me" and "Well, maybe." Now she points or contents herself with a single word when one will do; one word commands, frugal even to meanness. Even to penury: one of her favorite words; diction is a family game. But now she is stingy with language, seems almost to have lost touch with it. It is harrowing, isolating. I was warned, but still it is frightening to be with someone who hardly speaks.

I swallow and suggest we decide on a restaurant. Is she even strong enough to sit in a restaurant, can we make it to the car? Over and over she repeats "The Wellington, the Wellington." She knows exactly where to go, where she has ordered me to take her. Peremptory, certain, obsessed, beyond negotiation. But she trusts me: I am the one. And finally I have arrived. She knew whom to wait for. My god, this is happening. The worst thing is, I'm falling for it, going along.

And then Steven appears. Deus Ex Machina. He enters unannounced, he materializes. Did he know I would be here, I wonder? Handsome and charming and the light of her eye all these years, her golden haired grandson: "Steven is the son she never had," Sal said the other day on the phone. He will know what to do, I intuit, relying on his masculine presence, this man of the world, this young attorney; counting on the fact that he lives here in St. Paul, has surely been to see her here already, must have dealt with this himself by now.

Steven does something unusual, something on which everything that followed seemed ever after to hinge and depend: he presents an opening. And does it so casually, so easily, with such elegance and innocence: he does it with baseball. The Twins are playing tonight—why don't we go to Mother's apartment and watch the game, we can have dinner there. He gives us the Wellington, and permission, I think, the one permission I would long for but never dare to reach for. I do not even need to feel dishonest, though I do, assuming an equal nonchalance; disingenuous, feeling a rush of blood in my head. "Perfect, we'll run over to Lund's and pick up a lobster on the way, Mom, I'll cook our favorite dinner, we'll have champagne."

She is pleased with a perfect pleasure; mine is like terror. There is a small shadow of uncertainty about whether, since it's a home game, there will be a broadcast on regular television, but Steven even knows that if you call a certain number we can see it on pay TV since Mother has cable. Given Mother's idolatrous enthusiasm for baseball it is just the way to spend the evening in comfort.

It's an amazing suggestion, indulgence, temptation, to allow her to return home this once. Would they let us, I wonder? Apparently it is easy to arrange, Steven understands the whole procedure, the nursing home permits "responsible persons," to sign out its residents, even overnight. The game might be over late, this too is no problem; she could sleep in her own bed in her own apartment.

And then what happens? You bring her back—perfection of cruelty. No, take what you can get, live till you die, my mind recites, an artist's line, a gambler's. If there were just a way to make her live that way during every moment of whatever life she has left, if you could talk her into seeing it that way so that she would transcend the dour protestant self-denying air she has lived in so long, the basic, unimaginative puritanical and joyless atmosphere she has carried about so many years, that denial of vital engagement with experience which you fled in this town, this family. The good-time roll you have lived on all over the world, your own world: the Farm, the circle of women and artists, the parties and dinners, the hope you have tried to engender, the family of friends and lovers you have invented for yourself—all of this was your way out, your trail away from home.

Call it a lobster for now, it's something. And champagne even if it's only one taste in her mouth. Then Steven is gone, having disappeared as quietly into the dusk on the far side of the room as he had earlier materialized from a spot over by the door where Mother's roommate is supposed to be and thankfully isn't. We are alone now with our different secrets. I cheer her into her wheelchair with the prospect of the evening before us. "Remember de Beauvoir's theory of morsels, I told you about once Mom, morsels was her word for it, how she always ordered her favorite dishes even if she could only eat a few bites." Since it was for the taste of the thing after all, the essence of the dish, the relish of the quality of the cooking not its quantity she cared, because that was to savor life itself.

"Let's go for that while I'm here, Mom." "Okay," she nods, encompassing a whole new attitude and way of life in one word, different from the person she was, utterly different. I long to know what she has thought and felt here—I burn for her to talk to me. But she does not talk: instead she is.

~

In the car we are like two bandits. Even though we have the permission of the authorities, the nursing desk. Also the receptionist with her vast colorful Disneyland spectacles at the front desk. She will push a button that will allow us out another exit, one without stairs, one you reach through an elevator with a key presently in place, activating it. And because she presses the button we can leave without setting off an alarm, for when we reach the door on the floor below a notice informs us that an alarm would sound if we had not notified the staff. In pressing her mysterious button the receptionist has disarmed this alarm.

We have made it through all these obstacles and out into the fresh air, but when I signed my name under the words "responsible person" I already suspected myself. Once out we are almost hooting for joy, released with a bang like seltzer water. It feels like a getaway. "I hate this place," she said to me in the room, again and again, often with merely a frown, a thumbs-down gesture, a scowl perfectly descriptive if non-verbal. Just as Sally and Mallory warned me, she limits herself to monosyllables, refuses to go further into phrases. "Preserving her strength" is how they had explained it. After the trauma of surgery all her energy had to remain in her body to heal it; talk drains her.

Now her old reticence and politeness are entirely gone; her expression of distaste is absolute, her detestation for every inch of the room and the corridors, the very bricks. As if it were obscene, too gross and hideous to trust to language. I begin to inhabit her reality—she has broken out of jail. I am really her accomplice, her vehicle, her means.

Hardly a responsible person, I absorb her prisoner's high. Haven't I escaped the loony bin? She picked the right daughter. She knew whom to address with her purpose. She has said her "Get me out of here" to someone who's a sucker for a line like that. I have no idea what I have taken on though I understand beyond reason, at some purely instinctual plane of emotion. We are on the lam. It's a movie, it's the most unlikely American car fantasy, we are Thelma and Louise, this frail old woman beside me, and I some undefined criminal type: I light a cigarette.

"Oh no, you're smoking again," she accuses, but without much conviction or any of the usual force of disapproval. This is what the new haircut has done, this is what captivity has taught her: it doesn't matter that much anymore. Freedom has priority over decorum, she can let something be. I grin at her like a fellow offender: "If you're gonna ride with me, you're gonna have to live with it," knowing already at the most important level that we are escaping, that I cannot betray or force her back there, that we are on a tear now, that we don't know really where we're going.

~

By the time we get to Lund's I'm living moment to moment, fetching Mother's wheelchair out of the back of my rented station wagon, a beautiful new Toyota Camry. After I have carefully helped Mother into the new wheelchair—her own chair now—I discover I can't find the car keys anymore. Never mind, they must be in my pocket, and she's dying to get inside: you'll find them somehow. Lund's is Mother's heaven; hurry and push her into the store, she is back where she was never to be again in her Valhalla of first-class groceries, amid acres of gourmet shopping. Lund's was hard for her to get to even in the Wellington years after she had become lame and homebound. Once at St. Anne's it was certain she would never see Lund's again. But now she has the appetite for life, this frail creature, an appetite for food—which is life.

Still hardly talking, scarcely communicating in words, only through gestures, effusing asparagus and strawberries, commanding this kind of potato and not the other . . . go along with it, accept whatever she wants. It's her feast, her jail break. I alternate between frantically searching my pockets and just telling myself to forget the car keys—you got this far on pure cheek. I would love to tell the clerk at the fish counter that we've just run away from a nursing home and need the biggest lobster he has. Watching him open the peculiar little door behind the tank, Mother and I hold hands.

And when we are back at the car, the wheelchair stowed in the hatchback, Mother tucked in the front, her door safely closed, I see the keys still in the car door. I'm struck dumb by my own idiotic good luck—the car could have been stolen. I could be returning to an empty parking spot and liable for some $10,000 of corporate property. This is St. Paul, I breathe, not New York. But then I remember that time years ago when I brought Mother over to the University for an early feminist meeting, so excited to show her my world that I dropped the keys by the side of the car and we came back to discover it really had vanished. A week later the police found it gutted in Wisconsin: Mother's insurance gave her new upholstery. But for that week I lived in hell. And now I have done it again. And got away with it.

Once Mother is home she cannot really drink champagne, but it doesn't matter at all because she is home. The Wellington, her lobby, Dell at the desk welcoming her, other tenants saying hello in a confused way . . . didn't Helen Millett move out, wasn't she put in a nursing home, hasn't she disappeared into the chasm along whose edge they all stand? We ride up the elevator and along the hall serenely, ignoring that reality. I open the door to her neat one bedroom apartment: transformed after St. Anne's, magnificent now, luxurious, the height of comfort and efficiency and beauty. She is home again.

Her gratitude and relief are wonderful, frightening too. I am supposed to return her in the morning, supposed to take all this away and drag her back to St. Anne's. Neither of us mention it, we are here and now. We are so scared we dare not talk. Feeling like someone operating in an emergency, I find a big old enamel coffee pot and cook the lobsters, improvising. She rests in bed. I have given her this only to take it away? But it is something, it is living till you die, even if it is only for one night, one lobster dinner. We will have the good china, the real silverware—the wooden box that was to have been my object here found in her mahogany cabinet with the glass front. Even if she were to use it only once, once is something. I sure as hell don't want it. Not now, not yet.

I want to see this strange newly shorn head bending over its great red lobster shell in the crazy here and now which is everything. Then she will rest, then she will sleep at least this once in her new bed—for everything is new again, just as the building and the apartment, its chair and sofa, its table and silver and placemats are novelty and luxury without compare. Leaving St. Anne's I had a glimpse of the dining room: institutional formica and metal, dim little figures eating from plastic dishes on hard surfaces, aides bustling and feeding, the noise, the steam tables, the degeneracy of the public trough. We are sybarites here, fancy, genteel as the Wellington is gentility, a gentility I used to find both annoying and trivial. Realizing it is her whole world lost now, I embrace it. For her sake I love the good furniture and flowers in the lobby, every perfect inch of corridor and carpet, every service and convenience, its whole creation of dignity and security, its big glass doors and locks, its constant attendant at the desk, its courtesy and hospitality, its sense of honor and service, of paying your money and getting what you deserve . . . if only she could stay here. If there were just a way.

And across from me this game if depleted being, playing banquet with me, imitating earlier more possible feasts, lifting her glass and thanking me, devouring the lobster meat with gusto and appetite—there is still appetite, or there is appetite again—enormous appetite for life, all coming back. For what? For tomorrow's mass meal in that awful place? She didn't eat there, she says. "It was horrible," the frown, her hand pushed out in front of her. Do not ask her more: what was it like in jail Mom, how did that despair feel—tasteless to inquire. You wrote it all out, your own *Loony Bin Trip*. But she has no interest in recalling anything, offers no information, refuses to remember. There is no entrance to her inner self at all, communication is impossible. Only, only this moment: her exhaustion and her joy. Observe her rapture, be content with that, her relieved eyes fondling every object in her rooms, relishing the food and the table.

Hardly able to stay awake then, yet wishing she had the energy when finished, to sit a moment in her big chair. The one big easy chair; "her" chair ever since I was a child and there were his chair and her chair. And he is gone along with his chair, but hers has remained these fifty years, covered and recovered again, always still the same comfort, even identity. If she goes to bed now and you sit in this one easy chair—there is an antique rocker and a sofa, but only one easy chair—so if you sit in it, you are sitting in her chair. And you may do it only when she sleeps. Every moment she is awake or present in her living room it is her chair and hers only, the throne from which she pronounces and receives. When she is seated there her visitors are unaware that she can hardly walk: it is again her dais, her power, her ability to reign in her own home.

You can sit there and smoke cigarettes once she is safe in bed and all is well, but don't forget that this is only temporary. There's tomorrow. You're going to have to call those people in the morning: there was a nice social worker there, brand new, not hardened yet, a youngster with great sweetness of heart, Pam Keenan, nice Irish name. Would she help get permission for the weekend? Because I am already thinking of the weekend, already imagining ball game tickets, Sunday maybe. Tonight's game wasn't broadcast and even Mother had no interest in it. It had become merely our alibi, and once feasting we were beyond embarrassment.

Plan now, I tell myself: say that she just sleeps tomorrow, gets back her strength again, recovers from the trauma. To face one on Monday? Forget Monday, let's see how we can stretch it out. What would Steven think? Has he any idea what he has unleashed in the two of us? The authorities seemed relaxed about the overnight, they called it a "leave of absence," sounded like the army. So why not more absence? How does it go with nursing homes anyway: do relatives come and borrow those they have consigned to such places? Don't they just pay their obligatory visit and get out, bring the children, chat for an hour guilty or not guilty, and then flee? Are there actually occasions, family reunions, graduations, weddings, birthdays—moments where a resident is taken out, borrowed for a time? Wasn't the whole point to get them "out of the house?" Why would one take them back? Where would they house them when the usual rationale was that there was "no room" for Mother or Grandmother: "We couldn't keep her at home," "We couldn't give her the care she needed at our house, she needed round the clock and she couldn't live alone anymore." We have heard these phrases all our lives, the mitigating statement, the explanation, the justification, the excuse.

And of course how many nursing home residents, even in Mother's condition, still have their own lovely apartments just eight blocks away? Alas that will be over soon. What if you just went down and made sure? Sal thinks the Wellington will not have Mother anymore, have made it clear they would not permit her to return since she no longer qualifies as self-sufficient. What if you just dared to ask Edith? Dell at the desk is my buddy, always cheerful and a good sport. Edith however is the one, the boss. The residents used to say that Ellie, who preceded her, was nicer, cared more: Edith is all business, they had told me when she first came. Try it, make sure. Explain, tell her the truth, brave it. You can't be sure unless you ask.

But what are you asking? That Mother stay here? Impossible, there's the 24-hour care, which would surely be against the rules. Anyway, Mother could never afford that, she'd be penniless in months. Are you trying to ruin her? I'm on the sofa now, my sheets spread out, the last cigarette, the wildest speculations. Three times in three hours I have gotten up to help Mother to the toilet, it seems she cannot go often enough now that the opportunity affords itself, tiny emanations of urine, scarcely worth the trouble of getting out of bed and teetering behind her walker, so unsteady she is, so terrified of falling that she demands I hold on to her rib cage from behind. "Hold on tight, tighter," she commands. This must be how it was done at St. Anne's when she finally got someone to come. She never needed anyone before to guide her in her walker, far from being better than before surgery, she is worse, more insecure in her balance, more frightened of a fall. Are you crazy thinking of her staying here—who would be here in the watches of the night? Picture a night nurse dozing over a magazine, would she even hear the little voice calling out?

It calls out over and over and I hear it even in sleep, getting up from the sofa at eleven, then at twelve, then at one thirty, at two fifteen, at three something, four something else—no one could endure this. It is torture to rip oneself out of a sound deep sleep, time after time. The Russians have used sleep deprivation against prisoners for decades, it leaves no marks. It is very difficult to be good-humored by three or four in the morning, my body is in real pain for being awakened again and again. And hers? Imagine the insecurity over continence that wakes her repeatedly, imagine the urgency to preserve this wonderful new found capacity, the urgency to avoid wetting that perfect little bed with its dotted Swiss coverlet, its lovely sheets.

Mother's sheets are all the gifts of her daughters over the years, so that she would sleep in flowers. I know every pattern, have selected most of them myself, standing in the sheet section with my favorite clerk at Bloomingdale's in New York, deciding on tulips by Sonya or some bright yellow posies, this set would be perfect for Mother. The clerk, city-tough, bleach blonde and good at her job, is my partner and promises it will be sent out right away. Christmases, birthdays.

On the last desperate trip to the bathroom I catch sight of Mother's framed map of the Indies on the opposite wall, trophy of some cruise that it suddenly hurts terribly to remember. Mother once went around the world in one big go when she retired from life insurance in her sixties, circled the globe, traveling much of the time on her own. Later she took cruises . . . this cruise to Cuba, Haiti, Dominica, and the scattered romantic names of little islands in the paper sea around and below . . . how it all mocks us now. She will never travel again, never even see the Farm again, she will even lose her map when the apartment is dismantled next month, there will be nothing left of the great achievements of this old woman who had gone so far past the adventures of her forebears shipping out of Galway in steerage.

"Remember the steerage," she always says when it gets tough. It's tough now, that brave silly tourist's memento on the wall makes it tough seeing her unable to stand up from the toilet when she is finished. Carefully checking the toilet paper. She smells bad, she is not even clean for all her efforts—do they never bathe her there?

She is still wearing this dirty white woolen jacket, almost a coat, insisting on it, she will not remove it. Why I wonder, what does it mean? It was elegant once, expensive; now it is tired, eccentric. "It's Mallory's," she says, that's all she will say. As if her youngest daughter were embodied in this soiled garment, Mallory who nursed her all through August after surgery. Mallory heroic, almost hysterical with fatigue and defeat, Mother failing quickly as the time came for her and Thomas to leave. But they had to, they had to go back to California, they could no longer run their importing business out of a guest room at the Wellington, their lives were in disorder. So they left Mother in the Good Neighbor Suite upstairs where she would have 24-hour care for the few days until Sal came.

And then things went haywire? Did Mother feel abandoned, is that what the hypercalcemia represented, this strange visitation, this mysterious lethal condition we still cannot explain? What if it returned, how are you going to deal with that? Mallory left her coat. And Mother clung to it, all through her hospitalization, two weeks of it, and managed not to have it taken from her through the week she has endured at St. Anne's alone among strangers who must have been even more frightening as she realized this was not a hospital like the last place, intrusive and impersonal, but something of a jail, a place you could not leave. And when you called no one came. No, this was not a hospital, authoritarian and expensive as they are but full of expertise and perhaps help, this was a dumping ground, a place to wilt and die in, slowly and alone. "There are two things I am afraid of," she had said, "a nursing home and being a burden."

Mallory was right, there is no mercy in the hands of strangers. Would she take mother, would she come through? Sal seemed to think Mallory might never do it, wouldn't be able to get access to the flat next door for a long time, might be too busy with her own life; surely it would be a burden.

On both of them. The best thing of all is her own house, her own life here, the Wellington. Ask, ask Edith.

When I wake finally at six in the morning I hear her—Mother, all by herself in the bathroom, the click of her walker, the flush of the toilet—good God, she has gotten up alone, has gone to the toilet herself. Confronting her, I startle her, she nearly falls: "Why didn't you call me?" I say, guilty, afraid. "I couldn't bother you again, couldn't wake you again." "But you must, you could fall alone."

"No, I have decided to stand on my own two feet," she says, so small, so weak and unable, but she means it.

If she could do it, if she could make an enormous effort and regain her independence. If we could hole up here and just go to St. Anne's for the physical therapy—they've been giving her physical therapy everyday there—what then? I think of Edith, summoning the nerve to go down and ask Edith, is she even on duty today? "Rest some more, Mom, let's both rest some more, why not rest all day today." She is safe in her bed, she rests, I drink coffee and think about Edith. I have always been afraid of Edith, aware of how contingent Mother's tenure here might be, the contract and the obligation to self-sufficiency. As Mother's strength and ability drained away through the spring and fell off in the summer to the point where she needed both Carol and the Good Neighbor Agency, Mother entered into a fringe condition where outside help was a necessity and I became more and more afraid of Edith. Sally talked as if Mother's return was actually pronounced to be out of the question.

What luck, Edith is here today. I'm even invited into her inner sanctum, the room to the right of the reception desk. I begin, indecisive and shaking, daring to pose the question: would it be possible, under whatever conditions, for Mother to stay on? "Have you already rented her apartment?" Edith is downright surprised. "We'd love to have your mother back, her apartment isn't rented yet. Sally is supposed to be sending a letter formally surrendering the apartment, but I haven't received it so far."

"I thought your mother had been placed in a nursing home, St. Anne's, wasn't it? Isn't she there already?" "Well yes, but I brought her back home for the weekend and I began to wonder if there were some way she could stay . . . if we got the right help, don't you know?" "I see no reason why not," Edith replies, completely kind. I'm astonished. What about the rules? It seems the rules apply rather more upon entrance; Mother was entirely self-sufficient when she arrived three years ago. Once satisfied, it seems the rules can bend a little over time. Edith describes one old man who lived at the Wellington until he died. "Actually he died in the hospital, but he was only there a day. He lived here right up to the end and we were glad to have him. Of course for a good while he needed help, but there are people right in the building. Vera, for example."

I had noticed Vera at dinner and on the elevator; she seemed to have soul, a sense of humor, playfulness, imagination. There's Kay too, and there's Carol. I pull back a bit, there is trouble with Carol; Sally is contesting a bill, Mallory has complaints against her. "There's also the Good Neighbor Agency, who not only have a suite on the ninth floor, they have "floaters" throughout the building who give care to some residents right in their apartments. If you could put something together with them . . . and why not have a word with Vera, she's just come in for the day."

Vera is the sort people here call a "real good sport," warm, with a sense of fun, laughter and good times. I took to her right off, going on instinct and recalling the last line from an article on aging parents that I'd found in Mother's apartment: "Never hire anyone you don't like the looks of." I like the looks of Vera. She wears shorts and tennis shoes, is tanned and youthful but also has a beautiful head of gray hair she has refused to dye and arranges in a manner strangely reminiscent of Louis the Sun King. The effect is impressive and tremendously vital: Vera has energy, a sense of adventure, even mischief. And Vera would be delighted; she has actually said she's "had her eye on" my mother for quite a while and would love to have her as one of her "ladies." She took care of Mother's best friend Hap before Hap went to a nursing home: these days Vera's here to help Eleanor Bayliss, although only part time. But in fact, with this split schedule, she has to be in the building every day, seven days a week, from eight in the morning until eight at night.

"Aren't you getting married this week?" Edith teases her. "You bet, have a look at the ring; I finally got it." I wonder: "Will you still want to work such long hours?" "Hell yes, I've just got bigger expenses." She laughs. It might be possible.

In my enormous joy and relief I must still be practical. I like Vera: she's fun, upbeat, working class, real. And she would be kind, I feel instinctively. Mallory's voice goes on in my mind about how when you let these people into your homes, how do you know they won't steal things, they have keys, mother's jewelry, etc. Mother's jewelry is junk and her independence is beyond price, I answer myself. But how reliable is Vera, Sal's voice asks, undermining my confidence. Who does she have for "backup" if she were ill; she's an individual, not an agency. Sally tells me that all arrangements simply disintegrate, previous ones always did. Can you count on this over time? When you're back in New York? Months from now, they'll just call up and quit. They got another job, they moved, whatever. Could you pull this off, or are you just putting something together with Scotch tape?

You are only supposed to be here a week. Seven days from this very Saturday morning you are supposed to be on a plane for Toronto to speak at a benefit, you have a plane ticket leaving Minneapolis airport this Friday morning. Touch down at the Farm that night and be in La Guardia bound for Canada the next morning. You can't swing it. What if I flew out of Minneapolis for Toronto? The folks in Toronto would lose a cheap prepaid ticket and have to buy you another for full fare—remember it's a benefit. I remember all day long. I also remember that the following week I am to speak in Binghampton, New York in a staged debate on psychiatric drugs whose single advantage would be that I could finally meet my hero Thomas Szasz as together we would contradict the conventional wisdom of two drug pushers representing the American Psychiatric Association. I need the money, spent it already on my art show in Provincetown.

"Did you sell any pictures?" Mother asked me over lobster last night. "Four hundred fifty dollars in sales," I laughed, "and it only cost eight hundred to go there and to put on the show." "It's nice you can laugh about it," she concluded. "I'm only fifty-seven, Mom, just starting out, who knows?" It was funny last night.

Nothing financial is funny now. Time and money have begun to hold me in a vice. And there's Europe, my wonderful month-long trip to Europe, all expenses paid by the English publisher, the Spanish publisher, France just fifty dollars away from London, Irish Television would pay my way to see Ireland again . . . it is the chance of a lifetime. Four countries. There are elaborate preparations for *The Loony Bin Trip*'s publication in England, big public meetings, benefit lectures, interviews, groups of women writers to address, appearances at Oxford and Cambridge. I haven't had a British publisher for fifteen years, they were going all out, it could help me a great deal, it would be terribly foolish as well as rude to even consider canceling it, but it's so soon. How could I take on Mom's care and get there too, it's only three weeks away now. Don't consider it. Keep going, don't look right or left.

~

"Mom, Edith says you can stay," I burst in triumphantly, "maybe we can work something out." My voice falls off, seeing her gesture hopelessly: there's an emergency, I must call New York right away. Who's called, what emergency? She lapses into incompetence, won't talk, can't remember. I call the Farm, everything's fine. My old friend L.K. who manages the Farm, has everything under control: "Don't even think about this place, take care of your Mom." Who would be insisting I go back to New York, as Mother insists the caller has demanded? Did Jennifer call? "I don't know, I don't know anything," she sits inert and helpless in her chair. Has she invented this? Is it a test? Am I only complicating her life? Does she want me to leave? What goes on inside her? She is exhausted she says and will say nothing more. I help her to bed. Vera, Edith, it all seems silly now.

Helen Klett always seems silly, it is part of her charm, a carefully calculated act, like her glamor girl exterior, a work of art. Helen is eighty-seven and a working fashion model, a beauty with a studied routine of frivolous old lady built upon a firm foundation of good-looking dame. She has just survived a full course of chemotherapy for cancer, has the courage of a matador, the acumen of a general, the savvy and glamor of a diplomat. She is one of Mother's two oldest friends still living and by good fortune she lives in the building next door. There is no congregate dining in Helen's modest apartment house so she loves to be invited to dine at the Wellington where she has a great many friends. Mother loves to invite her and by the accident of this leave of absence, now extended another day, Mother can do so again tonight. It will of course be the last time, but Helen refuses to see that aspect of it at all.

"I never thought," she gushes. "Isn't it a regular registered miracle . . . isn't it the grandest surprise in the world to see you again in that chair . . . I never thought, not in my wildest dreams—isn't it wonderful?" Mother glares, she will not be duped into lightheartedness. Or even into sentiment; holding on hard, she listens to Helen tell her how she has walked by Mother's window so many times—it's just in the line of her walk everyday by the park and the River—and looked up, saw the darkness and wept, missing her. They are both named Helen, listening to them is like overhearing lovers forced to part. This is fifty years of friendship; how cruel are age and immobility that these factors could separate even over such short distances, the lack of transportation walling them away from each other.

Circumstances too, social arrangements, the expectations of those who are younger, entitled, enabled and mobile and in charge.

If Helen Klett had not masterminded the bus system so perfectly she might never have seen Mother alive again. Once buried at St. Anne's, visited by Steven and Joannie, taken out to dinner occasionally, maybe even permitted visits to her sister Margaret in Excelsior—but who would think to drive an old woman on an excursion merely to see a friend? This friend who was the first person she wished to see. Once you're in a nursing home everything goes, everything that is not family business: family blessed, family authorized, family centered. Bridge games go, tea parties, anything with peers or buddies, no one can go anywhere on their own and relatives think in family terms, have their own agendas and so little time. Anything outside the family is secular, frivolous. I adore Helen Klett's frivolity, her real love of whiskey, occasional cigarettes, hyperbole, Irish malarkey and brogue, the story of her own birth in a remote farmhouse, her twelve-year-old sister acting as midwife, the description of her mother's poor housekeeping and her passionate life-long composition of a book which was never published, even lost at her death, her relish for scandal in the diocese. This time it's not the archbishop who frowned on gay rights, I already know about him, arrested for drunken driving—it's the little bishop, the second guy down, caught in some vice or another. She giggles, don't you love it? We both do, working diligently on our scotch in the few permitted moments before Mother demands we leave on time for dinner, early even. Mother is always early and is going to insist on it again. She is not amused, she is serious. She has hardly enough energy for this meeting and has something to achieve through it. Taking her cue, as does Helen Klett, afire with inspiration—Mother should stay at the Wellington, why not? "You can get people to look after you," Helen's grandson has a girl friend who will be going to the University, needs a job, "This isn't insurmountable, why don't we figure it out. Kate says Vera could help, Kate says Edith will let you stay."

"I'm never going back to that place," Mother announces flatly. "Nor should you, they're horrible, we all hate those places," Helen Klett agrees smoothly, serving up her ginger cookies, still hot from her oven; there's more in a package to keep in the freezer. They begin with the assumption that nursing homes are the end: they know, as political prisoners know, as minorities know. It is part of their culture, the secret life of the old, the trail they follow among obstacles, pitfalls, diseases, forfeits, accidents that put you out of the game. Mother has been put out of the game, Helen Klett is game enough to try to get her back in. Against the board rules, she is suggesting the unthinkable, urging it on me.

It would take one of them, I realize, one of her own kind to put this notion into words so someone as obtuse and undependable as I could face the fact that Mother has already decided to stay, is waiting for me to co-operate or decamp. She is determined that somehow she will either manage to stay alive in these rooms or die doing it. And she is dealing with a daughter who will not override her, call an ambulance, deal with her through force, have her declared incompetent. Her outlaw daughter doesn't operate that way, but perhaps still cannot be relied upon not to decoy her back there through deceit, take her for a ride, drop her off, jump a plane. Therefore Mother enlisted Helen Klett, suggested the invitation, remembered the phone number, even made the considerable effort of telephoning herself. How I react now is crucial.

There's so little time, I have only a week here to put arrangements in place. Is it possible? I hardly dare admit how scared I am or why. In fact I'm scared of Sal, Steven, the authorities at St. Anne's, the system, all the "grown-ups," all the big shots who talk about old people as if they were absent or objects or children, creatures rarely consulted over the decisions that govern their own lives. And I'm also part of the traitor generation, the managing bullies who have put Mother in this position, may put Helen Klett there soon too. In their company I am painfully aware that this is cruel and stupid and I am ashamed.

Never mind, Helen Klett will beguile you with stories, will joyfully mock the nursing home's piety. "Did they have those plaster saints and all the rest of it, I'll bet?" She spins out an arabesque of talk. "My parents came from the old country, soaked in that awful reverence for the clergy, would you believe, my own mother used to genuflect to them on the street—the street? Yes, we'll just finish this and go to dinner, don't worry there's plenty of time." And at dinner Helen Klett is the life of the party while Mother sits ignored but out of the wind, not having to converse, a mercy since her deafness makes hearing others impossible in this large room full of talk. She can handle one-on-one in her own apartment, but here in the dining room under a high ceiling and the booming room tone of many conversations, she cannot follow at all. Instead, off by herself, she can concentrate on just getting through it, the shame of her fallen reputation here, her very frailty, her terror of vomiting at the table, dropping her food, choking. This is her first return to the living, the fast track at the Wellington, where everyone dresses up for dinner, converses in earnest, each exchange a proof you are still with it, not slipping. Mother's old table is the fastest set of all, even has men, a rare and precious element, for the vast proportion of those still running the race are women.

A new woman started at Mother's table last summer, very chic and able; Sally reported that she never addressed Mother at all. Finally Sally pointed out that Mother was unable to hear anything she said. The woman only laughed, deafness was beneath her consideration: sink or swim. This woman, Ceil, became the bane of Mother's existence, poisoned her mealtimes, became an element in her decline through the summer. Tonight Mother selects another table, the round one by the window, a different crowd, Marjorie Bordenave, whose daughter Barbara went to Derham Hall with me, though I can hardly remember her as well as I should, am overcome by her reports of Marjorie's children's exploits, her fabulous pride in them. Her son-in-law is flying in the Gulf War, my pacifism is needled with each report of his heroism. But I realize that behind Marjorie's barrage of family news, she is taking me in, taking Mother in as well. Forced to recall school chums I am slowly knit back to the town, woven into the table, to the streets and relatives and connections.

Deafness doesn't bother Marge Bordenave at all, her Mother was deaf since early womanhood, so learned to lip read, taught her children to enunciate carefully and look a speaker right in the face. There are others at the table who are hard of hearing and Marge keeps the whole conversation alive for them, she is doing it on purpose, out of an almost inexplicable goodness one has to accept as Christian kindness. She's an old friend of Mother's friend Hap too, and walks to Hap's nursing home everyday. So does Ruth at Mother's old table, but there's a dourness and disapproval in Ruth, much like Ceil's. Ruth goes by the rules, you're with it or you're not, deafness is a handicap. And to be brought down to dinner in a wheelchair as Mother is now, is to be out of bounds altogether.

I yearn for the time when Mother could come in her walker, I yearn for all her earlier capacities, envy the able-bodied. Even on the street I begin to envy youth, people who drive cars, run. I have never considered these things at all and now they obsess me.

~

Waking on Sunday morning I remember my own life, the Farm and books to write, feeling it slip away here. Life itself slipping away. I should lose weight, quit smoking again. I feel impossibly old, vulnerable, aware I will die. Finally realizing in Mother's imminent death the reality of my own, for she was dying while I was in Provincetown, raving between public phone boxes and the friends upon whom I imposed. The rest of the time I made a series of splattered drawings with words in them: "If they restrain you I will untie your hands," I swore in one of them. Big talk when you can't even free her and set her up at home. How do I dare risk it? At the last resort there is Mallory in California or my place in New York. Take her to the Farm if she can't make it here alone? The Bowery loft is five flights up and no elevator. Once there she would never be able to leave, go out, have any life.

Ten dollars an hour is Vera's price. How does anyone do something as hard as giving care to another human being for such a pittance? On the other hand, add it up, do the math, ten dollars an hour for 24 hours a day is $240 a day: at fifteen dollars, the going rate, it's $360. Times thirty days it's $7,000–$10,000. Mother hasn't got that, no one has. Then pare it down, do most of the hours yourself, make caretaking a job like the five hours a day we all put in to the Farm. And if Mother were at the Farm someone there might take care of her for pin money. Nonsense, these young artists didn't come to an art colony to take care of your mother, be reasonable. And for all the liveliness and vitality of the place, it is a place of the young, of lesbians and artists; not her place, not her life. Even if you got around the "burden" element, it would be utterly alien to her.

No, she must have her own life. As we all must. Make a stand for that. She risked her life giving you birth, laid down her life to support and raise you. Risk your own life a little. One day at a time. Call the bank tomorrow, get the Farm taxes paid anyway. You may have to stay a while and you have no bank books here, your little system of pockets, one account for this, another one for that, a method which has made it possible to actually run a farm on what it earns, while living a perilous existence myself on just $12,000, the $1,000 a month stipend which the Hamburg Institute for Social Research awarded a couple years ago to do the book against the torture of political prisoners. What do you need, they'd asked; "I can live on a thousand a month," I boasted. But they thought I would be done a long time ago, so I have added every lecture and mite of royalty and strung it out. It's four years, there are already nine chapters, the last four or five I was to finish at the Bowery this coming fall and winter, be done before I went to the Farm again next summer.

But last spring I already began cheating, writing three pieces about my Mother, one for each visit I made to her. A small private work for myself, doing it early in the morning or in bursts, still doing the other book, keeping up. It was over now, I felt, I have not even brought the notebook with me, no point in buying another: Mother's text is finished, it was just a portrait I did for myself; it would be absurd to see it continue.

Forget your damn books—live. This is life itself: this living room, its china cabinet and easy chair, the efficiency kitchen, old Maude Hill's rocker, the one bit of swag from our connection with wealth, how odd that Mother should inherit it or anything from her rich sister-in-law, this bit of Minnesota history, the chair where Maudie rocked while her son Louis Senior spent Jim Hill's booty on culture and fine bindings. It was Jim's own wife's chair and she rocked while she goaded him to his millions, Jim a driver like Patrick Henry, like Mother herself, this curious elusive creature I tried to put on paper. I never caught her character in my pages, never brought her talk across. Now she does not speak at all. Secret and silent. At the best of times, last spring, say, she alternated between the oracular and the trivial: "Throw the newspaper away, put the cream back in the icebox". Now it is simply a one word command, "trash" or "cream." But back then there were also moments of epiphany when I would sit at the footstool of her chair and she would face what's coming and make pronouncements, commandments: "After I'm gone, keep the family together, stay a family."

How, for god's sakes? when in following her wishes I would begin a feud, cause a fissure: Sally will never forgive me if I bring Mother home, expose her to a life without proper care, a fatal fall, an untended desert of loneliness and incapacity. Sal sees the bed at St. Anne's as safety, utterly essential safety. And the solution she has accepted with tears and anguish, finding no other, ill herself and her law practice hurt through her absences. This would solve everything, we could stop running to St. Paul and worrying; it would all be taken care of. And it's time now, past time, Mother was here on borrowed time all summer, left unattended as this or that caretaker didn't show up, couldn't make it, sent a substitute, charged for visits never made. How do you know what they're doing? Mother can't keep track, couldn't remember, was too ill to notice, too dependent to demand, helpless before these persons, did not even write their checks herself: they were paid by Sal. Who was sure there was a rip off somewhere. She has a quarrel with Carol which is perhaps becoming a lawsuit. She's "had it to here with the whole idea of these people, these agencies." As for individuals like Vera, independent contractors Sal calls them, she trusts them even less. No backup, Sally says in her attorney's voice, which is formidable.

Mother's independence I always start to say then, tentative, surely this is the whole point, it's Mother's money we are discussing and Mother's own life—is just over and done with, I hear Sal's voice declaring with terrible finality, as if Mother were dead already. For the Wellington is her life, the life she chose, the only one she regards as tolerable. If Sal can turn a deaf ear, I can't. And I'm on the spot, right here, listening to Mother's wishes—which I can't refuse. Sally probably couldn't either if she were here, storm as she might; Mother must have some way of dealing with this daughter as well. She appears completely without fear of Sal; but I am frightened of her. Her anger, her disappointment, her carefully laid and painfully executed plans. All messed up by her diffident, impractical kid sister.

Sal is the head of the family; we are like that: hierarchy, seniority. The eldest even usually inherit most: Aunt Dorothy observed that though Mother will not. In any case they have the most responsibility and so they are the boss. I am in the position of a mutineer here, a renegade. As always. But for the first time I am in alliance with Mother, the soul of probity and rectitude, the most conventional person on earth, I used to think. Now a little bandit on the run though sound asleep in the next room. While she sleeps, I take the opportunity to call her parole board and ask for another of their precious pills, dealt out one day at a time from a locked office. The whole apartment is full of pills in fact—the wrong ones. There was a paper bag at the door when we arrived from a prescribing doctor, a man whose name I have never heard of, some fill-in between the University hospital and St. Anne's. Three bottles of mystery. There are vials and vials of antidepressants which I have already consigned to the back of the closet. The less "medication" Mother takes the better; any foreign substance is a hazard now. But she really does need that synthetic thyroid she's been on for years. Go, get one, then start figuring out how to obtain a prescription of her own, her own bottle of the stuff to have at home. Control over the medicine is control over the person. And many of the medicines are control themselves. It is all so controlling, so authoritarian, regimented. When you get to St. Anne's, remember to be a lamb, all gratitude and grovel, cheerfulness itself. It's a locked joint, don't forget that, don't mess up Mom's picture, she is somehow—legally? (it's hard to figure)—in their hands.

They brandish Sally's name as if it were a sponsor's, the one in charge, the "admitting relative," the person they deal with. Then Steven, the power of attorney, a practicing attorney right here in St. Paul. I am a visiting lightweight, expected to stay only a few days, negligible, an artist whose clothes are not even correct, sandals and sweats and a jersey top my friend Marie gave me for a birthday present which comes in very handy now because the front of it has a big marsupial pocket for the car key and the house key, my most precious possessions while escorting Mother in and out of the car, the wheelchair, opening doors, her page and squire. In adolescence I used to be her knight after Dad was gone and I was the right age to lean on. I was thirteen, Mallory was only eight. A woman alone with two kids and no job, hardly able to drive a car. I grew up quickly, got jobs after school, emptied bed pans, sold stockings in department stores during the Christmas rush. I paid the utility bills, did all the laundry, bought the phone service. When mother did better I could squander part of my winnings on Christmas presents in fancy foil paper, a breadwinner showing off. In college I wasted my earnings on clubs and books, but I always came through, earned, spent, had my own resources. Ever since I learned about coke bottles at five years old, how a wagon full of them could stand the neighborhood kids to tootsie pops at Goldie's store while Goldie's son Benjy, a stand-in for Edward G. Robinson home on vacation, told us all about Hollywood. Money was fun, was something you got hold of and shared with friends and then you had a party, made life a party—the Farm.

~

All yesterday Mother slept. All morning today. Now the little voice calls out for attention. I've lucked out and gotten baseball tickets. We even managed to find the stadium, did the impossible and found a parking space near the Metrodome. Mother hung in for three innings before her strength gave out and we had to leave. The Twins were winning as we left which boded well. In fact they are winning a lot now, may be in line for the western division of the American League; Mother is excited, has hooked her star to her team. The Wellington bubbles with enthusiasm, a whole apartment house of fans, Edith is the greatest enthusiast of all, has season tickets, wears a Twins teeshirt and a hat. If the Twins make it to the playoffs the Wellington is planning festivities in their party room where they have a screen as big as a bed sheet; there may be betting at the desk.

I think of Mother watching her heroes at St. Anne's where the old women are lined up so that they are not even facing the television but the wall, a sight that confounded me when I went back to the dreary place for eyedrops and a few thyroid pills, her only medicine but dealt out as carefully as if it were opium. We have permission to stay out the whole weekend.

Steven drops by with Victoria, a treat for Mother, but an absolute block to serious conversation. Victoria is everywhere, goes at everything. Steven is like someone operating dangerous machinery; you can't talk to him. I'm running out of cash, need to write a check, dare not ask him for help. I would even love to sneak my mad plans and hopes past him—without committing myself, without getting called on it, just a trial balloon. But I'm wary—he is Sally's son, after all, a lawyer too, responsible to carry out her will. And careful to avoid me, diffident, noncommittal. We limit ourselves to drivel: how nice it is to see Mother home again, she seems better doesn't she?

Of course I will have her back by tomorrow for physical therapy, I promise, valuing the therapy, knowing that without it she may never walk, may never get the full benefit of the shunt surgery she has paid for so dearly. We do not venture further, we cannot speculate; he does not oppose me, but he cannot be my accomplice either. Even his neutrality is a gift, but I miss him so, even in his presence I feel utterly alone and afraid, would love to go off and have a drink with him, pour out my heart. Just what he is avoiding, so busy this week, his child, his wife, his job. Next weekend they will all be driving to Chicago for a wedding, Chris's brother. We can have dinner on Wednesday, all of us; otherwise every moment of his time is occupied. I feel so remote here, an out-of-towner no one has time for, too old for his age group of friends, his own life speeding past me. If only I knew someone to talk to, to consult with, a break, relief from the eternal vigilance of care, Mother's endless demands, commands, orders.

There are times I correct her now, ask her to preface her requests with please or thank you. Humiliate her with lectures on manners and phrases like would you please, do you mind, some icing upon her utterly peremptory manner. She apologizes and thanks me and returns to her one word directives. I must ignore it all, I must realize that "toileting" as the nursing regulations refer to it, is the most paramount thing in the world. I am as controlled by my aged dependant as Steven is by his infant. We look at each other across a chasm. But he has either failed to guess my desire or is ignoring it, is either innocent of my terrible proclivity or deliberately refusing to involve himself.

I live in a family where after decades of disapproval it is now permissible to be a lesbian: to advance beyond that to a kidnapper of old ladies is surely going too far, I figure, watching him leave, still having failed to make any contact at all. But if he understands, he has not chosen to stand in my way. Maybe it will work after all, maybe it will all come true.

~

Sal doesn't seem to think so. Though she does not categorically forbid me to consider bringing Mother home and undoing all she has done—in such illness and discomfort (it is pneumonia after all) and with such anguish and unhappiness: she had solved things, after all, by placing Mother in St. Anne's. Much as it was to be regretted, it was over, done with, suffered through. And there would be no further complications, no phone calls, no sirens, no "caregivers" finding themselves over their heads and calling ambulances, no part-timers quitting or failing to show up—this was total care. The family could breathe easy, could go on with their own lives. Mother was no longer a problem: the problem of Mother. Now I have made it all moot again.

Listening to Sal, I must regret what I have done so far and agree to its folly, even to have brought Mother home for a weekend can only increase her sorrow when she goes back to St. Anne's. Mother's nieces, my cousins Joannie and Helen Ann stopped by to visit after the game and could only cluck at the greater disappointment my poor Mother would experience when I brought her back, for I would have to.

If I don't believe Sally, I can call Doctor so-and-so at the University, a woman doctor and very good one. She has made it very clear, "disabused" Sally entirely. I admire Sal's choice of word: she is speaking with great effort, hard and fast and in detail, having considered every possibility already. Listening, I blush with embarrassment at my own naiveté, and feel a rush of shame as well as fear, my throat constricts to the point where I can barely speak at all, only mumble, yes, yes, to Sally's hoarse and strained fury in illness, her cough fighting with her need to explain to this nitwit younger sister, teetering on the edge of some mad scheme, questioning, operating where she has no understanding. Without facts or figures or even the names of the participants, caregivers, doctors, experts.

There is a notice here that Mother should have a routine annual check-up from her eye doctor, a petty detail to me, a great issue with Sal . . . If she only knew, I think, guilty, scared into panic, listening to Sal's barrage of arguments and priorities: the opportunity of a bed at St. Anne's as precious as its weight in diamonds in Sal's opinion—have I any idea how hard these places are to get into? Anecdotes about waiting lists, about inferior places that charge more: people have to wait for years. Have I any conception? The phone shakes in my hand—what if I lost the bed and then had to live locked up with Mother on the fifth floor of the Bowery trying to write between trips to the toilet. Have I even the most remote connection with reality? Sally's house is totally unsuitable, it has stairs; I listen remembering Mother's confidence that she would never have to go to a nursing home because Sally had told her she would share her house if the time came. Now it has stairs. Sally shares it with a friend. Steven has stairs, I have stairs, five flights of them. Am I crazy? Getting Mother into St. Anne's was the gift of the gods, never mind if she hates it or I hate it, it's the best there is. What madness took hold of me, has hold of me now, listening to prices and places, stark reality . . . guilty of what I dare not even mention, saying nothing, listening, being read the riot act.

By the sister I love, look up to, admire, have always followed and studied from—in high school I used to read her college text books just for the relish of what I would learn later. Sally is a grown-up, my senior and better, a lawyer, a woman of the world, someone who understands the law, the government, the system. Sally knows the actual world I have hardly bothered to pay attention to the few moments I was not in open opposition to it: mental patients' rights, that's my speed. That crazy liberation stuff Mallory called it when I gave her hell about the drugs. You don't give Sally hell, you get it; she's your elder, not your younger sister. You don't give Mallory hell either—she refused, from early childhood, to submit to the bullying I imagined it would be my privilege to dispense—having accepted it from Sal, now it would be my turn. Not on your life, Mallory made clear, Mary then, Mother's name for her still, she was breaking the chain of command and oppression. I had to admire her for it, I had also to accept the justice of her refusal. Permitting her to scream out her exhaustion to me on a pay phone in Provincetown, Mallory going on at a great rate that she adored her mother, would do anything for her, loved her more than anything in the world, how dare I question her judgment, in fact she is not even doing it for Mother, no she's doing it for God.

I listen and roll my eyes and she goes right on, Thomas trying to represent reason on an extension phone, the whole thing funny if it were not so terrible, if it were not a pay phone without a chair, if it were not my God damned telephone credit card. Mallory lives on the phone and has plenty of money. I'm running up long distance now listening to Sal; I called her after all, dialing the infernal string of numbers, my own, then the credit card code, which never works, so you spend more going through an operator, my life for the past month has been making calls I must charge because I am always gone, always somewhere else and not home to verify the call. Now this screwball reach to give my mother a home, her own home, the Wellington.

Not St. Anne's Home, no, not that awful place. A refuge, "Safety," Sal keeps reiterating: Mother would be unsafe anywhere else. It is dangerous and irresponsible to imagine anything else but the absolute security of 24-hour professional care. Yes, I mumble. Afraid as I listen and keep my own counsel. Mother has no intention of going back, that's clear. And I know I cannot force her there or betray her back through sleight. No more than I could fail to obey her when she said she wanted to leave and come home. I have no other choice now than to try to keep her at home, no matter how long or hard or even expensive it might be, I absolutely must try to do so. That is obedience. It is pointless to take this line with Sal; she doesn't obey her Mother, she expects her Mother to obey her, she sees herself as her Mother's investor, advisor and keeper. Has for years. Mother used to find this convenient. She may not find it convenient anymore.

At the moment of our elopement from St. Anne's Nursing Home Mother had two $1 bills in her purse. Let's see if I can improve on that. "I wonder about money Sal." "What about money?" "At the moment Mom's only got two dollars." "There's a checkbook in her purse." "Is there anything in that account?" "Of course, can she sign her name?" "I'm not sure, maybe we can work on it." Sal gives me permission to make an imaginary balance in Mother's check book; we slow down into practicalities and make a plan. I'm to send all deposits to Sal, who now remembers there's a rubber stamp for deposits in the desk: I should deposit any checks that come in directly. "What hypothetical balance should I make?" "Say, five thousand." "That's too rich for me, how about three?" "Whatever, just keep a good record of what's spent."

Wonderful, we now have a checking account. I have restored Mother to solvency from the destitution of two $1 bills, the two old pieces of paper in her purse when I found her. It had seemed the saddest thing in the world. She had that and an apartment. Go for the apartment. Sally at that moment had absolute control of Mother's money and very different ideas. But now Mother has a check book if you can get her to do a credible signature. The last time I was here in the spring, I happened to be in the room as Mother tried to write a check for the man who delivered her dry cleaning. It was illegible, deplorable: it was the first absolute proof to me that she was going downhill fast. All other infirmities were explained away, overlooked, politely ignored, compensated for, hidden by her public image in her easy chair, dealt with out of sight in the bathroom. This was real. I looked at the scrawl, surely a bank will not accept this. Not only was the sum written out impossible to read, but the signature as well. I begin to wonder how banks deal with old people. I can write out the sums for her but how illegible a signature will they accept, where is the line? Can she even hold a pen? I can't forge her name. This is St. Paul and I have entered into a bizarre elopement with an old lady.

Think of other routes to cash, go for broke. It's Mother's life, it's her money, I say to myself, feeling scared, crooked, desperate. What about credit cards? Sally tells me she has just destroyed them all.

There's a pause, I wait to hear that Mother will never need credit cards again, she lives in a nursing home and so forth. But Sal has destroyed them because Mother's wallet was left at the Good Neighbor when she was rushed to the hospital. "The simpletons took two days to find it." Sally was disgusted, she had to call Mallory and confirm that the cards were in the wallet and the wallet in safekeeping, but whoever Good Neighbor had answering the phone had sworn to her they have no safe; it took more calls for someone else to remember they have a locked box for valuables. Days went by. So Sal cancelled the cards. I wonder to myself if she believed they would go on a spending spree with Mother's credit cards, a bonded agency, but I keep quiet and am rewarded with the news that new credit cards have been ordered.

Great, I think, feeling like a bank robber or a gigolo: the elopement has funds beyond my own, which are entirely insufficient. If Mother has control of her own money, maybe she can live as she likes. I'm calling Sal to find out what we can spend. Since I will be hiring and making a budget, or imagine I will be, administering Mother's money in some way, trying to buy her what care she needs, trying at least to price it. And at sea—because, oddly enough I have no idea how much Mother has or can afford and have only the figure of what it was intended she would spend at St. Anne's, that incredible $36,000 a year.

How did Mother ever amass such sums? Thrifty as she is, she probably didn't spend half of that living here all these years. Of course that's the problem, the longer you live, the less you have. Mother must have been afraid to live too long, to run out, to get to zero and still be alive. A Bowery artist who has always lived pretty close to the ground, maybe I can arrange a better life. Surely I can get her a better deal than the imposing sum charged for what I rescue her from.

But it was at least a stated price and a sure solution as Sal must have seen it. And once you go broke the State takes over. But the solution deprived Mother of everything she had, of her very selfhood in depriving her of her independence. "Back of your independence stands the Penn Mutual," her insurance company logo read, over a picture of Independence Hall in Philadelphia. And we believed it, all of us, Mother most of all. It would make it possible for her to retire in security one day just as it would do for the working women to whom she sold high grade annuities as if they were the true religion. And somehow she sold enough of them to do well. She sold herself enough as well, and invested.

Still, the disturbing thing is I have no idea how much money Mother really has. Nevertheless, to have set herself up with enough only to be forced to squander a large sum for a few years on a place of misery you despise, seems altogether unfair. "It's her money, it's also her life," I dare to say quietly against the excellent reasons, the practical considerations, the reality Sal represents. I am trying to present it as matter of money and how one chooses to live. Sal sees it as care and what you have to pay for care because you cannot live without it. "But that place isn't a life, Mother is permitted no separate self, no will of her own. It's confinement, inordinately expensive confinement." "They give them excellent care." "It's a place of despair, I doubt she would live very long there, not past the Medicare months; I don't want to inherit her savings, neither do you." "St. Anne's will inherit her savings," Sal says drearily. "Well I'd rather she spent them as she pleases, living here. At St. Anne's I think Mom was on her way out, she'd already turned her face to the wall again." "Kate, she's got to be there." "Sal, she was losing her personality, her personhood, it's a total institution." "She has to have that care."

There's got to be another way, Mother's independence was always her very core, I remind Sally. Sally insists that Mother is too infirm to maintain her own life. "But she's physically, not mentally infirm . . . and she hates the place. She wants to live at home . . . people say it can be done." "Who says?" "Helen Klett, for example."

"Christ, Helen Klett is eighty-seven years old and dying of cancer herself." "She just made it through chemotherapy, she's sharp as a tack and knows a lot more about being old than we do." Immediately, I realize I have made an error in bringing up Helen Klett as my authority; it is only proof of my inexperience. "Edith says it's possible." "Edith! Edith is a business woman; they must have vacancies at the Wellington. These are people acting out of self-interest. Have you no understanding at all?" "They're filling them just as fast," I say, winging it. "Edith was truly kind. And there's Vera here who could take care of Mother. Kay is busy, unfortunately. And unfortunately we don't seem to be on speaking terms with the others."

Sally's quarrels and Mallory's fault-finding, justified or not, have eliminated certain caregivers and narrowed my options here among those available and on the spot. Caregivers who travel cost a great deal more than we could afford. The very fragility of my plan is defeating it and when my dumb little web of support falls through, Sally will be right as usual. And St. Anne's would be gone.

"Listen, if you put together some harebrained scheme and then take off for New York and it all comes apart over a couple of weeks—then . . ." Sally is beside herself with outrage, with grief, with pneumonia, and despair and even the hope I might be right against her own certainty I am wrong. Moreover time is against us always—the tumor. Mother will only get older and frailer. And the bed at St. Anne's would never be there to catch her. Sal would like to tell me it will be my fault and my fault only, my problem and my problem forever, she would like to cut me loose and Mother too, her heart is breaking and she has done all she can . . . "It's gonna be you then . . . you're going to have to be the one who gets on the damn plane and puts it back together." This is as close as I may get to permission.

Sally and I were in agreement when the hypercalcemia struck, and Mother had been stabilized but was still hopelessly ill in a hospital which insisted she now be discharged. But where could Mother go? A return to the Wellington in her condition was unthinkable. This made placement at

St. Anne's inevitable, Sally's only option. Sally herself was ill and alone and in a dilemma of enormous proportion. The placement at St. Anne's was not only a necessity then, it also put Mother close to the only people (Steve, Joannie, Rosellen) who could watch over her.

Then Sally's and my own recollections differ; since this is my version of events I must follow my own perceptions. I had understood that the placement at St. Anne's had been a permanent one: the prognosis so dim, the necessity of 24-hour care so intense, our grief over the decision so terrible. Although I was unaware of this then, Sally had respite at St. Anne's in mind as well and intended to return after my two-week stay and reassess things. In fact, Sally did not give up Mother's apartment, although I was led to believe this might be imminent, but continued to pay rent there all through the fall in the faint hope, which was Steven's as well, that Mother might recover.

Alone at St. Anne's, however, Mother had time to come to detest and reject the place utterly. It was this I had responded to. Perhaps Sally would have as well had she been with me. That interval was crucial, it formed Mother's own wholehearted refusal of the place before which I felt I had to accede now. Sally had not seen Mother's reaction and needed to continue to regard St. Anne's as a practical solution, temporary or permanent. I no longer could. I must have seemed utterly irresponsible in struggling to do what Mother wished by returning her to her own home. The fact is, I simply could not refuse my Mother.

Following Mother's wishes would put me at odds with my sister for a time, a hurt we both still feel. Unable to deny my mother's express desire, I had acted from emotion. If I could succeed in fulfilling that desire it would be due ultimately to Sal's own flexibility which I had tested now and had some hope of winning over. As time went by and I proceeded in a shaky amateur way I am amazed as I reread by Sally's tolerance and patience. Though she challenged me—with excellent reasons—every step of the way, Sally also generously permitted me to continue when she might easily have brought me to a halt. The entire project owes a debt to her kindness.

At once reaction sets in. I am scandalized at my own temerity. All these years Sally has been the one who took care of Mother, lived closer, visited often. Sal took the trouble, bore the responsibility, was the one Mother leaned on, was the one upon whom I shrugged off my own responsibilities, obligations, so many holidays. And now I have destroyed her arrangements, encouraged Mother's unrealistic hopes and am left holding the bag. Only fair. But I cannot betray Mother, I have still the habit of obeying her, pleasing her, cannot go against her wishes, cannot deprive her of her personhood and independence. The little apartment is her heaven; every trip to St. Anne's makes the Wellington look better. What have I got myself into?

Then I remember my friend Marie. An expert, Marie deals with age for a living; she is actually a nutritionist but has made it her mission to keep old people out of nursing homes. "That's my job," she reminds me, "I told you those places were awful. They're holding tanks. For death. Get her out of there, if you don't do anything else in life, get your mother out of that place, or you'll never be able to live with yourself."

But how, the costs, the uncertainty of home help, the regime I would have to establish, the obstacle of family opposition, the bureaucratic web I must enter, the complications of Medicare regulations?

"Bullshit. Just do it. I'll explain the whole thing, I'll send you the guidelines." I already have two copies, tried to read them and don't understand a word. "It's all on page twelve. At the bottom, and on the top of the next page. Your mother probably qualifies for everything they'll give. The rest you hire. Don't let anyone talk you down. You're doing the right thing. Keep in touch, call me whenever you get lost. Do it."

"You give me hope, you encourage me in my insanity, how can I thank you?" "You have to do this. This is absolutely real even if they run it like a game. Go for it, it's all out there."

~

But on Monday morning it doesn't look promising. Not in Maggie's physical therapy room. Maggie, the brave young woman who works with the old and infirm of St. Anne's, a shoal of dejected shapes in wheelchairs, their legs hopelessly misshapen and unable. Maggie doesn't think much of Mom, neat and trim in her little "companion" chair, immaculate in a monogrammed sweater. "Her legs are perfectly able, the musculature is there," Maggie shakes her head, probably at the tumor's effect, "But your Mother makes no effort and I cannot recommend her for Medicare continuance. They have to get better and they have to do it pretty fast, the government refuses to pay for maintenance. It's a tough system. Your mother isn't even interested."

Indeed she isn't, she is impatient to leave, has no respect or even tolerance for the place and its incomprehensible activities, resents the absurd requirements of these young people: lift her leg ten times, pull on those ropes—absurd activities without meaning, pointless assaults on her dignity. Seeing it from her point of view it is without purpose. And if it were not pursued with a vengeance it would also be without result: you would have to do these exercises over and over, once a day is scarcely enough. Once a week, which is all one could afford if doing it without governmental assistance, would cost $100 for an hour-long session. Which would have no effect whatsoever.

I ignore the futility and insist on it anyway: it's our only hope. So I pretend to a certainty I do not have at all. "We have to do this, Mother, and you've got to stop being so damn negative about it. Cooperate. Please cooperate." But she doesn't want to be here at all, she hates this place; it's St. Anne's after all. "We'll just come for the therapy and go home to the Wellington again, we'll live there and just run over once a day for therapy—this is absolutely essential." Then I decide speech therapy is crucial as well, we must come twice a day, I go on continuously praising the therapy, thanking the therapists, Mother still disliking it, hating to enter this building, afraid, reasonably, that each time she may be abandoned here, captured again. Only very gradually relenting, partly to please me, partly because she is improving, day after day, a little stronger as Maggie marches her down the hall in her walker.

I sit in a chair, watching, being in the way and underfoot, willing Mother to walk, to learn to sit up in the low bed where Maggie patiently teaches her day after day the correct way to raise oneself. Maggie, this slim young woman with infinite energy and strength in her nearly hopeless position, big Dave her assistant, and some temporary worker who wheels the candidates back and forth to the wards. How utterly difficult and discouraging their work, how fine and willing and indomitable they are.

Stronger even than Mother's refusal, her rude command on the first day that we leave at once. An irritated middle-class lady voice bored as she might be in a clothing store where nothing pleased her. "No way, you *have* to do this," I say, talking Bowery tough, artist tough, hard as the cobblestones downtown. "Don't you understand that if you want to live at the Wellington, you must become self-sufficient again, you must work at physical therapy the way you worked at the University, the way you worked at life insurance after Daddy left."

Telling this to a woman eighty-nine years old, dictating terms, the bottom line. "You have a goal, you're going to have to work hard, living on your own is going to be like having a job, going to school, you're going to have to put in hours and hours at this. Will you?"

"I'll do it," she says.

~

And other times she just tells me to shut up, she's heard this five times today. Because I am relentless, desperate, profoundly insecure. So are we both. Like people who have boasted that they knew how to ski when confronted with a mountain, indigents registering at a posh hotel, people sitting for examinations who have never read the book. We are impostors who hardly dare look at each other. As I attend Mother's speech therapy classes with careful and competent Mr. Olson, I am terrified she may not even have the wit anymore to speak in more than monosyllables, all through the day watching for proofs of intelligence, clinging against her silence to every symptom of wisdom or humor. Then we signed up for occupational therapy as well and to my relief Mother passed every test of cognition with flying colors, all tests of responsible decision-making too. Her mind is still perfect, wonderful.

But her handwriting is unintelligible since she can scarcely hold a pen: without the power to sign one's name one can't write checks, be an independent economic being. Sally is paying all the hospital bills as they come in, saving Mother the trouble for now by battling with the maze of Medicare and Mother's own health insurance. Mother herself will have to write checks to the women who care for her, have to buy things by mail or telephone, have to write checks for groceries when I am gone—no matter who, if anyone, fetches them.

Living off my resources, which are giving out, we eat our dinners at the Wellington because we can charge it. I think about cash machines, a little desperate to find one that accepts a New York Bank, but I still have enough to keep us in breakfasts if we eat them at home. Lunch consists of all the frozen foods Mallory left in the icebox. We get by, we work at therapy like a full time job, I have never been so busy. We live from day to day.

By Thursday Maggie begins to smile on Mother's hard won progress. Yet even that first day we got a break. As big a break as being able to keep the apartment. Coming upstairs on our way out after therapy on Monday, we stumbled into some social workers from the state of Minnesota who were here to do a procedure, routine we thought at first. We might easily have missed them, after all, we are only here for the therapy, Mother no longer lives in that room at all. The social workers are here to examine her "placement," in fact they are here to confirm it. Behind that, their real mission, "Pre-admission Screening" they call it, is to be absolutely sure that there is no alternative course except a nursing home. Ramsey County has appointed these two women to "double check" as it were, so that no one is put in a nursing home who could live any other way.

Because Mother was brought here from a hospital and as an emergency case, she has never been screened. Maybe there's a way out of "placement," I will take a chance and try them, nervous of authority, afraid of social workers and interference—but what if they could help? First cajole them into the only room in the place where one can smoke, a cigarette being utterly essential to my exposition, to revealing my intentions. "Look, the truth is my Mother hates this place and has a very nice apartment a few blocks away. Is there anyway she could return there? Because she's deeply unhappy here, she might get better at home if there were a way . . ."

By a miracle, this turns out to be the purpose of their special program. Standing in the hall they had seemed so officious. Miriam Otterly, the public health nurse, suburban and professional, Shirley Welch the social worker, so astonishingly beautiful one is in awe of her magnificent eyes and hair, her carriage, her open manner. Now, sitting down at a table, they seem warm, wonderful: I'll trust them.

Explaining the surgery and our hopes, the attack of hypercalcemia and our disappointment, Sally's dilemma, the possibility that maybe this place was a mistake and not "suitable" as a place for Mother in that she is so wretched here. It might just be that maybe Sal panicked, threw in the towel too soon, it may be that Mother will get better, will recover, walk again, those precious motor facilities promised through the surgery . . . if we give the surgery a chance.

In fact they both agree that people do better at home, all their experience confirms this. But there would have to be a support system and it may take time. "If you are willing to lay down the time, that is, if you are willing . . ." Shirley Welch looks me right in the eye. I hold my breath, recognizing one of the challenges of a lifetime, one of those few and unpredictable seconds where everything is on the line.

Alright, I say, already over my head, committed to so many impossibilities. She checks with her companion, the signal comes back; go to work on it, so they do. The forms, paper, lists. And then they outline a plan of care. Physical therapy, occupational therapy, the apartment examined and fitted with grab bars and every device possible for safety, even speech therapy. "You'll find these people—there are agencies. Medicare may pay for this if you qualify." They look at each other: homebound and post surgical, good categories for Medicare.

"The rest you will have to provide privately, personal care aides." "What does that mean?" "People who will take care of your mother, bathe her, dress her, take her down to dinner, put her to bed." Vera, I think. But what about the nights? The nights stump us entirely. Helen Klett had thought of a commode: they think of it too. Mother had made a face, but even Mother will endure the unsightly and undignified if her whole life is the return. "Does she only get up to go to the toilet, nothing else? Then a commode next to her bed might do the work of a night nurse and save a fortune. If you can make it all safe, soft materials, so that she doesn't fall."

I bring Mother into the room in her wheelchair, hoping that despite her mistrust she will speak up and confirm for them her preferences: will she realize they are not part of St. Anne's but a way out of the place? Instantly. And she is all charm, they are won over as is everyone by the carriage of her head, her dignity, her trusting little smiles. I find Pam Keenan, St. Anne's own young social worker, take the risk of appealing to her as well. Everyone turns professional and begins to talk of a "planning meeting for discharge." A week from today they say.

There goes Toronto—it's on Saturday—maybe you can reroute, go directly from Minneapolis. "If I must be away for twenty-four hours could Mother stay at St. Anne's the one night I'm gone?" Pam is sure that she can. Toronto will lose a lot on that ticket: perhaps they'd prefer to cancel. If I go there overnight I must come right back here rather than go home to New York. "If you are willing to lay down the time," Shirley had said . . . already it is coming true.

As we escape down the secret elevator and past the door with its alarm, it occurs to me again, as it so often has lately, how many thousand times I must have been an inconvenience to my mother, a cause for sacrifice. To begin with I was two weeks late in a record hot summer. From that point on, my very existence must have dominated hers until that extreme moment when she had to face the world and fend for me, sell insurance to people who didn't want to be disturbed those Saturday mornings when her tremulous and timid voice would intrude on their day off while she searched for "prospects" as a cub agent.

The situation has simply reversed itself, now I must fend for her. Just as we left St. Anne's an unpleasant young woman from the business office began to confront us with a bill; Mother, no longer living here, would still be responsible for the fee for all the days before release, beginning with the day she began her leave of absence. From that day, Medicare, which would otherwise pay for the first three months of her stay, will no longer pay. We must sign a statement that we acknowledge this. This is the price of her freedom: there will be something like ten days or two weeks she will have to pay for herself, as a private patient. Paying for days she was absent, not even there.

Ransom, I think, buying your way out. But we still get the outpatient therapy, so it is not without some value. The therapy, which is all she uses in the place, is still largely covered by Medicare; "Medicare B," Maggie explained. "You pay some small percentage, the government pays the rest, and it's worth it." Now Mother must pay for a room she does not even sleep in.

"But you are holding the bed, aren't you," this mean creature taunts me, full of rules and phrases, regulations and terms whose real meaning and consequences I cannot comprehend. How should I answer? I feel like a trapped animal. I must hold the bed until Mother is given permission to leave, until her plan of care is in place. There's a waiting list; give up this bed and if she can't make it at the Wellington, she has nowhere to go. It is injudicious to let go of the place here until you are sure she is safe at home. Already, what will Sally say? She looks on a bed at St. Anne's as the only sensible solution to anything, you can't let go of it without a cast iron set-up that won't, as she puts it, unravel, and she's right. So we are betting the cost of the room till Mother is able to do without it; then so be it.

More complex than that, there are different rates; you don't just pay for a bed, you pay for nursing levels. And Mother, this young bully insists, requires care at the highest and most expensive level because she is so helpless. "But no one here will be helping her," I argue. "Mother won't be in her room in the coming days. Except for therapy, which is paid for separately, she won't require anything. Since she will be living in her own apartment with me to assist her, she will need no nursing care from you at all. The minimum rate would only be fair. Just hold the bed, that would be $55 a day. Since she isn't even here, to charge us more would be unfair, unethical."

Alas, this has no bearing on it whatsoever. She's going by some higher regulation, the State of Minnesota's Uniform Care Act and according to the category representing the level of care Mother was awarded at entrance, a "G". Read here, it says "toileting with one attendant present" and so on. "She should pay at the G rate of nursing care" pointing to a far greater sum.

"Come on —Mother will get no services whatsoever for this money, she won't even be here." "Ah, but it won't be seen that way at all," my enemy swears, the law will work for her, for the business office, for St. Anne's. I better face it. It's a shakedown, I feel, outrageous to charge an 89-year-old woman for something she is not getting because they can manipulate a regulation. Pam Keenan suggests that it can be contested. It is clear I can't solve it now and I dare not give up the bed yet or make a scene. What powers do they have to hold Mother here? She was a permanent placement,

I had assumed. Keep your head down as you have all along. The main thing is to escape the place, even if it is ransom, a bigger and greedier ransom.

But the inequity of it eats into me—there is a difference of a thousand dollars. Mother never realized where she was going, didn't like it when she got there, had no way to get out, no way to hold on to her own apartment. A phone was installed in her room, great care put into the arrangement so that it had her old number, supposedly ringing both at the apartment and in her dismal room as well, but in the entire week she lived here the phone company never managed to activate the wire. So it was dead and she was, in effect, incommunicado.

When she said that she wanted to go home to the Wellington, she was fobbed off with disingenuous excuses. Pam Keenan suddenly realizes now that Mother's repeating the word "Wellington" to her a number of times actually meant something. But it meant nothing at the time; Pam's from Minneapolis, had never heard of the Wellington, had no notion of what the word might mean to the distraught figure before her or that it might mean anything at all. Now, Mother, here without choices or options, kept virtually, or at least effectively, against her will is supposed to pay over $2,000 to get out, half of it for services she will never receive anyway since she will not be here to receive them. And everyone knows it.

~

The more I think of it, the angrier I become. How straight arrow the Wellington seems—$900 a month for a good apartment and almost unbelievable services: cleaning and front desk, outings and entertainment and a decent library, jacuzzi and exercise rooms. For a nominal $100 more, congregate dining with excellent food and charming young student waiters and waitresses in a good-looking room. All this for about a grand.

St. Anne's is over three grand a month; surely for the two thousand difference I can put together a plan of care. Of course if I lived in St. Paul it would be no problem at all, I would have connections and be here always to oversee it. But the moment I get on a plane, I lose all control: how much capacity has Mother?

The other night she was sure that Amy would be fine to work for her, or someone named Rachel who the desk informs me has returned to Iowa: both of them work for Carol—and Sally is protesting Carol's bills, with good reason. What if Sally takes issue with Vera over her bills? If Mother paid them herself, she would have to write checks and keep track of hours. She can hardly stay awake, is ill so often, listless so much of the time, an object swept in a stream, the vigilance and defensiveness she would need in order to prevent exploitation from even the most kind-hearted and reliable persons now seems out of the question.

But what does she know, how foxy is she? Sitting there saying Rachel under her breath, already laying her plans, waiting till I get out of here to try to orchestrate what I find so insurmountable, she who can only walk a few steps at a time, has no energy to speak on a telephone, contents herself with silence or annoying one-word commands. Would Vera find her manner insupportable? I frequently do. Maybe she merely wants to be left in peace to dwindle here alone, some quiet suicide of letting things go, the least resistance. Secretive and solitary, everyday more unable and animal-like until she is dragged away as a disgrace. No, not her style. Her style is a lady-like indolence, just the necessary effort, none of your athletic therapy thank you, but a graceful ease that could put her utterly at the mercy of her caretakers: when they failed her she would be destroyed.

If she does not work at her walker and permits Vera to wheel her to dinner in the companion chair—so much easier and more agreeable for a caretaker; I used to try to talk her into it myself once when I first rented one for outings. Mother wisely insisting that she walk, the exercise was important—but now, if she cannot walk to her meal she cannot eat without this person's help in wheeling the chair. She could become more and more invalid, more and more dependent. Will she, when I'm gone, bother to make an effort, or simply slip into death? Is this merely an exercise in futility, is she wasting my time?

~

Mother herself is the issue, also the problem. She is stubborn and she is silent. Apart from any imponderable mysteries of her character, she is a physical invalid. She is the little figure who cannot raise her trousers, cannot pull them up or her underwear either when she rises from the toilet. She is hardly able to raise herself from bed or toilet, so terribly feeble. There is no strength in her arms, in her legs. Will therapy ever make it better, will healing give her more energy? She is barely able to creep about on the walker, demands I hold on to her from behind; tedious, infinitely tedious progress. I am as exhausted as she after she has used the toilet. There is no embarrassment now, her dignity has included me, accepted me here, measuring out and tearing off toilet paper, seeing her bare ass, her tiny wasted legs.

But she won't talk, still clings to the monosyllabic style, commands really. There are moments I hate her, moments I feel enslaved. Interspersed with moments of infinite tenderness, compassion and pity. Finally and always there is simply her need, that she cannot do without me. There are moments of gratitude, when saying goodnight, she thanks me, deep and terrible thanks, entire in her understanding of what I give. Moments too when her hand dismisses me, either because she can do it alone herself—wonderful. And we both feel it. Other moments when she dismisses me because she is just plain tired of my lecturing, instructing, insisting, willing her to a strength she cannot reach, an effort of character which she, with all her commendable lifetime determination, rejects, refuses to try for.

And then I go back to the kitchen, to merely serving her: the milk for breakfast, the dry cereal or the oatmeal, the banana. Often, to my surprise, I find she has already managed to stand somehow and reach for it herself and is absorbed now in her newspaper.

Because she has begun to read again. At first merely the headlines, the baseball victory. But this morning she has taken in the coup in Haiti and will discuss it in a sentence of summary clarity, understanding the defeat of Aristede and all his goodness and promise, the triumph of the old evil of Duvalier and the Macouts, the savagery in store for the people. Then there is only enough of her left to reach her chair and recover, put her head back, close her eyes.

"Why can't I get better," she says. Furious at her weakness, the limitations of her body, the tumor still there behind her left ear, incapacitating her whole right side, the pain of the incision, the itching—a sign it is healing I assure her, not all that sure myself.

There is no time to waste, we must get back for speech therapy, for physical therapy, I must somehow bundle her into her wheelchair and back into the car, for Maggie's unrelenting marches and weights, for David Olson's careful enunciation, his voice lifted to penetrate her deafness. It is futile and hopeless and she knows it, but I must go on lying to both of us, trying, making it happen or seem to happen. I have been caught in the wheels of folly, bravado, maybe even egotism—it would have been so much easier to take the silverware and leave. And now I am involved in this fairytale scheme, this enormous piece of self-deception, so that I feel like a stage mother in Maggie's room, egging on my product, my offspring, who refuses to perform. Or cannot.

For now she actually tries, either out of self-interest, having the goal of the Wellington before her like a bill to pay, or sometimes merely to please me, now she will pull the ropes of the meaningless device at the other side of the room. Where I have to lean from my chair to give her a look, make her do the whole fifteen pulls Maggie has ordered before she went off to work on another candidate.

Few of them seem to get better, there are far too many always. There is one woman with an amputated leg who does try and has a motorized wheelchair. No one else here seems to have any assurance at all, the figures in the wheelchairs, a flock of them at a time, nod off to sleep while waiting: everyone waits, there are too many of them and only one Maggie, one David, and the girl who comes and goes and brings more wheelchairs. Heads nod, mouths drool. There is a fairly lively old man who is supposed to sit on a chair and push the pedals of something based on the idea of a bicycle, but he has no enthusiasm. Still he is the only one who talks, who jokes back at David's teasing, Maggie's verbal encouragements. It is a place of stunning apathy, perhaps drug related. I am nearly asleep myself after ten minutes, but I can't rest, I must keep prodding Mother with a glance, a nod, a smile, the high sign.

We get nowhere. Then a little somewhere, a tiny improvement in the walking. Maggie admits that Mother is at least trying now. She managed to rise from the little practice cot almost alone. Almost. I can see her memorizing the instructions, her small face with the short white hair on either side and combed so carefully across the top, her clothes so pristine here, so out of place. The monogrammed sweaters, presents from Mallory, were noticed, possibly resented.

So today we put on the shocking pink sweatshirt I gave her, French and elegant; she needs all the encouragement her clothes can give her. This little shape struggling on a low bed, the eyes trying, her arms struggling to support her back as she slowly lifts her body. But the next time she is too tired. Maggie forgives and endures: rest and try it again.

Finally we are done for the day, Maggie will not yet say it's progress but Mother is someone to her now, a student, almost a convert, someone she can no longer dismiss and write off as she did that first day. I have used every possible occasion, every instant of attention I could coerce from Maggie to ask questions, get advice, and Maggie is so overworked she has few such moments. What would be the best way for Mother to have therapy; daring even to say to Maggie—what would you do if it were your mother? "One-on-one," she says at once, and surely that makes sense. Maggie has ten or fifteen aged and infirm women to take through exercises in the space of two hours, we can never arrive early enough to beat the rush. Ten minutes later I see another opening and ask very quietly, afraid to push, but having to, where could Mother get that, how could she afford it?

There are agencies, I already know that from Pam who has given me a brochure from a place over in Minneapolis, too far, too foreign, far too expensive. Personal care and home help—terms of the trade for dressing and breakfast—are priced at astronomical sums. And physical therapy is $100 an hour. Which is why we come here. But how long will they permit it? If Mother is discharged it's all over. Between two fires, I badger Maggie again. "Try a place called Optional Care, they're in St. Paul, I studied at the University with their therapist, Nancy Kasa, she's good, she could direct your mother's program. You might qualify for Medicare." I'll try them, I say, in dread of contracting with some bourgeois outfit that might proceed with the understanding we might get Medicare and then we wouldn't after all. Mother could be in debt for thousands, and we would be expected to be ladies and pay up, the manner of St. Paul, everything just lovely until the crash.

We leave for occupational therapy with Terry—all I can think of is a cigarette. But there won't be one, I cannot slip out the front door and relieve my tension, I must stay right here in this strange room and observe its curious mechanisms: the wooden structures where the afflicted raise a dowel from one set of pegs to another, trying to improve their upper body strength. We need to rebuild the muscles of Mother's arms so that she can make her transfers. Because everything is transfer in this world—life itself depends on it, that moment of danger where Mother may fall when moving from her dining room chair to her walker. Or rising from her easy chair to stand and turn herself and sit in her wheelchair. The seconds she is in peril, lowering herself to the toilet, having let go of the walker. Or standing up again from the toilet, grabbing for the bar below the picture of the Indies. That bar, really only a towel rack, is simply not solid enough—it is the first thing she would have me change. Somehow I will do it. Appeal to the management, the maintenance man, try to convey the urgency, the fact that Mother's life may depend on this, on her being sure it would always hold her weight.

I have already found a curious object in a closet left behind by Mallory and Carol, and finally discovered its use—it fits over the toilet, makes it higher, easier for Mother to lower and raise herself while using the toilet. Tyranny of the toilet, her million trips, still so insecure of continence, still so primary in importance to her absolutely lady-like perceptions: she must hold on to continence above all.

I realize that and no longer complain. Even wakened at night . . . but if we could get a commode, then she could do it alone in the small hours, the thing only a few feet from her bed. But she does it alone anyway now, I hear the walker clicking on its stealthy and unsupervised journeys, close my eyes in exhaustion and guilt and wait for the sound of her falling, her head split open by the hard surfaces of the floor, the vanity, the toilet bowl—her hip broken, that joint they never seem to recover from, a seam often parting even before it is sundered in a fall. Better get up and be sure she's alright. Only to startle her. I see her back to bed and wake up a few hours later, realizing she has done it again, is in her bathroom alone, actually preparing for her day.

I watch in bemusement as she tries again and again to push the lever on her electric toothbrush and succeeds finally in putting this crazy piece of American ingenuity into her mouth. She has three toothbrushes now and a raft of cosmetics, but this is the one her dentist has recommended and she uses it with gusto. It is the "stand on her own two feet" side of her, rising relentlessly at 6.30 or so, when I would desperately like either to go on sleeping, or for her to go on sleeping while I drank coffee alone and made my lists and plans, tried to imagine how to rearrange flights, run the Farm, cover the school taxes, or even just consider my predicament.

Every morning of this week I woke to another realization of how dim my hopes are, how unsafe she is in every transfer still, probably always. She will never be strong enough to live alone here, criminal irresponsibility. If Sally could see what I see every morning: Mother, still largely asleep, grabbing incorrectly for that walker, completely without balance, the familiar unearthly animal cry as she realizes she may fall, the terror real or imagined on her part, but unquestionably real on mine. My own judgment sees what the tumor has done, how it destroys her balance, gives her no referent in space, how it must achieve its work in sleep, and only when she is thoroughly awake can you trust her to walk without being held.

And here she is walking alone, all the way from the head of her bed, the far end of her bedroom, all along that wall to the toilet. What about moving the bed? Yes, that would work. We discuss it, Mother agrees. "Move it to where the call string is, that's where it was meant to be." Of course, she is right, the call string which protects each resident of the Wellington, an alarm system connecting them to the front desk. There is one in the bathroom too, but when Mother moved in, hale and hearty, she simply ignored it. Now it would be a lifeline. She has fallen once in this room and in her ferocious determination to rise but still unable, struggled so long there were dreadful rug burns on her knees, only now healing. That was just before the surgery when she was at her lowest.

That experience and the increasing incontinence must have pushed her toward death. Does she meet it again in sleep? in moments of dejection? for there are many. Her head back on the pillow, the piteous plaint of "Why don't I get better?" The frightening time when she put her head down on the dining room table and gave up. The exhaustion and depression after she has vomited, for she vomits now, sometimes from over-exertion, sometimes from stress, the fear of St. Anne's coming back. There are pains at night, nothing but gas I tell her, faking, hoping, having no idea in the world. Call a doctor, ambulance, the University hospital. Is St. Anne's inevitable then? You cannot deal with an illness, you don't even understand recovery and rehabilitation, you are winging this.

Try harder, you keep saying to yourself. "Mallory thought if she just tried harder," Steven said, "and she knocked herself out . . ." The hypercalcemia knocked out everything Mallory had achieved in a month of ardent nursing. You were going to have it easier, you would arrive after that dragon was slain, at a further point in her healing. But any setback, any complication, knocks it all into a cocked hat.

Things are already beyond me, I must admit, lying on the sofa in my blanket and without a pillow, Mother wants two now and another for under her knees, insisting, demanding everything be done just as she orders, commanding me to turn out the light in her bedroom even before I have been able to say good night. Her dictatorial manner alternating with heartfelt gratitude, long delicate moments holding hands and looking in each other's eyes—we held hands that first day in the car making our getaway, held hands until she told me I needed both hands to drive. Refusing sentiment and extreme gestures as she always does.

Today, between therapies I took her for a ride along the River. Pleasure, I thought, nature, the world beyond the biosphere of the Wellington, the meanness of St. Anne's. We find a sign for a little park just below the Nursing Home, on cousin Rosellen's corner. As usual Mother does not want to stop at Rosellen's, she doesn't want to see anyone, she is too tired. I must keep her going, fair means or foul, keep her up for David Olson only an hour from now, there isn't time to go back to the Wellington for the nap she needs and wants so badly. So we will just follow this little road down from the river boulevard and wind along toward the bank below. The Mississippi, I think, our river, her river, this place she is always telling me is my roots, homeland, entreating me to learn it, love it, carry it with me. Like the tapes of my aunts, her sisters, whom she insisted I tape years ago. Aunt Mary is already dead, Aunt Margaret is ninety-nine, the Farmington Minnesota past, the Irish immigrant past, her father Patrick's farm and their childhood there, remembered for the young writer with her tape machine.

Mallory got in the spirit then and bought Mother her own tape recorder:

she would tell us her life and we would cherish it. Alone, Mother would say nothing to the machine, it lies unused on the counter top that separates the kitchen from the dining room, mocking me on every visit. Perhaps it embarrassed her to address a silence. The River seems to embarrass her too. She's grumpy. Look at it, damn it, I think, take your mind off yourself for a moment, see that there is a big world out there, even your own past flows by you. And the present too, here's a barge, they still have barges, here's the great cement apron where hardy young men launch and then retrieve their boats.

"The ice is all broken up now," she says, out of nowhere. This is September, the ice has been broken up for months, we're just coming out of summer now into fall—"Have you forgotten the summer, Mother?" "I never had one." Of course, she was quietly going under to a brain tumor until we discovered it with knives and surgery and the peculiar plastic tube that is supposed to save her from future incapacity, relieve the spinal fluid that has built up, blocked by the tumor, send it quietly back through her body and produce not only relief but recovery, progress back to spring or the winter before or two years ago or however far we can drive her back into life. And she looks on the River, stony-eyed, refusing. I have desperate tears in my eyes from urging her back into life rather than mere existence, and I'm trying hard to involve her with the big water and the ancient trees, today's barge traffic, the little pleasure boats of young men. "Let's go back," she says. An order. "Let's see it," I insist, already defeated, merely angry. "I want to go back." "Damn it, look at it." "Take me back," she commands, perhaps even entreats; I am too angry to hear. But I wonder, even in my fury, if she was merely bored or resisting: life, the River, my tears. Her own. Everything.

I can hardly drive I am so angry, afraid of my anger, the anger I felt one day in Lund's when she was being particularly hard to please, and I discovered I was shouting and a woman was staring at me. This is the road followed by people who bash the aged, I thought, suddenly seeing that there was such a road and persons took it. Only with enormous effort can I avoid burning rubber right now, scaring her, bullying, threatening this little being with machinery over which she has no control. You're going to have to talk to her, you're going to have to confront her when you calm down . . . because you can't go on this way any longer, used like a chauffeur and a maid and otherwise refused and ignored, a mere instrument of her convenience till one day you let her have it.

So I prepare a speech to explain my sense of insult, my puzzlement at her closure; like a shell creature, she has retreated and refuses me any explanation, any language or communication, denies even feeling anything. "I know you're saving energy, I know you can hardly sit up, but why would you refuse to look at the River, just look for Christ's sakes?" "I can't." "Why? God damn it, why?" "No, please, I can't," her head shakes, refusing to go further. So small, so obdurate. "Is it that you feel nothing at all? Or that you feel too much?" The hard eyes are harder and then in tears. "So much, too much," she sighs, finally saying everything.

I'm sorry, but I'm glad too. I couldn't go on any further without a sign. I'd been watching for one during David Olson's lessons, as I listen to her recite, exploring what all these silly words must mean to her: butterfly, whale, flying fish. The fashionable ecological subject matter, predictably neutral, innocuous sentences prepared for the convalescent—yet each with a terrible force drawing her back to life, to the macrocosm of living organisms, all the other species, even the objects of human manufacture acquiring a new resonance. I find myself crying through dull sentences spoken in her voice, spoken only to test her powers of enunciation, projection, volume, the depth of disorder in her tongue and cheek muscles. But the very words pull me as they pull her, commonplace kinship terms or the names of birds and plants and animals, returning the sweetness and variety of life, its precious energy, the wave of visual experience, the enormity of emotional association, the desperate need of them we feel, for in these words are all we knew of life, all that can be referred to still in this dismal room. The very words dragging and crushing the heart, exerting an irresistible force toward life through mere nouns, the sacred names of things. We are people of the book, I try to convey to this man; my mother took a degree in English, made me a writer, her writer, she cannot lose language, she must speak again, naturally, in sentences, real thoughts, not riddles and bare nouns.

But she is already better, he says. And look at the writing, it is nearly intelligible at times. I look and try to believe. We force her through the ordeal of a series of signatures. Then he writes a word in the margin of a ruled pad and asks her to construct a sentence using this word. She writes them quickly, shortchanging us with idiotically simple sentences, but each one requires superhuman effort from her right hand, the tumor's withered victim. It is not worth it to try the other hand, it has no capacity for those movements, she was never ambidextrous.

We grasp after straws each day, he is beatific in his patience, his care that she see his mouth as he speaks: everyone else speaks out of her sight, their heads turned to each other, a hand or a piece of paper obstructing their mouths, their mouths pointed downwards and out of her vision. We go over the ground again and again, he has dated every scrawl, he has cleaned her hearing aid over and over again, we check its battery like people caught in a snowstorm for whom batteries are life itself. We scratch the bottom and start over, I am his apprentice now, Mother has always paid him careful attention: language is sacred. We dream of lip-reading lessons, he may xerox materials for me to use at home. As each day goes by she is patently improving: if she continues to read aloud, she will not need that much more coaching. But occasions for conversation are crucial; she could slip back into the slur again if she were alone too much.

It's the handwriting we go for now; it's doubtful how much of that capacity can be restored beyond a signature, and that will take effort to be credible. If she can never write, she will have only the spoken word and what she can read. She will be isolated into a narrow self-expression since the spoken language as it is generally used conveys so much less than the written. The prospect is withering; empty and lonely as a desert. Her deeper feelings which might have been committed to paper may never surface fully. I remember the long letters she used to type me, single space, full of amusing errors and news, the miraculous achievements of someone who learned the machine at sixty-five, took a course, practiced. Never mind the loss, forget your regrets, she is learning to talk again and doing it well.

So rapidly does she respond now that by the end of the week David Olson begins to see the end of his services. If she is discharged at the meeting on Monday, I can take over nearly everything he does. I see him slipping away and am afraid, and then confident and then over-confident: what if I found feminist friends at the University, somebody who knew somebody who could teach lip reading? It seems as remote as Chinese, as American sign language, which some of my friends know and adore watching when it is mimed at political concerts where the "signer" is nearly as admired as the singer. This is a novelty, of course; fads are not Mother's line and if she did learn to sign no one in her world knows this language so it would be useless.

She already knows some lip reading, David says, all deaf people read lips a little, sometimes unconsciously. Even the smallest progress in it would help her communicate, a "few more inches" of lip reading, as it were, and she could hold her own better at dinner, in group conversations. All those occasions where it is not one-on-one, where if she doesn't hear you will be made aware of it eventually, no matter how stupid or insensitive you are. Yet it never ceases to astonish me how people rattle on in her presence whom she could not possibly understand. And she endures them, fakes them out, scrambles to invent their meanings. For years Mother has placed her guests along her sofa and across from her, her deaf side, saving the ear that hears for the door and the dangers of the outside world. Figuring her necessities, managing her greater needs: she's a woman who lives alone. And besides, the furniture fits in one place, not in another. With some effort I have moved everything in her bedroom, the bed now near the door and the toilet, forcing her old battered desk out into the living room so that her bedroom will be spacious and comfortable, a place of leisure and ease.

How much will she permit me to move and rationalize in her formal and public room, the living room, disturbing her newly recovered nest, wreaking havoc out of theory? Do I contribute or only disrupt? There are times I see myself caught up in this, fascinated. How far can we get? How much could we wring out of this surgery, using every technique available? Then I remember I'm dreaming. Perhaps only interfering.

I lie on the sofa in my blanket, knowing that tomorrow I must go to Canada. Get up early, bring her to St. Anne's: the only alternative is the Good Neighbor suite upstairs which she hates just as much; due to Sally's dispute with them, they might well refuse her. So then, put her back into that hateful little room at St. Anne's again and promise to be back in twenty-four hours. The discharge meeting is Monday, I'm going through with it. Even though I know she cannot live here safely, even though I know she wobbles when she wakes. Only because I have promised and I hope. But it is hollow, mad, irresponsible, hopeless. Sure she's better, has mended each day: she is unrecognizable in only a week, is often full of confidence herself, believes occasionally, trusts and depends always.

But it isn't enough, it may never be. You are way over your head. Try to sleep. Impostor.

~

In Canada, I commune with myself in the basement where I am to sleep tonight. Up in the kitchen are the people in the movement who have brought me here, paid extra for a new ticket, have great hopes that there will be a good crowd, I have only a moment alone to change my shirt, to think about what I am doing. Not this here, but what I am really doing. I can't face it, so I use the toilet and look over my speech. They are upstairs getting ready, mustering their troops, old time anti-psychiatric workers, ex-patients each with a story, a whole history of working for a cause, leftists with decades of reasoned dedication. And I am off on this solitary screwball pilgrimage to keep my mother out of a nursing home, to rescue her. Of course they understand nursing homes: they understand drugs and confinement. But it is my own quest, need, almost secret mission, so private and isolated I am almost afraid to mention it and cannot bring it up until the next morning at breakfast. Between phone calls—they're trying to rent out the basement where I slept as an apartment, there were calls on it last night between calls for the location of the hall, the price of admission, inquiries about their speaker, the numbers they expect, the interest in the issue, feminists are joining the struggle, the day has come at last.

And now it's the next day and back to business, to returning the car they rented because among their own cars there were not enough seats to get us to the hall and back. The airport is the next order of business but I venture to bring it up, my present predicament, what I have got myself into, am returning to now. Wanting to stay forever at their table even if too nervous to eat, needing to cling to its wood, to them, their company, their certitude; fragile as it is, still better than mine. A few have experience with this. One good woman who is part Indian and now rigorously studying her tribe and its language, at one time a streetwalker, gypsy-like and warm and full of anecdote: she and two friends tried to rescue their professor of English after a stroke. The teacher lived out in the country, they had to drive a long way, could only come on weekends. They took turns, did it for years, she was recovering her speech and even some movement when the next stroke came. Then they had to give up, the professor went to a nursing home and died very soon after. The worst thing was that the original stroke had been fortuitous, was the result of a botched operation she never needed anyway . . . they had pursued this malpractice tirelessly, all of them. But they never got anywhere, a long recital of Canadian grievance boards and appeals. I listen and crumple, here were people who tried, who gave all they could give and got nowhere.

By the time I get to Detroit to change planes, I have bought a notebook and can tell it nothing, sitting in the one permissible smoking section of the waiting area. I watch a large vital black man, then a soldier kiss his girl—they are life. I am going back to death, age, futility. Feeling so old myself I cannot ever remember kissing anyone.

Yet I am waited for as if I were the solution to something, to everything, by a tiny figure in a nursing home, my hour past. The baggage was slow: I am late. Has she given up on me, does she imagine by now that I deceived her, ditched her, dumped her in this place. Does she doubt me by now?

~

I sure doubt myself: coming into the room to see her lying in bed, staring at the ceiling this time, but eager to rise, to get out of here, this instant. Into whatever nebulous arrangement I am committed to concoct but probably cannot. She is so glad I am back, so delighted with me. "Did you doubt me?" "No," she says and probably means it, probably believed more than she disbelieved, what choice was there? I must go over everything with her now and be sure: does she really want the Wellington? She has had a night here and can compare. And if she decides to leave here, can she do it, will she work hard enough? The discharge meeting is tomorrow morning. Are we doing the right thing?

She has not slept all night. She couldn't sleep here. But she knows, she knows for sure. She is certain, she says. She refuses this place. But how certain that she can make the recovery and work at the therapy as if it were rocks to break or a marathon to win: will she get lazy, prefer her easy chair, backslide? Twenty years in retirement, doing just what she wants and nothing but, what about her own character, her gentility and lady-like weakness, her feminine excuses, the very permission of her years—who would urge this effort on someone eighty-nine? Will the sedentary comfort of the last two decades just steal over her when I am gone? What if it did? You tried, she tried. Will she try hard enough? Take the chance.

We revisit the River. And this time it is good. She does not avoid or evade it, lets me take her out of the car and push her wheelchair along the walk by the bank. She sits there absorbing the sunshine and the life before her, the speed boats, another barge, children and bikes. Life is a kid on a bike, just that, we conclude, as I sit on the grass at her feet, watching the water, like time, the past in the present. And we are still here, living on, absorbing the energy of the young and the water, the working dads taking their boats out on a Sunday, launching or winching up on the causeway. Without warning and wanting not to, I am overcome by a recollection of that day they took me out on the water after I won my insanity trial here years ago; my good civil rights lawyer had a little boat and we went out on the St. Croix for an afternoon to celebrate. I had a glass of whiskey and was sitting at the stern when it all hit me suddenly and I cried like a nut, still crying downstairs in the cabin as my hostess prepared a beautiful dinner—that my own family did this to me, I said to her. Only realizing it then, when I was safe. Safely past it now, I can even remember this here and let the memory fall harmless from my hands.

The nightmare lifts from me entirely and does not threaten her.

For a long time Mother and I watch one barge as it makes its way around a series of curves; this is the tricky place where the Minnesota joins the Mississippi, there are islands and shoals, this is water for a careful pilot, the invisible figure at the wheel must bank and tack around that dangerous turn ahead. We hold our breath and admire, worry him through the turn, and feel victorious when he has managed his double load, for the boat itself is pushing another flat before it, the thing so unwieldy it is impossible that he could make that turn, the weight ahead must be managed perfectly by the force behind—and then he does it. We nod to each other in perfect harmony.

Mother is in a rare mood of optimism and good humor. We should go back to the Wellington and have a little party, she thinks. Angel food cake and iced tea she says. I smile at her definition and am delighted to comply. We already have tea, I'll just stop at the grocer's for the cake. Mother surprises me. "You don't need to buy Angel food, Joannie brought some over yesterday." This seems odd, if Joannie came to visit her she would have seen her at St. Anne's, how would the cake end up at the Wellington? Joannie has keys, Mother says, beginning to sound a little unsure. Has she imagined it?

In fact, there is no cake in the apartment. "We will have tea then," I say, keeping an appearance of gaiety. "I'll make the tea and while it's cooling I'll just run over to the store for some cake." I should have bought it anyway over her objections. Perhaps Joannie brought cake once in the past and she mixed up the occasion. In all these months of hospitals and nursing homes, losing and regaining her own apartment, how easy to be confused. I'll ice the tea and be back in a moment. Then I see her head down on the table in despair. She is humiliated, she has made a mistake, been disoriented, all the things they watch out for. Not me—I don't care.

But of course I do, I was as frightened as she, as caught by the throat. Her "marbles"—realizing that had been my bottom line. If she were senile and wanted to live in her own home, wouldn't she have just as much right? Maybe, but I would not have been able to wage my war if I could not believe in the absolute integrity of her intelligence. And I reacted to one little slip of memory as if it were a direct hit, a catastrophe. Now I must talk her out of taking it so hard.

The cake when it arrives cannot rescue her; she tries, but the party is over. She wants to watch television. Then she wants to go to bed, without dinner. "Everything has gone wrong," she says from her chair, her head hanging. "Talk to me, be honest, talk about what you feel and what you fear, what your thoughts were while I was gone." But she will not talk. "Come on, we're giving up the bed at St. Anne's tomorrow. Everything's alright. You're very brave, don't you see that?" Urging her own heroism on her, the terrible, almost adolescent risks we are taking, our wild scheming, our recklessness, all of it dependent upon her final courage and determination. She shakes her head, nobody's sucker, "I wasn't brave tonight," she says.

I put her to bed and hold her hand, the enormous affection we feel for each other now: it is a new relationship, utterly compelling for both of us. But for this risk we have taken together, will embark on tomorrow like children jumping off a garage roof holding onto umbrellas imagining they can fly—but for this accidental adventure, we would never have been so close, so entirely spirit to spirit, dear, unutterably dear to each other, this strangest love affair. "I'm scared," she says. "Me too."

~

When she sleeps I watch a movie on television, *Longtime Companion*. I've seen it before but I need diversion and it is different here than it was at the Farm where I saw it with other gay women. Everything is different in Minnesota, at least this corner of it, a retirement apartment complex of impeccable respectability, here in this prim living room, an invalid in the next room. When one watches, sitting in this chair, her chair, the gay men in the film seem doomed from the first frame; their lives of pleasure and sex are transparently vulnerable, a hedonism built on even shakier ground than their jobs in New York or their afternoons in Fire Island, scenes of parties and bodies and swimming, their laughter and youth stricken by a plague easily predicted in this cold climate. How did you ever think you'd get by with it? And they might have been right after all; the puritan force I feel here has always won merely by default; often no one has fun because no one dares. Of course life could actually be a triumph of pleasure and imagination, the great parade of resurrected friends that closes the film. But there was death. Just as there is the tumor in the next room.

"Catastrophic illness," my friend Fitzgerald reminded me in Provincetown, lifting his eyebrows. We had been discussing Mother's brain tumor.

His father had one too, but Fitzgerald implied something else as well: the young man who had champagne with him on my deck the night before whose wrist watch went off to remind him to take his AZT. The three of us had been standing in the moonlight watching the lights of the harbor and the ocean, the luxury of all this and the pale champagne in its clear slender glass, and then the noise of a small alarm on the young man's wrist. He is dying just as surely, certainly. Our two worlds met as I watched the finale of the film, the gay world dying so visibly and young, my mother's life as threatened now. Seeing them assemble again by the ocean in the last frames, all the people who had died in the film alive again for a moment of wild rejoicing and reunion, I am joining her fate with theirs, no longer aware of contradiction. Nor is she, we have talked of AIDS often in these last visits, her sympathy is real, she has transcended a lifetime of prejudice and has gained a great compassion. I am not so out of place anymore.

~

Steven calls to say that he visited Mother while I was gone and found her transformed: she talks now, she chattered like a jaybird, she was wonderful. I've wrought a miracle in just a week. If he only knew. But he doesn't: instead he is all ready for tomorrow's discharge meeting, the social workers have set it for ten o'clock. I imitate confidence and feel none at all. Walking into the kitchen, I am assaulted, as one is from every wall here, by photographs: Mother at Lisa's wedding—she was okay then, just a year ago last summer; Mother as she was once and will never be again. We risk her safe haven tomorrow.

I walk around the apartment in a state of terror that lasts for hours, realizing, here, just at the brink of winning—just how wrong I've been. She can't cook, won't eat once she's alone. Can't cope even with help. And the help she can afford is so scanty, insufficient. I grasp after phantoms of 24-hour care, someone to sleep in her living room? At least she'd be safe at St. Anne's, might not fall; she will inevitably fall here. I have not been responsible, only romantic, responding only from my own experience, the wrong, inappropriate responses. Steven was deceived. I have deceived myself, but now I better face the truth. If she didn't sleep last night out of fear she would be abandoned at St. Anne's, how will it be tonight as she lies there exhausted with the fear that she cannot live at home? Jackass, you have walked into a river, you're drowning.

It is as if my little personal quarrel with death—undertaken months ago when I started propagandizing Mother for life over death, an aesthetic choice, a fling on a trip, a sideline—has now caught up with me, dared me to a showdown, a commitment to the last day and dollar. Remember when you decided to picket *The New York Times* over the want-ads till you won, not till you dropped, but till you won? But you are too old yourself now, too compromised, too overextended—you no longer have the strength for these Quixotic gestures and you are alone.

You can't fight death with youth anymore, with snobbery or disbelief, because you believe in it now. You finally believe in death, have seen it prefigured in her. And you want to run. Grab onto what is left of your life and career and a trip to England and run. You are losing your own life here somehow, your life energy, maybe even interest in your own life. Hers has become more interesting, a challenge. You sidestep your real responsibilities, take a big running jump into this great romantic project. Everything goes to hell in your own life, but you have a great excuse. Your Mother, for god's sakes, your sacred Mother; nobody talks back to that, it has the power of religion on the one hand, lip service on the other. These days one stops less and less for the fallen. My exit was there from the beginning: pick up the silver and beat it.

Of course you can't abandon her, you know too much. Unfortunately, you know death now too. It's breathed on you and you're scared. It's finally real, hypnotically real; you stand like a drunk looking at a rattlesnake, unable to move. It is her death you are supposed to be fighting off, but now that you finally believe in death it's sickened you too, like an ulcer in your mind; you're gotten so shitting scared you even think you're dying. You've felt its breath, that stench, that nausea. You know what you can take, you know when you have to cut and run. Turncoat, double-crosser, you're gonna have to let her down, jump ship. You can't face the time it will take, the work. And you can't face losing.

And if you fight and wrestle with it, it will get her in any case, but its hand will burn you, wither you. It's too big, you are too compromised already, let's admit it, you have been more than half in love with easeful death, you've had big time depressions, six-month bouts with self-annihilation, and you feel that familiar return, the proximity of all those sinking moments, the stack of failures like unanswered mail. No, not that route again. This is a trap, I'll never make it out of here alive. Unless I get out of here now.

~

It's the same in the morning, a running terror, a sense of unreality and folly—I want to bolt, can hardly stay inside the apartment, the old claustrophobia that used to drive me downstairs to my den in the guest room, to compulsive reading, to escape the town itself.

Ten o'clock is only a few hours away. Tell them you've made a mistake, you can't go through with it. It's all wrong, I am taking part in a charade. This will be play-acting, the most outrageous dishonesty. Face it, you would traduce yourself, you cannot do something so dishonorable. They'll understand: you changed your mind. Probably she has too, probably she is just as afraid. Will you go into her bedroom, pretend to be judicious: hadn't we better think again—let her down? Or do worse? String her along, go through the entire procedure in bad faith and then collapse on her?

Steven had said it was worth trying, even if it failed. I cling to that, having nothing else to believe in now. Playing for time now, hedging my bets, a conscious duplicity. Mother starts the day very down: "I hate this day," she says, admitting she is very afraid. Could I play grown-up now and get her off the hook? Lying in bed, her thin voice, "Why do I still feel so weak?"—a new day's weakness assaulting her on this of all days. "I'm no good," she says, dismissing herself altogether. Move in on this? Adopt a sugared voice, conciliating, controlling—you've watched them do it—overcome her with reason, obliterate her for her own good. It would be so easy. The traitor in me stands ready, on the jump.

Walking her to the bathroom my eyes fall on the titles in her bookcase, an index of irrelevant detail: stuff I've borrowed to read aloud to her, my own books, inscribed copies, as meaningless as the mysteries or romances or reportage in hard cover editions that come at Christmastime. Nothing means anything. The whole idea was crazy.

If I succeed in duping these people today I'll lose England, my trip, my wonderful month in Europe. "Laying down the time": that sure was a trap. So is the charade of the meeting, the earnest circle of staff, Pam, the social workers, even her boss has shown up. And David and Maggie who can stay only a short time. We proceed hurriedly, without making any sense at all. No one sees through us, we do not see through our selves; they never even suspect me. They are about to relinquish my mother into my hands. Mother herself looks on in amazement. We are a parody of common sense, I am almost about to tell the truth and give up when Steven enters.

Gorgeous in a camel-hair jacket, charismatic as a political hero, the women take him in and react as if to enchantment. I feel we are rescued by a magical force, enamored of him, proud of him. What has he done to exert this energy, this presence: mere beauty cannot do it, surely there is effort and understanding here as well. And he sounds so sensible, so well spoken, the commanding way he carries his head offset by his gentleness, the wonderful power of his green eyes disarmed by a still youthful humility and goodwill. Of course he is reasonable, we will go by stages. This is a kind of trial we will set up, partly dependent upon what services can be found for Mother to enjoy at home, partly dependent upon her own progress. He is neutral, patient, willing to take time and experiment, never headlong. And wisely deferential to the Home, its schedule and regulations, its institutional ego and sense of propriety. It is a masterful display of St. Paul good manners; I remember New York in its full foreign incivility. One might be watching diplomatic technique as practiced here during the early decades of the century, perhaps even some old-fashioned European tactician exercising his perfect skill on a modest scale. Steven's ease is gracious and generous, he seems to overlook whatever costs are involved. In this he is the perfect negotiator: there is no place for quibbling.

Now it is up to them. Fortunately Pam, the best of them, rises to the occasion, conscious of how deeply all this mannerly behavior could affect Mother, even aware of the uncertainty to which such leisurely trials would subject her. Each therapist gives an appraisal: there are movements both forward and backwards but the consensus seems positive. Pam goes for it: "Today is Monday. If we start now, discharge could be set for Thursday. Kate has an appointment with Optional Care tomorrow for a total assessment of Helen's case which will determine what services she needs and what Medicare coverage she will be entitled to. All that remains to be established is the personal care plan."

That's my job of course, or rather Vera's, since Vera may be only the beginning, and seeing this thing done now, this improbable series of suggestions accepted as a reality, I, who was once to lead the revolt and declaim in passion or to give up in cowardice and call a halt to it all, realize I have made it through, hardly saying a word.

Mother, it is discovered when the other authorities have decamped and David Olson checks her hearing aid, has managed to sit through the entire performance without hearing anything at all. Her battery was dead. A good thing or otherwise, I wonder, appalled all over again at how little part she is ever permitted in her own fate. I overhear her with Steven, fascinated to know what she will say to him after her great occasion, but I only catch her asking him, "What have they decided?" The helplessness of it all. She sinks further, telling him that she will abide by his judgment "Whatever you decide," she says, humbly. I grit my teeth: it's what she said in the University hospital, it's how she got to this lousy "visitor's parlor" in St. Anne's Catholic Home to begin with. It's surrendering to youth or masculinity or a law degree. Beyond its transparency it isn't even necessary. "No, G.M.," Steven answers staunchly and sweetly, "It's what you decide." She decided a long time ago. This may be merely a performance of little old ladyhood, a gesture once she has put us through her paces, a form of flirtation. Steven is Mother's late-life romance, during his years in law school he virtually lived in her house on Selby, she spoiled him, he doted on her.

It is only natural to collapse after victory. I do so in the car, snatching a cigarette and a moment with Steven to divulge my own timidity and loneliness, desperate at the assignment before me, the weeks of rehabilitation I have taken on in such faltering faith, such outright doubt. All this time there has been no one to talk to, no companion, no drink or dinner. I've been imprisoned in my mother's age and illness and it has seemed isolating and unnatural. But there will not be much relief.

As Steven sees it, he's here to pick up the pieces when Mother's daughters are gone; when they are here it's better that he remain off duty. He has no time to socialize or hold my hand through this: I got what I wanted for Mother, now I have to make it work. "And she's got to get off the roller coaster she's been on for so many months: from one bed to another, ambulances, uncertainty everywhere. She needs a daily routine, the certainty and security of a regime." For himself, he wants no more harrowing phone calls like the one telling him Mother was being rushed to the University barely alive; there must be no more emergencies. A tall order.

He has performed his function as figurehead, for the moment that's all he can offer. It's tough, but clear enough. My adoration takes a tumble, I treasure Steven, have always felt particularly close to him in the family: we have the same birthday, I have known him since he was a very little boy, saw him off to Europe as a lad. I am stung hard. I feel personally rejected, held at a distance. I struggle with annoyance at the way he appears to protect his time and effort, a privileged young man attached to a prestigious firm who has a fast-track lady lawyer for a wife, a new baby. This is how it is: he has this life, these responsibilities, these other loves and interests. Mother and I must not intrude, we are to remember our place in his life. Recognize that Steven did not thwart us; he wishes us well, but we will be going it on our own.

~

I'm in this alone. There will be no respite: the duties of the wheelchair, the keys, the phone calls, the maze of agencies and informants, the leads and possibilities—I launch myself into this sea precipitously and by one o'clock, when I finally reach Shirley Welch, I am struck by an attack of diarrhea while talking on the phone. It's a long cord, I go on anyway. Mother sleeps soundly after a good lunch at her favorite Chinese Gourmet. I have located a Lifeline, the mysterious device recommended by all my advisors, so that if Mother fell and were unable, as she was before, to reach the Wellington's own emergency pull cord, she could call for help by merely pressing the button on a necklace she will wear at all times. It gives off a signal which, through some clever technology, dials up the emergency ward of St. Joseph's Hospital, who then ring her back to see if she is actually in danger. If Mother were unable to answer that call the emergency team would not, fortunately, jump into an ambulance and siren over to frighten her and her neighbors, but prudently call the Wellington staff (very much as the string would) who would then bring a pass key up and enquire after Mother. Lifeline rental is a minimal expense and could save Mother's life. I feel efficient.

I have also located Meals on Wheels, a group of volunteers in the neighborhood who deliver a big hot meal at lunch to the homebound. Delivery is free, the lunch is inexpensive and would assure Mother a large daily portion of cooked food even on a day when, through her own indisposition or Vera's, she might not make it down to dinner. I have lined up Mother's old friend and retainer, Ollie, her cleaning woman for twenty-five years, to come and do up the place and have a good visit: Ollie and Mother haven't seen each other for weeks. Things are returning to normal. I am getting good at my job and learning the system.

When Jane Winter calls, a friend of the Farm, even a friend of Mother's, since Jane lived in Minneapolis for years and used to visit Mother on Selby Avenue, she reminds me that this chance to be together with Mother is profoundly important, an opportunity one rarely gets before death: I could have missed it.

It beats England too: I have canceled my trip. "Wouldn't you be wiser just to postpone?" my agent demurred. Perhaps she's right, but there were simply too many scheduled meetings in public buildings to put on hold. This is fairer to the sponsors since I don't know how long I will be here. "You don't?" the voice of New York, astonished anyone might linger in Minnesota. I hear myself confessing that I have no idea how long this will take.

Then I go ahead and say it, that I'm going for broke, that I will never have another chance to try for fullest rehabilitation and that any date only confines me, sits like a wall in front of me, penning me in with further worry and responsibility when I already have more than I can bear. I must do this without any parameter, any boundary. Realizing only after I have said it how far I have come.

Mother is happy now, believes now, has set her face to the future, is optimistic and affectionate. The Twins win again. She will begin to have physical therapy at home today and a young woman named Ellen McKenna has arrived to give her a bath. Our new agency, Optional Care, provides a bath and a bath lady each time the physical therapist is to deal with a client. I am amused by the precaution of cleanliness, but I am delighted that

Mother is getting a real bath where she can sit on the floor of the tub rather than on a mean little stool while being showered with a hand shower, equipment we have for ease and safety. Ellen is kind enough to pass up these half measures and undergo the physical effort and risk of a real bath instead. Under her pampering, her shampoos and pedicures, Mother prospers, grows back into her flesh again, becomes not just clean but indulged. Which is like being loved. As I love her and Vera loves her, with lotions and back rubs. Each time she is dressed now she is caressed with moisture and fragrance.

When Mother permitted the first back rub that first weekend, I found hope, spied an opening in her wounded selfhood that might point the way back into human society. It was in touching her flesh that I could first really nurse her body and her spirit in her body. Otherwise, all that I gave her spirit in honoring its wishes, believing in its intelligence and respecting the sanctity of its autonomy, was still cerebral and theoretic, dry as talk. If she would trust me with her flesh, she would really trust me.

Now the flesh is back. It will rule her whole regime in fact, since the person in charge of her case is not a nurse, but a physical therapist. What Mother needs most now is strength, muscular rehabilitation. She accepts Nancy Kasa as her Maestro with a professional's regard for another professional, but there is one characteristic moment in their first interview where Mother asserts herself in a way that is both amusing and admirable. Nancy is standing by the bed, beginning her instruction: "Now when you lay down . . ." "Lie down," Mother says, without even thinking. She has corrected the grammar of those around her all her life, used to teach these rules to schoolchildren. Nancy is her physical therapist and in charge of her now, but she is also fifty years younger and has just made an error in grammar. There is an instant where we all pause. Nancy smiles, Mother smiles, I laugh. Suddenly we are all terribly happy: Mother perhaps is a "character," but it is just her character that has made us cherish her, work so hard for her. Nancy is visibly impressed by this sharp old lady with a sense of humor, her professional surface relaxes, she asks Mother what goal she has set herself. "To get rid of this altogether," Mother says abruptly, nodding at the walker. Nancy and I exhale audibly together; I nearly whistle. "It is not entirely inconceivable," I say to Nancy as she leaves. "You know, with someone this determined . . ." She grins, not ruling it out.

Now that I have entered upon this role, I begin to enjoy it—the laundry, the dry cleaning. The dirty white coat is clean again. I perform errands with a sense of pure triumph, I have found a source of cash in the machine at the grocers, I even have a whole roll of quarters for the spotless laundry room at the end of the hall, a convenience I have never enjoyed at the Bowery or the Farm. I spend hours on the phone, finding things, learning entitlement. My plan of care is working, will work. We will give up the bed at St. Anne's on Thursday.

I write to Sally listing every particular and bragging of the free benefits (worth $2,400) I have already secured for Mother from Medicare: two baths a week, three sessions of physical therapy, two of occupational therapy. I'm going to try for a case manager and a speech therapist next, both dependent upon young Doctor Conroy's permission, a delicate matter since he is now on vacation and after that will be on jury duty. I also intend to soft-soap Sal into writing one of Mother's checks to pay for a commode. Unfortunately Medicare does not see its way to cover this particular sum, but for just $100—yes, it's a bit steep, but imagine, we will save over $100 every night—the commode is Mother's new night nurse. When we give up the bed at St. Anne's on Thursday we will still have the safety of the waiting list but we will also fight their bill.

On my sofa, I smoked a last cigarette and realized that the grudge is all gone, the last shred of resentment against Mother, the loony bin trip, whatever. Every difference is gone, over. Fight the tumor now, win or lose, everything is possible, fear is gone. Also all the despair and claustrophobia of Sunday night and Monday morning. Just fight that tumor. Try to sleep, don't worry about overdrafts at the Farm, the deficit going into harvest, the new septic going in, the rents not paid. Still awake as the hours pass I notice that Mother can now sleep six hours without waking, without stirring. This will make her strong.

Tonight we arrived late for dinner downstairs. Our new table was full and we were forced to huddle at Mother's old table, feeling Ceil's scorn for the unfortunate and imperfect, visited by example upon the person of Eleanor Bayliss, Vera's other patient. Eleanor suffers from Alzheimer's and senility, though as Vera points out, Eleanor can still beat everyone in the building at bridge: it is only recent memory that suffers, short-term memory, the forgetting of her house key or some other detail that brings her back down again to the dining room during the second sitting, our sitting. Ceil maliciously pities her reappearance: "So confused, the poor dear." It is a voice completely devoid of fellow feeling, completely suffused with self-satisfaction, as if every point Eleanor lost were Ceil's gain: like a bridge game, like money. Absent-minded or not, Eleanor is always elegant, full of wit and compliment, quick, charming. And Ceil, a diabetic, is as close to death as a stroke, fears blindness even before death, rides the edge of a precipice herself.

Nevertheless Ceil excoriates the unfit in our hearing; each remark demeaning Eleanor is meant for our instruction. Ruth sits next to Ceil, backing up her point of view, scolding always, a librarian who insists on the rules; she imagines Mother transgresses them by riding in her chair, having my help, Vera's when I am gone. We will not sit with Ceil again, we will always be early and take our place at the round table with the kind ones that endure us, accept Mother's pariah state. The pecking order of the aged, the hierarchy of the well at the Wellington.

~

Mother begins her days now with declarative statements like "I'm gonna stay up all day today. No nap even." Then she tries too hard, ends up vomiting in her armchair, her beautiful clothes ruined, her beautiful confidence.

The therapists see. Mother is overcome with shame and exhaustion. They are polite, gracious. More gracious still, Mother endures them, their foreign presence, even when she is exhausted and would like to clear the place out. The occupational therapist and I let her rest and go over the apartment, trying to think of everything. There will be many changes, beginning with that grab bar in the bathroom opposite the toilet. Another grab bar for getting in and out of the tub, Sarah has several we can try. The commode is still not really a working event: Mother is too unsteady to get on and off, we must think of something. Sarah has an idea, something she's seen in catalogues but never had the opportunity to use yet—a vertical pole, wedged between and floor and ceiling. It might have come out of California. A long shot, but let's try it.

While I rehearse signatures and simple sentences in handwriting with Mother, I am interrupted to have my ears burned about bills by Sally over long distance. When I try to obey Sal's orders and fight the phone company's charges for the phone they never installed at St. Anne's I am interrupted by the little voice in the bedroom: "Katie I need you." If I were to live my own life I would go to the gas station for sunflower seeds, trip out on this addiction and read my life away as I always do here, but fortunately I have a sixteen-hour job. It is only when it stops that I notice how strange this life is, tonight for example over roast beef with Chris and Steven at the Parker House out in Mendota.

Steve drove ahead to show the way, wearing sunglasses and a plaid shirt crossing a bridge my own father built, bringing us into the kind of old-time bar Dad lived his life to live in. Only when I have a drink and am with people somewhere near my own age and interests, only when she feels like friends and have that younger-generation urge to sneak out together to a bar and play together, away from one's elders—only then do I realize that those days are over and this is just a break because the routine of duty is reality now. It wasn't till Chris and Steven got up to leave, bearing their own responsibility, tired and cross little Victoria, that I remembered to reassume my own: put down that drink and drive your aged Mother home. For a moment I'd forgotten.

Safely home I drink more scotch and forget still more, resuming through booze some memory of my usual Lower East Side view of things. My old world does obtrude on the telephone late at night, an earful of awful unreality from Jennifer, unreal New York effluvia, followed by a surreal description of my friend Skippy's New York opening where everybody showed up but no one bought. Call Naomi, you need to pay the rent on the Bowery, you need to pay Jennifer's rent as well since you have promised to help when she lost out on a cheaper place and despaired, just entering her first year of film school. Everything from New York is so implausible here, everything here would be so implausible in New York. I am about to recite my life here in Bowery artist terms to someone like Chris who would find the language novel, the point of view colorful, and instead find I am coming unexpectedly upon my own fury. What if I did all this work, the nut artist and black sheep they have locked up and found disgraceful, what if I even pulled this off and then Sal came to town in November, took one look and said, this is absurd, Mother can't live here alone, look she's falling down, has fallen down, will fall down. Off to St. Anne's; thank god we kept her on the waiting list. By now I am quietly drunk, but venting alone, at least I have had my fit in private.

It goes back and back, includes every slight, real and imagined, but of course offended most by those two occasions when my family turned me over to the state to be incarcerated as crazy, occasions of great and total rejection. That a group who had treated me thus should so need my services now is strange—but not to be regretted, a good thing actually. It permits me to heal the breech with good works, forgive where I have been abused . . . the other cheek business, which, curiously was the biggest part of what I learned in those little social hells.

But there is always a moment when you think—fuck 'em, the bastards continue to screw me over—enough at last. Mother has shot right past that, a victim now as surely as I ever was. And I have at last laid down any "attitude" against her: simply consider her frailty and helplessness, her vulnerability to every exploitation and I have to let go, any and every trace of resentment falls from my hands, my soul, my eyes, my heart . . . I am free at last. With the others, I am also free to drink more and rave at them in the middle of the night. Silently. In solitude.

Then just get up and do your job in the morning. Mother has had a bad time overnight. She had worn fancy stockings to go out to dinner rather than her usual cotton ones. Getting up in the middle of the night to go to the commode, they betrayed her. She slipped and could not right herself. Leaning against the bed, finally, exhausted, she slid to the floor where she waited until her voice could wake me. It seemed to take a very long time. She blames the commode, I blame the stockings. Together we find a pair of "totes," extra warm slippers made of fabric with velcro on the bottom to prevent slippage: she will wear them to bed every night. This cheers her up and when she has finished breakfast she is raring to go. "Let's call someone up," she says, delighting the speech therapist in me by volunteering to talk on the phone, invite people over, be sociable. I want to give her a hug, listening to her social patter with her favorite nieces, "You don't *mean* it," cousin Joannie booms at her, busy in her office, dropping everything at the sound of Mother's voice, "This is you, actually you—why you sound wonderful." "I'm absolutely *floored*," cousin Rosellen says. It seems Mother has not telephoned anyone on her own initiative for a long time, didn't have the energy, her voice was not even strong enough to carry.

I balance the hopeful signs, statements about standing on her own two feet, yesterday's proclamation when she got up that she would stay up all day, not even take a nap, the moments when she has saved up enough energy by reading quietly in her chair to announce that she will now practice walking in the hall. Balance them against her wobbliness on waking, how she is still bound to fall if alone. Of course there remains the dictatorial character of her constant commands, the megalomania that interrupts all the time, her preference for a life of leisure. And the tumor, the tumor, the tumor.

I am supposed to judge today between Vera and Denise of Good Neighbor. Despite our quarrels with this agency, Sally prefers them to Vera since they have "backup," can be held responsible to a greater degree than Vera who is a freelancer. "Vera says she has backup too," I dickered, preferring Vera, guessing that Mother does too. I have an appointment to meet Vera's backup, but have also made an appointment with Denise. She arrives and we proceed in an awkward way, Denise vowing to give excellent care, displaying her best manner. Mother sits through it all calmly, noncommittal. I attempt the manner of an employer, inquiring about hours, substitutes, billing procedures. There is only one problem: I instinctively dislike Denise. Something about her strikes me as false, maybe repressive. I do not relish the thought of her being in charge of Mother, I spy a bully somewhere, fairly or unfairly. But I have orders to find the more reliable source of care. The Good Neighbor office itself never returns my calls, they're right upstairs but they never call back; perhaps I must call the head office somewhere out in Edina on the other side of Minneapolis. Denise really wants this job; I feel obliged to take her, dismissing my own misgivings for Sally's reasons, accepting them too, almost afraid of Vera's easy good nature.

Mother is giving off no signals at all: I stall for time, but still give Denise plenty of encouragement. More than I should have, it's clear the moment she's out the door. Mother's thumbs down answer is in the wave of her hand, that remarkably eloquent gesture reserved for St. Anne's and other opprobrious intrusions on her helplessness. We look at each other and smile, guilty, perhaps uncharitable, but in perfect agreement. "Funny isn't it, Mom, I felt the same way, something about her . . ." Mother will not bother to put her reasons into words, doesn't need to: she will have Vera and that's that.

There have been so many times I have wondered if her judgment was solid, worried when she would wake from sleep, still dreaming of the house on Selby Avenue, mumbling about a paper bag in the basement, or wondering irrelevantly where all the children are. These are only dreams, I reassure her, scared at how nursing home attendants or any hostile stranger might interpret these scraps of sleepy talk. You can lose everything through a few stray words. And then she nails me with her perfect intelligence, her unerring instinct. Reminding me politely but firmly that she is the employer and not I. Now I must face Denise and take away the job I seemed to offer her.

I am struck again by the stoic character of Mother's dignity, how naturally everyone defers to her—none of your Mother McCrea stuff—she's a tough little nut. In her man's haircut, which she cannot wait to be long enough to restyle, even perm. But how strong it makes her face, the hawk like profile, the fine shape of her head. Is it how she carries that head, I wonder, weak and frail and tiny as she is, all the energy left in her being is concentrated in that indomitable carriage. She was gentle to Denise, far more honest than I, infinitely polite, genuinely kind. But never taken in, beguiled, won over. "Sally wanted us to go with the Agency, you know," I say afterwards, nervous over the decision. "I will take care of Sally," Mother says.

After lunch my speech therapy "class" concentrates on the issue of the commode: I present Mother with my essay on the subject to practice reading aloud. I have summed up my arguments, beginning with economic reality: it cost only $101, it will save an hourly wage for a night nurse at whatever figure times eight hours times thirty days times twelve months a year. It could save your life. Then I change gears into the rhetorical question: "Is toilet training worth dying for?" A pyramid of logic: "Is it worth risking your life so that: (a) the linen doesn't need changing? (b) you are not embarrassed? (c) someone might see the commode and know?" Closing with this peroration: Use the commode and live . . . better yet, use the commode and live independently." My summary a pithy clincher: "This object is a small price to pay: dignity is living as you choose."

She glares and then she laughs, reciting my propaganda aloud as her lesson. There will be other nights when she fails with the thing, cannot get back into bed by herself, complains of the offensive object to her therapists, dismisses it as a bad idea. There will be adjustments to the vertical pole until we get it just right and she can swing from bed to commode and back again with an agility she will come to take pride in, there will be another morning when she wakes to announce she will never use that thing again, and strike terror into my heart, for my whole scheme depends on the commode replacing a night-time attendant she could never afford. But I have made my essential point and am not willing to back down and she knows it. I will not relent over the therapy either, she knows that she has come to depend on my obduracy; it will suffice when hers weakens. We are a team.

Certain days we have to forgo our rides around the city to see the fall leaves: therapy took too much out of her, or Mother vomited during another of Sarah's visits. We had to leave early during the first big game party when the Twins beat Toronto. I stay up to watch on Mother's set as they win in the last inning, conscious she has made me her substitute; she herself is conserving energy for the playoffs. Speech therapy the next day starts off with Mother's increasingly forceful voice reading the columnists' praise of Jack Morris's pitching. We close with Moberg's description of the immigrant Swedish landings in New York. She composes simple sentences on random words like "tapeworm" and "Coca Cola": concluding with "Who will win the World Series" in desperately shaky script. We practice palmer method funnels and uprights. We try to see writing as calligraphy, as just a form of drawing, but five signatures exhaust her. The sentences have to be short and pointless and are still so hard to read . . . if there were a way around this . . .

"Why not try the typewriter?" I say. She dismisses the idea with the habitual hand movement. But she can't stop me, in a moment I have unearthed her Smith Corona portable electric from the closet, my face burning to remember how the second day I was here—still in the stage of taking the silverware and making off, seeing every object in the apartment as something Sal would have to pack and ship pretty soon—my eyes fell on the typewriter and I thought to myself, better find some young relative who can use this, some college kid. Hadn't Mother's beloved microwave already been shipped off to Sal's daughter Lisa, handy thing to have around with the new baby?

What if I had been stupid and interfering enough, brazen and arrogant enough to have given this away, this possible treasure. I open it up and turn it on and it works. "I'll never remember how," she says, "I haven't used it for a long time." Not since the tumor began smothering her life and her grip began to loosen, but now, after surgery? Now, when it is clear that she may never write an intelligible hand again, will be lucky to arrive at passable signatures on checks—why not go for the typewriter? Typing could transcend the problem of the great coordination required for handwriting altogether, give a vent to her soul, her inner self. "Mom, try it, even for fun; you'll be terrible at first. I am too, the computer has ruined me altogether. It's just practice, you might have to stick at it, but what if it worked?"

Then she's excited, yes, she'll try it. Of course it is slow and difficult. I leave the room to give her space, privacy, everything writing demands. I can smoke in the hall, for I am now considerate enough to have given up smoking in her apartment: the odor offends even me, the rooms are so airtight, small, carpeted and draped and upholstered. Smoke never seems to leave and opening windows is a further intrusion since she still chills easily. When I come back there are only a few words on the page and her face, watching me. Was she good enough? It's pretty short, the sentences are disappointing, true. But it cost her such effort, she is about to be so proud of this little note to an old friend, Glady Gilbert, housed in a nursing home now, the sorrow of it, Mother's gallantry in directing her first words in freedom to someone now without it. I celebrate with her, address the envelope, put the stamp on; wonders of the civil life, things you'd never find at St. Anne's, one's own desk and a good supply of stamps. I run downstairs to mail it.

From that point on, the typewriter is the highest note in our lives, our best shot, our proof of every possibility. Seeing her pride in it, I wonder still at the difficulties and shortfalls, she needs hours of plain dull practice, just copying—will she make that effort? And composing, the letters must grow to greater length, fuller disclosure, real ideas, the inner self. Cool it, the point is that she has done it, dared to sit in front of the thing and face failure, found the strength to try, found the satisfaction of her little conceit over it now, telling Nancy and Sarah and her nieces that she's "taken up typing again."

~

One morning I glance at the headlines and find the right-hand column proclaiming that "Sexual Politics Invades the White House." It seems that a young law professor named Anita Hill has accused Clarence Thomas of sexual harassment when he was her boss and head of the Office of Economic Opportunity itself. Thomas is President Bush's own inadequate candidate for supreme court justice, put forth to succeed the great Thurgood Marshall. Through weeks of hearings Thomas has concealed or denied his real opinions, a conservative of such vacuous duplicity that he has become an increasingly embarrassing choice on judicial grounds; now it seems on ethical ones as well.

All day I watch Anita Hill's face on one television set or another, at home or out doing errands—the whole world is listening too—a beautiful face saying outrageous things with the most amazing integrity and courage. At Radio Shack, while I buy Mother a new coaxial cable fitting and try to get her tape recorder repaired, Anita Hill calmly and with a great dignity one can only call "lady-like" describes Clarence Thomas describing the size of his penis. She has to be telling the truth, no woman would dare to enunciate such things otherwise, certainly not this kind of woman, not on national television. Not even if they were true: and in fact she replies with a powerful unwillingness to the unsavory curiosity and skepticism of the senate committee.

There she is again, on the car radio while I search out a welder who can make brackets that will lower Mother's bed so that her feet will touch the ground when she sits on the edge of it, so that she is less likely to fall. I drive through desolate streets by railroad tracks listening to these astonishing statements: Thomas's penchant for pornography, his fascination with "large-breasted" women, more boasts about the size of his penis, Anita Hill forced to render up details for Senator Arlen Spector, forced to explain why she did not "come forward" earlier. She hardly wants to now, did not volunteer colorful details to the FBI when they first and routinely interviewed her, does not want to repeat even what she has just said, having said it with loathing, with hesitation. Hardly able to believe her own voice, these words in the senate, on television all over the continent, the millions gasping and enjoying. Yet having to believe her. It is impossible not to.

Mother watches from her chair. "I believe her," she says with finality. At dinner Anita Hill is believed or disbelieved according to political affiliation: I hear Ceil at her table saying this woman might have made it up. At the round table we believe. But a number can hardly accommodate what they hear, so appalled are they at the fact that it is said out loud. We are a modest town. What impresses even the most dubious of the elderly women is the candor and grace of Anita Hill, her own embarrassed femininity, daring to speak these words. She represents the very upright behavior they most admire, the gentility, the correctitude, the integrity and forbearance. But she is another generation altogether. She is a lawyer, a woman of greater education and civil stature: her very race in a racist society testifies to the excellence of her achievement, how remarkable her gifts must be, how extraordinary her poise and dignity. Everything they esteem. And daring to speak this truth. You bet they believe her, they know what she risks on every side, the enormity of her loss, her inevitable dishonor even if she were to be believed. And already they perceive that she will not be. Not now, maybe never. These women listen to Anita Hill and hear the future and know it has not come. Hearing this much truth, they are afraid that a punishment will come down on all of them. Like factory hands hearing the union organizer talking back, cowed, doubly ashamed to be hearing courage just as they realize their own cowardice to support it, to risk the consequences, their hearts sinking as they hear the scapegoat begin to speak.

She didn't really mean to get herself into this. Anita Hill, like any brave or honest woman never intended to be this brave, surely never this exposed. It happened to her little by little, a combination of refusing to lie to senate staffers, forbearing to elaborate before FBI investigators, begging for confidentiality and being denied it, put before the millions like Susanna before the Elders. This solitary womanly figure, vulnerable but proud, humiliated and refusing to be humiliated, mortified but determined—done down as we have always been, defeated and undone by the perverse sexual aggression done to us. And refusing the guilt even as it is poured upon her by the eyes that watch, the ears that hear what they have known but never heard said aloud. It is a magical act, she has stood her ground with a courage and grace all women admire, watching; a courage and grace beyond every one of us. Who among us could have mustered this much unimpeachable virtue: if this woman will not be believed, surely not one among the rest of us could hope to be.

~

When we went upstairs Mother and I felt isolated and defeated. "Those fools will vote on Tuesday," she says, knowing it all already. And when the vote came in the senate she left the room, would not stay to hear the count, took to her bed, refused to be engaged in sanctioning the defeat of truth, even by observing it. Nothing prevented her from optimism on the private level, however. Cousin Laura stopped in for another session of encouragement. For over a year now Mother has been coaching Laura to give up real estate and try to paint. Now Laura has rented a studio, goes there and faces the possibility of failing and then retreats a little, stops in to be told again, Mother in her chair like a sibyl, her voice in difficulty but determined: "Do what you want to do with your life." In her age and illness illustrating the point, embodying the courage Laura finds it so hard to master for all her youth and beauty and privilege, Mother herself the proof that there is only so much time, so many chances. Then you missed it, it's too late, you betrayed yourself. And in denying and cheating oneself, saying one did it for others, you may even cheat them: they never needed your soul, in failing to develop it you have impoverished them as well, made their lives smaller and dimmer too.

Mother has thrown up her food once already today, I am afraid that if she exerts herself further she may do it again; each episode sets her back, exhausts her strength again. It has come to the point where I even regret the loss of sustenance, eighteen hours of nourishment lost in a plastic dish. Meals on Wheels arrives with her lunch and I wish she could eat it in peace, wishing Laura gone, fearing that if she tires Mother further she will lose this food as well, it will grow cold, she will not be able to keep it down. This morning when she vomited up she apologized: I was ashamed, listening. But I know Laura's need too, the vulture impulse of that necessity, the desperation that cannot stop itself.

The Thomas hearings have gone on day after day like a soap opera of "he said, she said," a form of national public entertainment. By the second day they are competing with baseball. Kirby Puckett has driven in Hreblok to tie it up at two and two. Like boys the players chew gum and blow bubbles even before the camera eye that exposes them to millions. But they behave modestly and keep their tempers. On another channel Thomas is furiously denying, claiming "they" went through the country, looking for dirt: "give us anything," he snarls, having cast himself as an aggrieved black man, actually using the term "uppity." He calls the inquiry into his probity a "high tech lynching," posing as the victim of the most terrible form of sexual persecution, a comparison with the tormented and castrated victims of the past that is utterly disingenuous, a historical farce. A clever lie that will steal a seat on the Court from bewildered white guilt.

I turn back to watch Kirby Puckett execute a beautiful double play and retire the other side. This magnificent plump little athlete with sloe eyes and the wisdom of a buddha, crossing himself at bat. Mother's darling and hero: pity she's asleep and cannot see this. I watch for her. Watching the hearings for myself, where an egregiously vain young black man named something Blodgett the third, graduate of Yale and Harvard business and law schools, with a Wasp's privileged pomposity is trying to persuade the world that Anita Hill is something of a neurotic dame who probably had the hots for him because in fact he is irresistible. You respect the satisfaction of his generation of black achievers, their sense of mission, their need for mutual protection, but realize it is still the boys versus the girls and the boys are out to win. He would be happy to dishonor her but makes a fool of himself instead. In another world of black excellence it's the bottom of the ninth and Alomar gets a single. The game goes to extra innings and an ordinary player given a chance to pinch hit, a man named Pagliarauda, puts it right over the fence for the Twins who are now ahead by one home run. Kirby strikes out but manages to catch Toronto's last fly ball ending the game. Our home team are close to being champions of the American League and a chance to play in the world series. I wake Mother for just a moment to tell her the news: she goes back to sleep utterly contented.

Alternating channels between the surrealism of the Thomas hearings and this, I must admit American baseball still gives satisfaction. How alienated the political life is now, how unreal and dishonest. I begin to see things from the point of view of the residents here, who still love baseball and are capable of a fine cynicism about the rest.

~

There comes a night when Mother puts on her lipstick for dinner and takes note of a $649 dividend from the Dreyfuss fund. A woman of business, opening her mail from Penn Mutual, the Company. She sees who has paid their premium on policies sold years ago, each client remembered, the residuals there for her on the bottom line, tables that had been incomprehensible to me—till now I had been sending them on to Sal who perhaps couldn't figure them either.

How mysterious are the lives of others when we are faced with them in their absence, how problematic. Every detail of an existence is like this, essential to the owner, extraneous to the intruder. Like the furniture in the apartment: Sally is to inherit the sofa but already does not need or want it, shipping and reupholstering would be too expensive. Whereas for Mother, her sofa is perfect, just the way it is, just in that spot, so perfect that she doesn't want it exchanged for the convertible sofa bed I might wish she'd buy so that I could save my back, a hope I have already surrendered, realizing that the change would be totally unacceptable for Mother, however temporarily convenient to me: it's her home, not mine—we've agreed on that.

The sanctity of my mother's existence is monumental to me, it must not be disturbed. Being this close to her death, either literal or civil, has given me grave apprehensions for my own: where are all my negatives, could I find them? My drawings never catalogued, the whole mess of my life there at the Farm—who would ever understand it, sort, preserve, respect. I do not want Mother's existence sorted and labeled and consigned away, however carefully. I want it preserved for her, here in this room. Seeing her finally take up her mail and sort it, read and save or consign to the trash, I observe a miracle of restoration. All big steps back to life, independence.

The night before last she called me at one in the morning to have me watch her—"But you mustn't touch me"—swing on her new vertical pole from her bed and to her commode. Valiant and fragile. Back on my sofa I am so satisfied I cannot sleep. Sal now calls me Mother's "coach," asked if I had thought of a career in rehabilitation, a joke Mother turned into a compliment by taking seriously. Mother's old friend Louise White stopped by, bringing homemade chicken soup and "bars," as brownies are called here. Louise brought her daughter along, a nun who runs a priory: we planned visits there and to Lakeville, where Louise lives alone now, her husband Bud dead a year and she is still not used to it, a woman of great beauty with magnificent white hair. Surgery gave them an extra year and a half she said, even a trip to Ireland. Hearing this I am happy for her as well as sad: living till he died, there was this much.

Maggie's assistant Dave is substituting for Nancy this week while she is out of town. Since he has observed Mother from the beginning, when she was first at St. Anne's, he is probably the best judge of her progress, which delights him. "Can I get rid of my walker?" Mother asks him. The huge young man laughs down at her: "At the rate you're going, it's possible." Yesterday he and I lowered Mother's bed with the new brackets I had the welder make: now her feet touch the floor. Dave gave us the next day off and we went to see Mother's friend Hap in her nursing home, a visit Mother dreads. Hap may have too much against her to make it out of this place and back to the Wellington. She is deaf and going blind, she has a catheter she had preferred we didn't know about on our last visit. Today she will admit to it: "Means I'm wet all the time and mad. Mad as a wet hen," Hap grumbles and performs her life like a comedienne. She's going back on physical therapy next week.

Ruth is there as well, giving off an atmosphere of prevention, discouragement, finality: her very manner proclaiming to Hap that she will never get out of here. It was impossible for Mother and Hap to talk privately. After Ruth has departed, I put their two wheelchairs together and left them to themselves. What I did hear, the two wheelchairs face to face, were simply the words of one condemned to one who would survive: Hap asking "Can you make it on your own?" Mother nodding, a small tight voice, "I plan to." "You'll need help," Hap says, a blessing almost, a farewell. I have been trying to persuade Hap's daughter to follow our course; Mother wants Hap back across the hall. But everything depends upon another generation's judgment. Mom stiff uppers the last goodbye. When we leave, Mother comments in a matter of fact way that she looks better than Hap. "That's not very charitable," I say, disappointed. "No, it isn't," she answers, knowing it's not about charity but chance, fate, luck. A bitter knowledge, simple truth.

Then we drove the town, seeing the leaves, Summit and the River Road a maze of gold, an ecstasy of light, we held our breath and didn't speak as we drove along, sharing a cloud of golden mist as the leaves swirled around the car. "Don't you love Summit," Mother said, saying everything in this one statement, surely not a question but a confirmation. I pushed the River at her once, now she pushes Summit, our great boulevard; bestowing the town on me, home and homeland. The leaves churned around the car, the wind picks them up and blows them like a rain of yellow light around us as we glided down the avenue of old elms and younger maples, surrounded by grace. We were holding hands.

~

Drinking coffee I wonder what it will be like when the leaves go. The sadness of this landscape then. Arriving in September, I didn't bring a coat. I think of L.K. at the Farm, harvest preparations. I worry over the twelve thousand I must put together soon to get through the coming year; I have only four thousand eight hundred of it now. Top of that, the Farm may need as much as three thousand for the septic and probably more. Did L.K. ever collect the cottage rent? The taxes are paid at last but soon there will be bills for propane and electric. No one is buying landscape trees because of the recession. How will the Farm survive, how will I? I sit here scared, so far from my own world. The Canadian geese are flying, I feel a terrible pull to go home and take care of business: the Farm, the book on political prisoners I should be finishing.

It is all part of being here, the strangeness of being here, the sense of being a blank, an empty thing. So alien that as I sit around and socialize, with the Wellington crew or the cousins, I am acting a part, eager and delighted if I can do something real like fetch ice cubes since I am otherwise merely a big stupid pair of eyes, an awkward body without identity, past or present. In fact the longer I am here the more I disappear, become someone with no idea who she is; I forget my name, my hard-won definitions.

On Saturday there were cousins discussing the Thomas hearings and I talked as a feminist, said that the man was not on trial, but a candidate for a job—"The Supreme court—that's Something," as Mother had put it. He's an office-seeker, therefore the presumption of innocence (today's spin on television) is irrelevant. "This is not a trial, there's no danger he'll be convicted. Only that he'll be confirmed." No one heard me. The tide has turned: the president has spoken, the polls have gone to work. After passing a polygraph, Anita Hill has yielded to pressure—how enormous it must be—and cancelled further panels of witnesses. It becomes a question of air time finally; her last press conference was blacked out, reduced to a mere snippet. After all those grueling hours of testimony. Today all anchors proclaim a victory for Thomas. "We will never know the truth," I hear my cousins say. Even here. But Thomas has every reason to lie, Anita Hill has none, I argued. No one listened. When Steven left I confronted him for a moment in the hall: it has been this way all my life in this family, I tell him, recalling the Loony Bin. He is offended, surely he has never—"Of course not, or I wouldn't complain to you."

I am the outsider here still. Strangely enough I am also the one who is at Mother's side now, trying to assess her character, that mixture of indomitable will and timidity, the bossiness I have resented since adolescence, the nagging, the habit of getting her way even if she is obeyed through coerced "respect," telling me to see visitors to the door as if I might not, instructing me. I become a clod, a disgruntled teenager being taught manners. There is also astonishment before her dividends; at eighty-nine she still knows business and the world, understands people, sees through things.

And then her vulnerability appears again, like a ghost, like the frightened woman from long ago calling "prospects" on Saturday mornings. Will she be helpless before her attendants now? Is the attitude of command her only defense before the world's callowness, the betrayals of age replacing the original ones of gender?

Oddly enough the usual erasure of the self I experience here, that familiar disappearance into invalidation, has a quite different effect this time. That constant sense of being no one which used to enrage me here—buried and silent and hidden and then erupting inevitably into a quarrel and guilt and sorrow—is, paradoxically, the perfect thing just now and uniquely qualifies me for my job. As no one, a cipher, I can perform one hundred percent for Mother, become a machine, a force to heal her and bring her every conceivable benefit the social system affords.

Even when she wakes up tired and grouchy, actually tells me to "shut up" when I give her directions about how to position her walker safely when rising and sitting, I am amused more than insulted. And I love her spunk. It is less delightful to wait upon her hand and foot as she eats breakfast: impossible to eat with her as she orders me to since every time I sit down, I am instructed to put the cream back in the fridge, fetch her a spoon, put her stipulated three prunes in a dish, bring the sugar when you come and so forth.

There are a few days when there is no speech therapy from "Dr. Millett," days she is simply canceled, a washout. Even at my best I get a second-rate reception compared to the real professionals; it is hard to get

Mother to concentrate, to put the same effort into working for me as others. I even let her off the hook sometimes.

But other times we are in rapture. For days now we have been reading Tennessee Williams' great "Overstuffed Chair" story, perfect for us. Almost too perfect, especially as Williams comes in time not only to hate his father's drunken and loutish behavior (Mother approves) but even to understand it (less approval, hard truths to face) and finally even to replicate it. The fate of someone who in the course of producing Shoe Sales—in his progenitor's case, or literature in his own—is merely a machine that makes something. A man who ought to love and give to others, but after doing his stint of words, has no real energy whatsoever left for life itself; mere living, mere people. This honesty shuts me up. We both love the way the man is personified by his chair, his laziness, his surrender to its misshapen womb. His ugly old-fashioned tassel lamp amuses us still more and we laugh until we cry while reading these passages aloud. Their resemblances to our own family skeletons, our own family alienation, father who drinks, kid who writes, are tonic and painful, make us alive through reading together. We get high, transcending the usual genre of feminine romance—Mother's preferred form—and the general banality of the television news, *Newsweek* and the *St. Paul Pioneer Press*. I treasure the moments I can make her feel through language, even if it's the bittersweet of nostalgia. At this point anything she reads about is likely to be looking back, not forward, aware of loss rather than expectation. Some things she refuses utterly, Annie Dillard's description of her father's infatuation with the Mississippi and New Orleans Jazz—surely too much of Dad in this. But then she will perk up and marvel over a paragraph in a biography of Edith Sitwell called *Portrait of a Rebel*, a paragraph which characterizes the mind of Lord David Cecil, his manner of listening, his manner of speech and reaction to what he's heard; the thinking process and habits of mind of this erudite and subtle scholar is something Mother can relish, feel positive affection for. Whereas Dillard's father's interests represented something raffish and dangerous and like my father, Cecil does not threaten, he is the charm of the thought mechanism itself, wonderful, neither male nor female but pure process.

Lord David was around at Oxford when I was an undergraduate but I have no recollection of him beyond a lisp, which I do not contribute since he is already such a hit. I watch Mother's reactions to a description, a bit further on in the text, of Dame Edith's eclectic mixture of aristocratic populism and formality, waiting for Mother to be impatient with the privileged, to frown or jeer at the great lady posture, the heartiness toward the lowly. And am outfoxed. Either by her tolerance. Or her wisdom. Or her West Britain tendencies.

For Mother is a curious blend of plain homespun honesty with a certain lady-like fastidiousness. Of course all these years living in the city of St. Paul and away from Patrick Henry's farm and the villages where she grew up and taught immigrant children, she has grown wonderfully fond of comfort, fine soap and cashmere sweaters, less rigorous now against all the tedious petty bourgeois niceties she must have found phony or oppressive once. Her compromises with convention both in the name of good manners and good diplomacy fascinate me. All her honesties, all her possible dishonesties and foibles as well. For she is an interesting creature: ethically, aesthetically, socially; parti-colored, by no means simple. Mother long treasured a toffee tin with the pictures of the Queen Mother of England and the little princesses Elizabeth and Margaret. Odd behavior in a daughter of Galway whose favorite song and only prepared composition for pianoforte during my own childhood was a lively rendition of "The Wearing of the Green." Hammered out lustily in her heyday when this was a fighting song. Calculated to inspire warlike race memory even in little girls suddenly ardent to grow up into amazons or patriots like Maude Gonne and Con Markewitz.

Driving over to do the brave and still possibly reckless thing, to cancel the last connection with St. Anne's, to give up the bed and close that door, though we do have the waiting list as a safety net, I chew on the ethics of freedom. Pitting my own homemade existentialism against everything else, all bureaucratic social systems, St. Paul's indigenous puritanism and pessimism, its narrow always constricting margins, its ruthless and routine manner of flunking out possibilities as they arise. Go on, rail at the place, hate it as you love it, demean it at one moment as you idealize it at another. Neither are true: the truth of the place is as banal as its little avenues of houses, as dear as the random names of its streets, each one a tree and summer in childhood. Even so, you are taking on the place now as you drive, this time cutting and running, you have made off with your own mother.

Make an equation then of your resistance, it will help you analyze your own errors in logic. If the fright you feel is represented by A and the action you take nonetheless, is labeled B, then does A prove B right or wrong? Justify? Exculpate? Such terror as you experience certainly takes all enjoyment and pleasure out of the exercise of courage. But does timidity function to "excuse" and palliate activity that could be called rash as well as, or instead of, almost brave?

There are a few last things to get from Mother's sad little room: photographs, the chair, the television. Adelaide Behan, Mother's roommate, is there in her bed, the woman left behind. I am a little ashamed before her. Adelaide Behan wants to go home, her family keep telephoning, wanting her back. I hope so. "When will you go?" I ask, accepting her story that she is merely here to convalesce. "It's been months already," she sighs. "I may never get out of here. Except in a box." Perhaps things are worse than she had first led me to conclude. "But I keep wanting to get out. Would you believe it, I keep wanting to go dancing? If I could go dancing . . . my husband and I, we were the best in the world at it, the old time dancing, do you know what I mean, the shoddisch and the polka."

"Then goldarn it, the Good Lord took him." There's a long silence in the room, for what do you say to such love of life, such a terrible ripping need to be out on the town, such futile desire, such thwarted vitality? She will never be allowed to dance again. The picture of St. Francis where he looks like a hippie has been moved to the chapel, there is a new last supper relief in its place in the front hall. I notice a plaque attesting that St. Anne's was given a special award for care. I catch sight of the little woman who had been asking the attendant for her social security check last time, asking in vain. I wish I were mean enough to photograph the discouraging statue outside Mother's door, her desolate room. Document, you ought to document, I'd thought. But then it seemed overkill and I left the camera behind. So I just load the car and then go back to face the last interview with the authorities.

Cornered in a basement office with Pam Keenan and her rather forbidding boss, Kim, I feel a stricture in my chest while professing gratitude. Of course there is a little problem with the bill. I had the distinct impression that Phyllis Kirk, the nursing supervisor, promised me in her office the other day that we would be charged at the minimum level of nursing service. Pam and Kim don't think it will be quite that easy, since the business office will have a different view of things than the nursing staff. Therefore they have prepared the papers for me to lodge a complaint and petition the state of Minnesota for relief. I stare at a mess of forms—not this too.

Moreover, as part of my appeal, they have taken a copy of all the nursing notes made during Mother's residency at the home, a record generally secret and particularly unavailable to the individual whom it observes and records. For this occasion, the filing of a petition, I am permitted to read it. In view of later events it is surprising how the whole idea bored and annoyed me—my chief interest in this interview is to butter up St. Anne's so that, if utterly necessary, if Mother collapses at home—we could get her back in there. That's what I've been told to do by both Sally and Steven. And today, seeing my bridge burning brightly, I too want some secret path back to safety: if Mother were suddenly taken very ill, she would need the place.

Therefore, feeling grave and adult, I elaborately write Sal's name on the waiting list, Steve's, and my own, complete with both my addresses and phone numbers—so that I will be notified before any action is taken and no one sneaks Mom back in before I hear of it. There, everything is covered. Mother is protected in the case that she is well and competent; in the opposite case that she is unwell and incompetent, there will be refuge here. How long till the next vacancy, I wonder idly, how many times through this winter will we deliberate and then pass up the great opportunity to secure Mother's existence at the expense of her autonomy? This could be hell, this could go on a couple times a month, every time someone dies. Well, at least I have acted responsibly, I congratulate myself.

So that later in the afternoon, reading the nursing notes out of a pallid curiosity, it takes a while for their meaning to intrude on me. For all the different specimens of handwriting to become legible, even for their odd jargon to register as language. And out of their barbarian abbreviations, their tedious repetitions as one observer informs the next that Mother is deaf, that she has had a shunt bypass, that she requires one attendant present at toileting—out of these banal observations, my own mother appears a stranger in a strange and terrifying place, who calls out "nurse" and "toilet," terrible and disturbing acts which are reported to annoy her roommate, break the silence and serenity of the place. Moreover, she does not cooperate in taking every medication put before her—not by now—and even strikes the hand that would administer, refuses many blandishments, is not adjusting. An unwilling resident, who from the moment she entered the place seems to have provoked the admitting nurse, who responded by asking Sally, the admitting relative, to give the Home permission to use restraint. Specifically a black belt, a great hunk of rough fabric like a huge karate belt with which one is tied to the bed and made immobile and helpless. Sally refused categorically. The admitting nurse is undeterred by this altogether and makes a note at the bottom of page one that she plans to begin the campaign for restraint the next time she sees this daughter. But for Sally's refusal, Mother could have been subject to restraint at once. For the moment however, the double-railed bed is thought to be sufficient.

Until 2.30 on September 19th, when Mother was perceived as "trying to leave the building." This wreck of a creature who could then hardly stand, scarcely walk with a walker, was apprehended near the elevators. Odd, how this elevator already had special vibrations, even the first days, was familiar to Mother, she knew that once she was inside that elevator door . . . but they caught her first. She was taken back to her room and put to bed. Restraint, the usual black belt, a contemporary version of the strait jacket, is forbidden them thus far. I have seen one and told myself it was to keep someone from falling out of bed or a wheelchair. Since restraint is unavailable to them—so far—a "wanderguard" was ordered.

It took a phone call and a visit to establish what this word meant: in some embarrassment Pam explained the wanderguard device, the electronic eye it triggers at both doors, the loud alarm it sets off. Over the phone Steve called it an electronic jail—I remember hearing about such devices in certain new schemes of imprisonment where the state has hit upon the process of "jobbing out" its prisoners to corporations who incarcerate them for profit, an "advance" in the criminal justice system.

It takes a while to absorb it all, but St. Anne's changes with each page, each revelation. The "wanderguard" was ordered September 19th, the day Mother tried, with such lovely courage—how would she ever make it those eight blocks back home?—to leave a place no one had ever informed her she was forbidden to leave. Was she supposed to know? And having committed this terrible indiscretion—or so it appears in the notes—she will be punished with a tracking device. We might have been told all this by telephone, hear only their side, not hers. How easy to persuade "the family" then that she is senile, dangerous to herself—all those little phrases behind which you lose your freedom and suffer substituted judgment, so that whether by formal commitment hearing or not, you enter the confines of the mad or irresponsible, the senile or just "absent-minded"—a loose cannon that must be tied harder and harder.

Permission for restraint would not be hard to achieve now with the story that Mother wanders, requires a tracking device. Worrisome long distance ultimatums; the institution could demand this for insurance reasons; they do not want to be sued if Mother walks across the road and is run over. Sally could not hold out forever, who could? Either give permission for restraint or remove your mother. We would have had no place to put Mother by then, her apartment gone, her behavior described as difficult, unreasonable. Restraint would soon be "indicated"—always of course only for her own good. From what I read here its eventual use would be inevitable if Mother maintained any spirit at all.

Restrained then, tied into her bed, an entire prisoner now, she could be drugged as well. Would "have" to be, in fact. If she is a disturbance calling out "nurse" or "toilet," imagine what it might occur to her to say when tied down. Perhaps something ominous like "help" or the names of her daughters, her grandson, pleas, cuss words? The institution requires silence. And gets it now in the age of psychiatric medication. So that Mother could be drugged. We would be scolded into silence with some story that she was consumed with anxiety, might do harm to herself, is deeply agitated, in need of sedation—whatever it took to make us believe. And who would question these reports, investigate these so convincing even embarrassing details? How does one question a doctor's judgment—the home would surely have his cooperation. Here too they could threaten expulsion of the resident who has nowhere else to go.

So that for $36,000 a year you can be tied to your bed and drugged. It is all legal. It is permitted and practiced in America and elsewhere; you can spend your last dollar on it. After that's gone, this enslavement continues free of charge at state expense, under slightly worse conditions in a smaller, darker room. You could live years like that—Mother had perhaps enough money to endure three years of this imprisonment. Of course the heart breaks first and many die long before the 120 subsidized days of Medicare are over. Imagine abandonment under those circumstances.

I look around Mother's apartment and swallow hard. She was on her way. This isn't what they do to everyone, only to the harder cases, the ones who don't cooperate, don't want to be there, are suspected of escape, fail to adjust, refuse to. And my infinitely polite and conventional mother was one of these, had, it turns out, been labeled not just "G"—needs help to the toilet as I had been told—but additionally "H," which is "behavioral problem." Mother Millett a behavioral problem, for a moment it is funny—then it is sickening and I am so angry that I'm glad I never knew this before. Certainly not while jockeying to get her out of there with everyone's permission. Today the social workers seemed to infer that the permission of Mother's physician is required for her to leave; otherwise she is "discharged against medical advice" which is a category in itself and with legal ramifications which might adversely affect her benefits and payments, etc.

In any case, one doesn't discharge oneself: Mother is out because I got her out. Steven's cooperation must also have been crucial. Damn good thing I never guessed how this place could have abused her, how these places routinely permit themselves to abuse the aged sick. In perfect legal impunity. These are the terrible prerogatives of force they reserve for themselves: drugs and methods of physical coercion which amount in effect to both torture and slavery. I would have blown the place apart if I had known. I could never have been civil, still less kissed ass. And I needed to. If I'd started mouthing off in a place where Mother was already so labeled, so endangered, I could have been forbidden the premises, my own record as a certified nut resurrected, matter for an injunction if necessary. One fit of temper and the management might have lit a fire under Sal, then what?

How will she react now, I wonder? Steven suggests that I may wish to withdraw my own name from St. Anne's right away. He'll have the nursing notes typed and when he's read them, come to his own decision about the place and its waiting list. I want to circulate the notes in the family together with a covering letter interpreting them and explaining why I now find St. Anne's or any institutional facsimile completely impossible—no option whatsoever. Which leaves only the choice of Mother living at home as she wishes to do. Failing that, and Mother *acknowledging* she fails that, Mallory and I can both offer her our homes.

The nursing notes are a turning point, having understood their consequence has left me no acceptable moral alternative than to reply with what is in effect an ultimatum: St. Anne's never. And since Mother's present regime is viewed as merely a respite from St. Anne's, a temporary evasion of the eventual and inevitable answer of this or some other nursing home, I have dropped something of a bomb.

But I have dropped it on myself as well. To prevent restraint I may have to rebuild the Farm. Maybe even build that stone house I used to dream of making for Mother as a memorial, something like an Irish cottage with a view of the sunset up on the hill. No, too isolated, you will have to build a wing on the blue barn, wheelchair accessible; it would take time, will I have time? All traces of bitterness and rancor over the past are healed now, I feel an overwhelming urge to protect her—will do anything to save her from the fate I have foreseen here. To prevent restraint I will go the whole way—stay here all winter if need be, through harvest even. What if Sal were to come after I'd left in November as planned, take one look around and decide Mom's arrangements were inadequate and she should go back to St. Anne's? So I can't leave, I can never leave. But there is the tumor, growing, growing; what if Mom is a vegetable eventually—no, not even vegetables should undergo restraint.

I admired Mallory's generosity in offering Mother her home—now I must join her. If Mother is ever too debilitated for the Wellington I'll refurbish the Farm: whatever has to be done I will do it. I had no idea when I sat in the car after leaving St. Anne's today, parking along the River Road for quarter of an hour just to celebrate that it was over, everything packed and loaded and out of there. I just sat back for a bit, filled my eyes with the color of a red maple, let the music on the radio get inside me, a country boy singing "Who needs you, I got Mexico," grinning at the blow-it-away hedonism, wishing I could ever give her that, toasting freedom with a Marlboro—I had no idea how close a call it was.

~

Steven's measured response to all this is disappointing. I had hoped his indignation would take fire at once. But he is a corporation lawyer, he is supposed to cultivate neutrality, must feel he represents his own mother here and cannot be certain how Sally will respond. It seems wise to circulate the nursing notes in the family and wait for reactions. I have Mallory's vote over the phone already, that makes it two sisters. As to what Mother herself wants—and the full truth of why she feels the way she does—that is surely clear enough. But will it be respected? Especially since two attorneys are in question: Sally and Steven.

Now that Mother is out, I must see to it that she is never put back again—the full danger of the place is clear to me. Perhaps most of us are like the neighbors around the concentration camp who were never very sure and therefore could always hide behind their uncertainty. Reading these notes is a watershed: there is now no excuse at all. One is no longer hesitating over the loss of personhood (putative, subjective), one is confronting physical bondage, psychological toxicity. I have been on psychiatric drugs against my will. Even if my family have not, they can imagine being tied to the frame of a bed day after day, never allowed to move without permission; even to urinate one must be privileged by a captor. How much imagination must this take? Yet when you mention these facts to people, they hardly respond. Yes, it's awful what happens to the aged, they say. As if old people were not quite people to the extent that we are, so that inhuman treatment for the aged is only a shame, a "pity," not an outrage, not a crime. Tolerated routinely it no longer surprises. Rather like the sufferings of women, one takes such things for granted. Like all crime perpetrated against the helpless, easy and predictable, cruel and unfair, but emblematic of how things are, the public may regard themselves as helpless to protest. It does not now occur to them to object. Yet this is our own fate before us, the world is getting older and older; these places will be stuffed.

"Not my mother," Mallory says, a tribal ring in it. "These places are crammed with everybody's mother," I say to her, "And they can't get out 'cause they got no bread." "That's lousy, for sure; but not my mother." I hear it and know this absolute refusal is mine too. We are the younger sisters, we are not attorneys. I wonder if we will be listened to. Because we are engaged in a refusal now, not just a change of plans or a postponement.

And as St. Anne's is demoted from the better and more sensible choice to what seems a kind of moral anathema, upon the discovery of its underside, I now fear Sally's reaction. Though she played no part in it, forbade their brutality from the start, Sal's unequivocal refusal constituting Mother's only safety against the staff's desire to restrain her—until Mother's own gumption got her into the line of fire—Sal might still feel judged, implicated, criticized. Will it make her stubborn, will it make her hold out for St. Anne's, will it make a fight and a great fissure down the family face? I must make damn sure it doesn't. Nothing would give Mother greater anguish than to have us quarrel now when she is so ill and trying so hard to recover. Stress makes her vomit, so keep her out of the wind, prevent a storm altogether.

How to insure that Mother's never dragged back there if you mustn't even mention it? So mention it, but don't let it threaten her. She's got to know if St. Anne's is calling Sal or Steven with each vacancy, presenting a temptation, a solution. Wait, I had her on the waiting list too. Yes, before I knew the half of it. I must protect her from any return to a place she experienced as such misery that she will not speak of it. A place which, by the accident of reading these notes, I now happen to know even better perhaps than she does.

~

"Did you know they use restraint?" I came out and asked my mother after her nap, afraid and embarrassed but finally needing to know what she knew—if only to protect her. A frown and a deprecating gesture of her hand says no, but it confirms her disgust to hear this. So she did not fathom this side of it; she escaped this narrowly. Mother is nobody's activist. I cannot automatically assume she sees this politically. On the other hand, she makes oracular statements like "This is a big thing," when we talk about her friend Hap getting out of a nursing home and coming back to the Wellington.

It was not really till she read my covering letter. And I wouldn't have put her through that, or the nursing notes at all—why bring the place up to haunt her now that she's working so hard to live at home, is so easily upset, eighteen hours of sustenance is lost in each attack of vomiting—if it had not been for the damn power-of-attorney issue.

Sal needed one to pay Mother's bills, certain Medicare procedures demand a power of attorney. Steven also has a power of attorney for Mother, but he is here in St. Paul, handling the quarrel with Carol, whereas Sally is receiving and paying Mother's great mound of medical bills forwarded to Nebraska. For convenience Sally must now also have a power of attorney of her own.

~

It was nothing at first; since we were having lunch together I asked Steven to bring Sal's power-of-attorney form along with him, Mother could sign it after the banquet Vanny was giving her. For Steven has mediated a great treat for Mother, something sure to boost her spirits and remind her of her palmy days in business. Her old friend Vanny is now the vice president of a powerful bank and Vanny wants to honor Mother by staging the bank's best luncheon in its board room overlooking the Mississippi and the whole town, capitol and cathedral spread out in a sweep before her.

Mother is pleased but as the luncheon proceeds her deafness isolates her with her food; Steven and Vanny and I happen to be talking among ourselves when Mother's attack of vomiting begins. No, I beg fate, not now, not here, not in her moment of glory and recall to the world of big time activity, the movers and shakers, the pomp of fancy office buildings. Vomit is seeping down the front of Mother's beautiful sweater as I run to help, devastated to see her triumph lost through her body's betrayal. Yet somehow her unshakable dignity even manages to encompass this. In fact Mother and Vanny transcend together through feminine tact and Vanny's perfect manner. In Mother this power becomes a kind of miraculous grace; I have never seen her more stately, immanent, almost shining. One can only marvel at her poise and sense of what is valuable and important, her wisdom.

But as I say goodbye to Vanny, she presses my hand and assures me that my mother was one of the smartest women she has ever known—her use of the past tense is painful. Vanny understood events only so far, failed to see that Mother was even smarter now. The entire experience disappoints: we had looked forward to this so. It was to be a moment of recognition which would compensate for all the indignities of the nursing home and Mother's recent near dismissal from her world. The polite farewells depress me unutterably. No one understands the real extent of Mother's courage and sagacity. Even Vanny, caught in the lesser world where smart is making money.

What had been at first sight so satisfactory, the swank of it, the affluence of big business here at home, originally even quaint, acceptable as friendly and "ours," is suddenly as hostile as its parallel in New York. Even a little more smug, more comfortable and unaware. Suddenly the self-importance of these brand new office towers, the hell of getting a wheelchair through their tunnels and elevators, the labyrinth I had to struggle with just to get us there, this entire day, seems like insult. Relieved only by the radiant beauty of how Mother handled her fall: that single insight.

The power of attorney is a good excuse to visit Steven's office, and of course he wants to show it off, the great window, the big view, the other members of the firm both male and female, the jokes and introductions in the corridor, the prestige of Steven's own spot there in what one colleague teases him is the "high rent district." For Steven's sake Mother and I are more than willing to be impressed by the grandeur and appointments of the room. Then Mother sits off to the side, looking at the document she is to sign as Steven explains that it is nearly the same as the previous one, only a few small changes have been made. Since there is the possibility of a suit with Carol, litigation has been made a category now as well. I see her accepting the explanation and signing out of complete faith in her grandson, hardly reading what she signs, the picture of trust, a trust I share.

But I must remember too that I am her advocate and I carry with me the nursing notes which Steven will have typed by his secretary. Diffidently, without conviction, only a notion that such a question is pro forma, I ask Steven if the power of attorney will have any bearing on Mother's rights. I'd asked him before, over the phone and he had teased me "She'll have none, none whatsoever": I'd laughed out loud, Steve's imitation of judicial obduracy was so perfect. It is less amusing now that I ask in Mother's presence, and somewhat awkward since his old secretary, the one who worked for him when he first joined the firm, called in now to notarize Mother's signature, is listening: this is family business. Mother signs and the woman leaves the room.

This is a legal question after all, I remind Steven gently, Mother's rights are not that well established yet. She's just come out of a nursing home where she could be placed, I assume permanently, against her will. No one intended harm thereby he assures me in defense. "Of course not, Sal must have felt that any one of us might have done the same."

"I wish you'd tell her that; it would make her feel so much better." "Of course, Sal went through hell, I know it." What I must explain to Steven is that once in St. Anne's—a place where Mother was miserable and as we see now, in real danger as well—no one would preserve her rights. Once inside, how was she to get out? "Mother could still be there, if I hadn't come. If I leave she might be put back there. It's essential she be protected from that."

Steven stares at me: he is getting angry. "What I'm trying to say, Steve, is that Mother is free now but I have to be sure she's safe, that she has rights and that her wishes will be respected. In asking these questions I'm acting as her advocate." Coming up against his annoyance—he will not explore the idea—my throat tightens and I realize I must actually speak up like an advocate: Mother is the client here and these questions must be answered.

Steven appears to be outraged; he must be impressive in court. I kept quiet and waited to pursue this until the notary left, but now we are family and in private. Unfortunately, Mother, the object of our discussion, is too far away to hear us—as always objectified, discussed and not consulted. She cannot grasp the topic but senses something wrong. I try to make a stand but feel myself slipping into embarrassment, incoherence, suborned by Steven's mounting ire, his expertise, the prestige of his office and his sense of insulted rectitude.

I read the document granting power of attorney while the notary was in the room, even as it was being signed. It frightened me very much; its scope is enormous. One is warned at the top of the page to look up all its implications in some arcane section of Minnesota law. But there's a lot to make one nervous just in its plain English, particularly the clause at the top of the second page, checked off on both Steven's and Sally's copies where, in one paragraph Mother has given assent for them to act on her behalf without restraint in the case of her becoming incompetent. In the next paragraph they are permitted to transfer any and all of her funds to themselves for administration.

Then it had seemed simply a matter of principle that one inquired at all: there are two such powers of attorney in existence now, Sally's as well as Steven's. Could they, would they, have any bearing on Mother's rights and her wishes to live where she liked? Is there anything here that might, under some circumstances, hinder or subvert her choices, put them in other hands? It is my job to be sure her wishes are honored. Is there any danger for her in having signed this? Any conceivable danger?

Steven reminds me that no one can declare Mother incompetent without a court procedure. But I know how treacherous such events can be, how defenseless one is before them, how the victim can be drugged and fail to understand, how the court-appointed attorney can fail to represent a client who is generally a stranger to him. Mother does not in fact understand what we are saying about her now. I stand between her ignorance—not wanting to make a scene—and Stephen's anger. "Look, Mom was just put into an institution, a place from which she couldn't remove herself on her own, without help," I argue, feeling foolish; Steven helped too. "But all this was done without recourse to the power of attorney," Steven argues back. "Just what I mean, people do whatever the hell they want to with old people. Even families do. I have to be sure her wishes are respected and this piece of paper . . ." He has got to understand that when I ask if her freedom is jeopardized by such documents I have real reason to be vigilant. Our eyes meet across a tense silence: I'm deeply sorry and terribly embarrassed, but I must defend her: "These are ethical questions and you're a lawyer; it's your responsibility to answer them Steve." I say it with the last energy I have, humiliated before him, afraid of his anger, afraid for Mother before all the machinations of paperwork, the very fact that she cannot even hear or comprehend this discussion, which now seems to become a quarrel between us, rather than an open and reasonable airing of the issue in the presence of the one concerned.

Steven sees me as having questioned his honor and he is responding with a high baronial rage: familiar, like a Millett. He feels his integrity is impugned and is failing to see the issue entirely: the rights of the elderly, Mother's own future, whether she will have control over her own decisions. Which must after all depend upon her having control of her resources. Sally presently administers her funds, what if she refused to pay Mother's rent at the Wellington, argued over Vera's salary? "Mother's independence rests on her having access to her money, don't you see? Isn't it a fact that whoever controls one's money controls one's life?" Begging him to understand, not take umbrage. "It's about her freedom . . . I have to ask . . ."

My forehead hot, how crazy that acting in Mother's interest I could ever be potentially at odds with Steven, with Sally: we are all supposed to be working together to help her. Why has everything gone wrong, why are we talking about her when she cannot even understand us—what have I done wrong, what several things? First I have been a coward before Steven's anger; hurt and frightened. It has taken all my courage merely to state my case: I am twenty years older than he is and his aunt. I have outraged him in ways I cannot really understand, though I suspect he may be protecting his own mother's judgment just as I protect mine. But it is shameful that the person we discuss is not even admitted into our short, almost dishonest squabble.

It is all my fault, I think, going through the maze of elevators to the parking lot, guided by Steven, though aware I could find my way by now without him, deferring however, "making nice". Steven must be thinking me paranoid or vengeful over my loony bin trip, engaged in some private quarrel with his mother, my sister Sally, and determined he will have no part in it. That was never the point, the issue now is Mother, the very specifics of her rights. Which I fear could be violated at any moment, even obliquely—anything that threatens her little set up at the Wellington, any hassle over fees for example. What if there is a snag, or a controversy and it is alleged Vera overcharged? I consider Vera's humble $10 an hour—here in a warren of lawyers who make $250 an hour and never do anything as measurable and material as dressing an invalid.

Steven admired me today for the speed and ease when I cleaned up Mother's vomit. However, when I played advocate I was suddenly someone he intensely disliked, towering over me in his barely controlled fury, a theatrical outrage that must be extremely successful at trial. I felt cowed, mortified, thoroughly intimidated. And loving this young nephew as impulsively as I have, I also felt despised and hurt in my very heart, spurned as one who loved him, imagined herself a comrade and a friend. Something in me was broken by what I felt to be Steven's bullying, something of hope and affection and trust.

It was not only his refusal to see Mother's vulnerability before the institutions around her, it was his annoyance that I should dare to raise such a question, stand apart from the tribe and its inner directed and emotional manner of making decisions, and adopt a neutral, outsider's view. The very thing professional legal advice is supposed to provide. Steven was acting like a family member in fact, not like a lawyer: it must happen a lot. And families, imagining they are saving money or using their own resources well, must frequently err in having uncles and cousins see to things they perhaps cannot see clearly.

I had imagined I was only up against Sally's family rule, which may or may not permit Mother to live her own life: to make sure of the latter I may go head to head with the former. But Steven as well . . . and the shock of masculine domination that emanated from him, the surprise of that, the pain of it.

"What is it that made you so unhappy in Steven's office?" Mother asks as we get into the car. I postpone but finally I must explain, hesitantly, irresolutely, that the power of attorney worries me, having such powers over her purse is having power over her person and if she wished to continue to live at the Wellington and Sally deemed her incapable of doing so, she might ultimately, in ways one can only still guess at, be at some risk legally, financially, through the power of attorney. It may be only potential but it scares me.

"Steven says I can revoke the power of attorney anytime I like," she answers, having absorbed a great deal of this matter already; she is a woman of business after all. "They don't jump to your assistance with notaries in places like St. Anne's, Mom. Once institutionalized you probably would have no opportunity to revoke a power of attorney unless the family wished you to do so," I remind her. The management defers consistently in the family's wishes and seems to prefer their interests over those of the residents who tend to be discounted as senile and mentally incompetent whether they are or not; their residence itself is taken as evidence of nonentity, substituted judgment and civil death. "I heard a little lady asking over and over where her money was—her social security check—they answered her in bullying voices that it was 'safe in the bank,' probably withheld to pay for her keep. But the point was that though they had her sign for her money every month she never had it in her hand. Maybe she just wanted to squander it on a grandson, a great grandchild. It was once supposed to be her money to spend as she wished—you see what I mean—she never had it in her hand." Mother sees perfectly.

If Mother were to revoke Steven's power of attorney he will be angry and his feelings will be hurt. There would be hell to pay. It is easy enough to do it, Edith downstairs is a notary. Mother says that Edith notarized Steven's first power of attorney, the one he replaced this afternoon. Mother could revoke his second one with another form purchased at a stationery store and never even tell him. Easy to revoke now, living at the Wellington, safe and independent. True, you risk Steven's displeasure if he were told, but were she to wait and be institutionalized it would be too late; she might sacrifice her entire freedom to avoid his pique.

How do you hedge your bets, I wonder. Having no idea and very afraid of offending Steven myself, for he will logically find me the culprit here, planting doubt in his beloved grandmother's mind, poisoning her delightful and entire trust in him, insulting him as a gentleman. That there is a principle of law, that there are real questions of human rights—I bleed to make him understand, to convey the hard sharp consciousness of what it would be like to lie tied down in restraint, insensate with drugs, struggling to maintain conscious thought. Your vanity has no place here, I want to explain to him, you have never been a prisoner, suffered indignities; you insult my experience of them in your grand big office. You have never been made as helpless and afraid as the aged or persons accused of insanity, those perfected states of the female condition, the stomach like water, the forehead hot. What does your masculine and privileged existence lead you to know or imagine of this? I am forced to question on Mother's behalf.

Steven needs a power of attorney now to pursue Mother's interests in being overcharged; Sally needs to pay Mother's bills. This piece of power, so easily delegated, so difficult to retract if circumstances changed and it became a danger. I have to admire Mother's sang froid, her serene conviction that we are all just children and will do as we are told, even now, even after St. Anne's. Tonight there is Sally, who will be at the Minneapolis airport for an hour between planes, on her way back home to Nebraska after her college reunion in California, with just time enough for a drink and to pick up her power of attorney . . . I was supposed to bring it to her. Mother decides that I will not; I will say that she requires time to read the document and think about it. How pleasant that the decision is out of my hands and I do not need to stand there being quizzed and punished, which if I were to defy Sally, would surely happen. And I would surely lose: I have lost for an entire lifetime. I cannot imagine any other outcome.

Aged and infirm, consumed with her own recovery, Mother must still rule her children and run her life—yet how much richer she is in this than in letting go. It didn't work for Lear either, I think, driving to the airport, saying to myself—you must persuade Sal it's an adventure, a mission. Driving in real happiness, realizing I am living a book, which is always more fun than writing one. I must convince Sal, I must make peace; when she reads my comments on the nursing notes she will have to agree. My letter and the notes are long winded, take time to absorb, if I brought them up now it might cause acrimony and argument.

Sally and I have a pleasant visit, she is very cordial and gentle, the big sister I have always admired and depended on, the smart and practical self: we are fellow feminists denouncing Thomas, cheering for Anita Hill, excoriating senate hypocrisy. In my haste to be on time I have forgotten to stop at the cash machine and have just enough for the parking lot so must ask Sal to pay for my drink. An embarrassment, but there are so many embarrassments over money in these circumstances, so many occasions when I wish someone would just say, "how are you fixed for cash?" or even some deeper insight: "Gee, this must be costing you a lot, staying on here all these weeks, renting a car. Here's something to help out." My own circumstances are a bit different from the others in the family: Mallory and Thomas have a business worth $6 million, as Mallory told me several times that day on the phone to Provincetown, an occasion when her wealth and importance were somewhat overwhelming for both of us. The rest of the family enjoy a professional standing that puts my bohemian existence in a rather unflattering and even hazardous light: I have no employment, live hand to mouth on a small sum each month. In four one-week visits this year I have spent four of these sums, using up the money I was to live on over the winter, now I must figure out how to replace it. I have just loaned the Farm another $3,000 for a new septic system, money that may be returned to me at harvest, if we have one. Meanwhile I am not there building better Christmas tree signs, I am here, skating on thin ice, having just covered the school taxes.

Life is rather exhilarating at this rate and I try to get all the fun I can out the stein of beer Sally has ordered, stoically refusing a second. My mission has in fact become so all consuming that I have nearly given up drink altogether, have been for weeks without booze of any sort, remember the custom of a drink before dinner as if it were in a past life. Tonight I report soberly on Mother's progress, satisfying Sally that I am doing things correctly, practically, earning her confidence. Sal describes Mother's habit of ordering one around as "imperious" and we delight in our sibling understanding, sharing our love yet capable of criticism.

My impression of Sally tonight is of great goodwill, reasonable, kind, very different from Steve today. I say I don't like nursing homes, and register the hurt on her face—"I've read Mom's nursing notes, I'm sending them to you with a letter." We leave it at that. The whole meeting is mellow and hopeful, our affection as sisters warming slowly into life, taking heart at the prospect of planning a ninetieth birthday party for Mother at the Farm. A wonderful idea, Sally's idea.

Her idea too that Mother should pay all her caretakers herself, personally, so that they are aware they are working for her. Yes, how astute. She has a handle on another possibility as well—say that Mother were too ill to live at the Wellington but didn't want to be consumed by Mallory's life or mine. There's a middle ground, a new system, they call it "assisted living" or something, her friend Jinx's parents live in this kind of scheme. As you go along, every level of care you require is made available: you have an apartment and then whatever you need in home care comes to you. As you need more it's provided or is already on the premises, there are floors with hospital beds and nurses. Jinx's folks bought into this thing, it's fancy and expensive and Californian, but there may be other less expensive versions too. She charges me to look into it.

In fact I had heard vaguely of alternatives to nursing home institutionalism, independent living schemes which one social worker mentioned while laying out the entire spectrum of care to me. But I had my eyes on the Wellington only since Mother did and wanted to limit myself to making life possible for her there. "For the future," Sal says. I promise to investigate. Sal is giving up St. Anne's I think, good.

The last sad moments in the waiting area now, out of the bar and onto little plastic chairs and no smoking, the moment before Sally goes, really goes and I don't want to part with her, both of us tense with the loss of each other. I need her so and she is going: what would Sal think if she saw Mom unable to manage the vertical pole? I mention our occasional troubles with the commode, a better solution for night-time but still not perfect. If she knew how shaky it is—if I dared tell her. What day does Sal come in November—it affects how long I stay—should I stay till Mom passes Sal's inspection? Sal may still imagine this is an experiment, but with what I know now it's a necessity. Should have brought my covering letter for the nursing notes. But it seemed absurd to subject Sally to three pages of single space in an airport, so I just say, very gently, that St. Anne's is out of the question: I have made some discoveries about the place that make that so. When she reads my explanation she will understand. "We have to find another way, Sal." Already she seems to have found one. I watch her go and want to run after her.

~

On waking, Mother pats the bed and I sit down next to her. We are chummy and have a lively discussion of the power of attorney, what it means to independence, independence as money, one's own money. I read the form itself aloud to her. We discuss her ability to recall it. At breakfast I tell her I don't want her to go to a nursing home, so if need be, Mallory and I will take care of her, the first time I have ever said this to her. She touches my cheek. "How?" "I'll redo the Farm." "Get me a spoon," she says, remaining in the here and now. "I told Sal you didn't like St. Anne's and she understands," I say.

The bath lady and Sara the occupational therapist both arrive together, the little apartment is full of people: Mother vomits in the confusion and then is humiliated. I negotiate an arrangement so that Mother has her bath and Sara comes back later. But after the bath Mother puts her head down on the table in despair—"It is all too hard." Of course, everything is coming at her at once and her future is still insecure—damn this legal nonsense.

After her nap her legs don't hold her as she tries to hoist herself from the bed to the commode. Back in bed I give her water, persuading her to sit up and clear her windpipe. I'm in haste and fail to be gentle enough; "Let go of me," she commands. "Get away from me." An excellent response. Thank god she is so hard to push around; it will go well for her. Still I'm sorry, desperately sorry. She forgives me but this is obviously a down day. I spend the rest of the afternoon on the telephone to her surgeon's nurse trying to find out if the vomiting is to be expected with a shunt or something we can stop with the help of Mother's internist, Doctor Conroy. Sally has a client with a shunt who has vomited for twenty years. Dr Heros' nurse is confident the shunt does not produce the vomiting, it must be something else. Like stress.

There is no going back now, Mother is in charge now, questioning the power of attorney is "standing on her own two feet," fulfilling her vow. But what if her body betrays her, then what? Her will was weaker before: being so ill she let go her hold, agreed to go anywhere and was taken to St. Anne's. Where she learned too much to let go again. So frail and still she must fight so hard.

My buddy Naomi calls from the loft in New York. "You're becoming involved," she says. "There's just this one chance," I explain, "It's a gamble. But it's getting a little complicated now with powers of attorney and stuff like that. Now I have to make sure Mom doesn't get jugged again. These places are awful," describing what I have learned and how nervous I am for the future. "I have to get some real legal advice, maybe someone at the University, what does this piece of paper really mean, what consequences could it have?" "Go by your instinct, your experience. But get some outside help."

It's night-time, Mother is asleep in her room; I'm in her armchair. Sally calls to tell me that there will be problems with Vera and social security, withholding tax; mysteries to me. Mother's credit cards are on their way. I feel happy, secure. Have I sent the power of attorney yet? An awkward moment: afraid of my big sister with an old fear. "Well, Mom had some questions about it and I thought I'd find out . . ." "Fuck you, if I can't be trusted with a power of attorney, fuck you." She hangs up. I'm shaking, terrified. I have offended Sal and Steve and Millett honor, their professional expertise. I want to cry but am too scared even for that, I sit paralyzed in Mother's armchair. Sal calls back, "Listen you asshole, till you got involved Mother trusted me. You came along and sowed seeds of distrust." There are tears in her voice, there would be in mine too if I dared to speak, but I don't want her to hang up again so I let her go right on: "I'm sending all of this crap back for you to do—you take care of the bills—the whole mess." The very responsibilities I had hoped to avoid. I can't do all of it, was so relieved to be spared part of it. "You've made Mother distrust me," Sal's voice hurt and I want to stop the hurt. "Wait, wait, she doesn't distrust you, she loves you, me too. Sal we've got to stop this . . ." But she has hung up again.

Nobody gets the point. Don't we learn? And why can't one ask a lawyer a question, I say to myself, powerless in an armchair, wanting to call Sal back, make peace. Apologize, humble myself, explain or take all the blame, whatever. I cannot proceed if they are angry with me, haven't the strength.

Having to stop myself—this isn't you, this is Mother, her fate—you've got to protect her. That means outside help. For the first time I will have to let them be angry, not call back. And then the strangest call, my German translator, Erica Fischer, calling to have the last puzzling details of *The Loony Bin Trip* explained, easy things at first: "Drambouie," Japanese "kana," "Mother McCrea," the "Wabash Cannonball." Then harder things: crossed locks, crossed sticks, coaches and horses—references to the capture of witches, the burning times, recollections or race memory while a prisoner in the bin at Ennis, dying to escape but doped to the nines. The strangeness of it. Maybe I am nuts.

What after all is the relationship between literature and life, the written and lived? As literary references the witches make every kind of sense, but psychiatrists would make "madness" of it, absurdity, irrationality, "grandeur" or "flight of ideas"—wonderful term—just what a writer dreams of. Are things alright in books, but not in life? In "reality". I am at the moment in the reality of another quarrel with my sister which I already know I do not want to write about. Because I love her and she might not "look good" therefore I should not write it, since she still smarts over *The Loony Bin Trip*, having long ago regretted what she did, having become a good civil rights lawyer since, having helped others, clients, to escape the fate of commitment. So that what happened then is not even true in the present.

I do not want this to be taking place; we must not quarrel. But it is happening, it is there. "Did it not happen?" O'Rourke, my old movie teacher, shouted the morning after she had filmed a quarrel between me and Mallory—did it not happen? Sure it did, but quarrels don't have to be recorded. I can't write this down, therefore I don't want it to have happened since I'm writing this adventure with Mother as a book in my mind, the ending unknown. Things were "working out," it might have a happy ending, but now—bang—the inadmissible enters.

I would like to call Naomi again, Sal again, but instead I just sit in my armchair disintegrating and beginning to wonder, with Sally and Steven so angry, could my record be brought against me here? Am I safe? Imagining the knock on the door, an injunction to remove me from Mother's side, she must be protected from me. I'll be off to the bin, she'll be back to St. Anne's, the hard justice of the system will be done. I would love to laugh at this, to make comedy of it to my pals on long distance but it is too surreal for play.

Sally was instantly angry. Has she talked with Steve? Last night at the airport I was so assured by her good faith and her real need of a power of attorney to settle bills that I thought I'd let it pass, mail it as soon as we had gathered a little information on the thing. If Mother hadn't asked about the power of attorney again this morning I might have been inclined just to send it on. After speaking with Naomi I thought I'd ask a lawyer, the feminist network here, maybe my niece Lisa. I'm not the only radical in the family, Lisa took her infant son along on an AIDS demonstration: Nathan wore a teeshirt which said "small injustices count too." I'm proud of this niece: she will hear me. Even if I ask for outside help, I could use another point of view inside the family: I'll call her in the morning.

This is all a misunderstanding, these paranoid feelings and fantasies: it was power of attorney at some future time that made me uneasy, not the present need to pay Mother's bills. It was some possible moment way down the road I feared and it would have been so easy to reassure me: just no more St. Anne's, that's all. Such a feeling of sadness: I wanted to be part of the family again, not estranged once more. For Mother's sake I have had to oppose two people I love. One cannot be underhanded: revoke their powers on the sly. One cannot be unguarded either—all I did was ask questions.

At one in the morning Mother wakes and insists on going all the way into the bathroom, refusing her commode. She also doesn't seem to make sense, talks about the fruit cellar in the basement of the old house again; she was dreaming. Is she lucid—I hit rock bottom, what if there were hypercalcemia again? It was Sal's phrase that Mother was only "intermittently lucid" which caused me to assent to St. Anne's; later I learned it was merely a symptom of that condition.

In terror of Sal's wrath, I can't sleep: smoke and read trying to block out Steven's scorn. "Listen, if it were not for you, your Mother would still be at St. Anne's," Naomi said tonight. "You were the only child who would listen—I wonder which of my own children would," she mused.

But I cannot be at war with my kin. The years I was at war were blighted. Then I began to build a peace with the reunions at the Farm. Then *The Loony Bin Trip* was published; everyone read it first, did not object. But when reporters began to pester, there was resentment. Now we have made peace again around Mother. And since I arrived here, working carefully and diplomatically, I've come a long way. I've also had a great deal of help. When we embarked on Mother's return home Steven called it giving it a try. Sally had called it temporary—we'd resort to St. Anne's when the time came and it would. Even I wasn't sure how long Mother could hold on to her independence, much as I wanted it. And of course I am not yet sure she will be safe alone.

But the nursing notes changed everything. I had been very sure when they read the nursing notes and my covering letter, the whole family would come to my view of nursing homes and close that as an option. But they haven't read them yet. Instead we have entered upon this quarrel over Mother's future through the power of attorney. We have forgotten the point, lost our place. Mother still faces her twin evils, the burden and the nursing home. As for the burden, Mother does not want to live in my house, she wants to live in her own house, beginning with her own decor and ending with her absolute independence. Which is by no means assured yet. Get help.

At four in the morning I hear Mother resorting to her commode, I come into her room, considering her by the glow of our new night lights: "How would you handle this scene in a play?" she asks humorously, looking down at her rubbery legs. "What play?" I ask, not getting it. "The one that starts again tomorrow morning," she replies serenely. I ought to rethink the fruit cellar and the paper bag in the basement. Mallory was right, Mother always does make sense. Was the hypercalcemia merely abandonment, not being able to cope, wanting to die, willing herself? She's a long way from that now. "Vera's coming in the morning," Mother says as she falls asleep, eager for another tomorrow. Funny that she'd call it a play—I don't write plays, but the theater was her form, she taught theater.

And don't forget the Harvard man who said if you couldn't write it down you didn't know it. Since I've been here I've feared forgetting: the armchair, the rocker, the map of the Indies, the blur of the little plastic night lights which imitate the design of cast iron lanterns in a way that is both hopeful and depressing. But since Sal's outburst it's a matter of being afraid of what I know, of being unable to write it down.

At five I am still awake and ought to sleep: to have patience one needs sleep. I make coffee and open my American Express bill, happy to see that I can pay it. The proceeds of my show also went directly to Am Ex. I had asked my dealer to address my check to them and it has covered my ticket to Minnesota. There is still the rental car to pay for. Ask the machine for your balance today, attack the mail, pay the Farm electrical bill, write letters of apology for the meetings you are missing at your co-op gallery and your neighborhood council. Surprised I can concentrate. By 6.30 I have done a lot; by 7.00 I am almost caught up with my own life.

Speech therapy today will have to be spilling the beans: "Don't put your mother in a baby-crib," Naomi had lectured me over the phone. "She's feeble in body not in mind, and by now she must understand she's out of that awful place because you're the one person who would listen to her. So stop being put off by your siblings. It's her life." "I was afraid to upset her over this power-of-attorney business . . ." "Level with her, she'll be up to it." Now we'll see. After asking Mother to read aloud from an article on the persecution of AIDS victims and a new attempt to repeal St. Paul's hard-won gay rights bill, we swing right into the fine print of the power of attorney. Mother doesn't flinch. I explain the reasons Sal needs a power of attorney and how she has taken offence at it not being sent right away. Sal is hurt, but the stakes are higher, or they could be. What makes me nervous is not merely a matter of money but control: the second page and the references to competency and the transfer of funds and property might be something to consider. "Sally feels I have caused you to mistrust her, which was not my intention, but I do want you to be aware of possible risks. I want you to be perfectly safe."

Then I read her my covering letter to the nursing notes. At the passage "Then on September 19th, only one day before I arrived and six days into her stay at the Home—Mother 'tried to leave the building,'" she nods. She doesn't smile, it's too serious for smiling, but there is a little acknowledgment in the nod. Staff reported that Mother was apprehended near the elevator or "Angel" entrance and brought back to her room. The sinister import of the euphemism "Angel" bears in on us; a back elevator for the gurneys of the dead. And it is also strange to be reading to her about herself, in the third person; there is something distant about it, almost rude. Like some slander reported, an unkind remark, the bureaucratic impersonal self others see which one is shielded or prevented from knowing, as medical records are generally most unobtainable to the very persons they describe.

There is something gross too about repeating all the references to restraints. True I had told her before that I had discovered them in use, but I did not tell her how close. But for Sal's determined and excellent refusal, the Home might have had the permission they sought in order to use them on her. Ollie is cheerfully cleaning the apartment as I read; Mother perfectly content should she hear. "But don't leave that paper around now, get it typed nicely and send it off. I'm going to take a nap."

It turns out to be an excellent day: Mother had a fine session of physical therapy with Dave and can look forward to a good evaluation with Nancy on Monday, we talk happily for hours after her nap, her hand patting the bed: "Sit down and visit: I'd rather talk to you than anything." I realize how lonely she must have been in her silences. Now that she is "there" I realize too how much I missed her, how hard it was to go on with only the failing animal and the spirit in despair hiding behind anger and peremptory monosyllables.

Mother would not, could not, tell me what she had been through; instead I have discovered it, which is better. We have a drink before dinner, like old times before the tumor. After dinner we pass up television to have another talk, our plan unfolding for her life after I leave: tonight she is sure of things. As for Sally—"I'll take care of Sally," Mother says with the old authority. "Can this be the bundle I found at St. Anne's?" I tease her. She goes to bed happy and then throws up all over the new rose covered sheets Sally had given her. Since these sheets were put on this morning as a kind of propitiatory magic: "Sally's sheets, I want Sally's sheets this week,"— I run them right through the washer and dryer and will have them back on the bed by morning: nothing must harm her security and confidence in her eldest daughter. I refuse to lose ground even after a second attack of nausea; her spirits are too high to permit dejection or setback.

Sitting up alone while she sleeps I marvel again at her independence, her self-determining instincts—so perfect they are nearly comic: "I'll take care of Sally," meaning she'll just phone her when she feels up to it. How she surpasses me: there is so much less taint of dependency and self-doubt, all that made me a patient of the "mental health system"—the broken spirit, the broken wing. "We should change those X's," Mother says simply, referring to incompetency and transfer of funds in the power of attorney, quite undaunted by the idea of annoying a proud authoritarian strain and bringing down wrath, everything I tremble before. Mother doesn't duck, has not invested her opponents with magical powers—in fact they are not adversaries at all (she has no ideology here) simply wrong-headed children.

~

Mother easily understands and honors Steve's preoccupation with his own new family, Sally's with her new home and her companion Ruth, her extended family of children and grandchildren. But does Mother also intuit that there might be a temptation to pass over her now (older and less interesting) for the miracle of a next generation? Has she grasped that this impulse might go further than merely ignoring or neglecting or preferring and, in a last gesture of taking notice, become a dangerous form of taking charge?

She is used to being left alone. Not called on Sunday, visited fleetingly. There have been decades of this. Surely this was my style, a queasy mix of guilt and sentiment. Alone there was plenty for her to do: she has never sustained herself from her children. She has always delighted in her own peer group, her circle of nieces, a wide acquaintance over generations, even chance encounters in hardware stores or supermarkets. Long before she ever became a salesman, Mother could strike up a chat with any stranger in the world; people of all sorts fascinate her. My slender and fleeting social skills come entirely from her and I sometimes wonder how I would have survived without the example of both her polite conversational style and her knack for the witty remark addressed to anyone at all which opens hearts to her everywhere. Mother can amuse herself alone beautifully; she has done so during all the decades since we left and grew up. Forty years she has lived alone and loved it.

Then illness made her a responsibility, the bogey of age, the certainty of her mortality presaging our own, our generation caught sight of its own end. How would hers come? Would she fall? Would she call out and suffer, would it be our fault? So, like the insurance industry, the urge for actuarial took over: security, the urge to control. If you put her in a box she'll be safe. And we could go about our business, free of the generation passing, we can turn to the next generation, free of our past our careers can soar, we'll finally be grown-ups and on our own, come into our heyday of glory, unencumbered. Because we need all our time and attention. And she is in the way, cluttering, making demands, all these trips and calls and interruptions, plane tickets, rental cars.

To put her away would solve every problem. She would be stowed, parked, filed. We would visit when we felt like it, found it convenient, when the prick of conscience occurs we could step in. She's safe. In place. On the shelf, waiting like an object; for her own protection and our convenience.

It was just that process that harrowed me, that through institutionalization she would lose her selfhood and separateness, since her existence was so utterly predicated on her independence. Does she know she was put away? Perhaps the impertinence of the idea prevents it from penetrating. That much insult is hard to absorb. Who would interfere in a life so private and self-sufficient? Mother dotes on Steve and relies on Sal. Harder to imagine what Mallory and I represent: pride and entertainment value, probably consternation as well.

Does she know? She knew when she was a lump of dejection on a bed at St. Anne's Home. More than the staff's obdurate power in preventing an escape, she might have been broken by the final intelligence of abandonment. Wearing Mallory's white coat for luck. Fortunately this period was short: she has no scars, is not enraged as I was, not twisted or deformed by a righteous fury which festers and scalds when the world refuses to acknowledge. And she is not corroded by self-doubt.

At least not now, not with a team to coach and cheer her on—dejection cannot win out. To be realistic, I must admit how easily it might have won—when she puts her head down on the table—if she were here alone, every setback would mean more. Her whole effort to rise from the bed, the exercise she performs many times a day now but still with great effort, that struggle might have been abandoned without the team of therapists jogging her on, my dogged insistence. In the first weeks my assurance was desperate and phony, unreal and fantastic: I couldn't go back, I had made this mistake in public, before the family and the authorities, couldn't retract it now, was too much a coward to admit my courage was only rash naiveté, movie versions of health work, descriptions of recovery reprinted from novels. Not very good ones at that. In real literature you deal with error and death, poverty and the final galling bitterness of life on earth; the animal dies and defeat is cosmic, essential to life as the coming of winter. Coming now, and I just ignored it.

But so did she. It takes two for a *folie à deux*, this unlikely and irregular affair. And so we go on. Until it is safe for me to bow out and she skates off alone. Can she? When if ever is she safe? And this strange new relationship: we ran off together, I will never just walk off as once I might: we have bonded. I will be there.

Late last night she said she wanted to see the Farm again. A.D. never did. Simone de Beauvoir did once, and it changed the place and my life; she blessed it, believed in it when it was a failure and a fraud during a bad summer and her blessing and faith transformed it so that it is neither now, almost a success and very nearly true to its promise. We'll have your ninetieth birthday there I said. "Sal and I were talking about it night before last. Last night we were fighting"—we both laugh—"but the night before we were drinking in a bar and talking it up." "How will I get there?" she asks, and I realize she means it. "An airplane of course. Vera will put you on, I'll pick you up. If Steve's coming, he'll take you." Of course it is not that simple because Poughkeepsie is at some distance from New York and it is a long and very taxing journey. But she means now to make it. "Last spring you said you'd never see the Farm again. She winks and gives assent with a pressure on my hand.

Something in our natures, always so far apart these many years, something has met and blended at last. But now they have entered a lasting accord, knowing how precious the time. I outline the rotating daughter plan, as I outlined it to Mallory and Sal. "And how was that received?" "Well, Mallory has this phobia about airplanes and will have to reserve rail tickets months ahead, but she approves in theory. Sally will be relieved now by the two of us." "I'll take care of Sally." "Remember her feelings are hurt." "I'll talk to Sally, don't worry." A woman in charge of her life.

Now and for how long? When the institution and its machinery take over, when hospitals and insurance and the lawyerly mode set in? These pieces of paper, these instruments of control. Should there be a revocation of the power of attorney made and just saved for contingency? In case? So that you can take your life back when you wish? If only we just had to deal with vomiting and rehabilitation, not legalism: the authoritarian and masculine, the state and its engines. It seems so unfair in illness, so unnecessary a complication. Oddly the struggle that exhausts me makes her strong today.

Has Mother still not measured the force of institutions? I saw St. Peter's

Asylum when I was eighteen, bought candy bars and rolled cigarettes for destitute geriatric prisoners, vowing my Mother would never see such a hell-hole. And found her in one. "You seem to take all these things so to heart," she says as I sit on her bed, chatting. "You're always for the underdog," she used to say, almost as if there were another dog to root for. As if it were a fault. But that carping side of her is gone now, these days she has the same empathy she had when I was a child and she backed the Blacks and the Jews and Mahatma Gandhi at the kitchen table when the newspaper came before dinner. "You taught me," I say, our eyes focused deep into each other's, "St. Peter's was my first cause." "Good, it's come in handy," she says, succinct as the fine skull under her short haircut.

~

"Haven't you got anything better to do? Why don't you get out of here and go shopping?" Mother says on Saturday, sending me off to the antique stores. Now that I have moved her old desk into the living room it's obvious she will need a nicer one; she's redecorating. Today she is fascinated with *Newsweek*'s special on the 500th anniversary of the "discovery" of America. Mother has recovered her interest in life to learn that Columbus never quite got here at all, though he did bring the horse and consumption, came back with syphilis and several important foodstuffs. Not just corn but the potato. Starting a population explosion and the invasion of the New World by the poor of the Old. This is interesting and morally problematic. He also started an industry in slaves: this part is devastating. *Newsweek* has provided diagrams of the slave ships, the method of stacking the living bodies like cargo: Mother is sickened, outraged. She is looking at the New World from an entirely new perspective, that of its native peoples. "I can't believe this," she says, the scales falling from her eyes, coming upon the Pre-Columbian world for the first time. "I wish I could go to school again," I hear her sigh, fervent with appetite for life. I recall her first attempts to bestow some notice to the headlines, weeks ago, even her curious skepticism that first morning she received the *St. Paul Pioneer Press* in her hands: "Is this a real newspaper?" an irony capable of many interpretations though at the time it seemed like the voice of Lazarus risen from the dead.

~

In an attempt at peaceful enlightenment I telephoned my niece Lisa, wanted a lawyer's opinion on the power of attorney, but got a relative's, a mediator and a compromise, a plan for a conference call. We can all discuss Mother's future next weekend. Perhaps a real civil rights attorney would insist upon the revocation of both powers of attorney: but I am not an attorney, I too am a family member, wanting peace and cooperation. I do not want to hurt or insult Sally or Steven: revocation would do both. They are perhaps not being attorneys but family members, working on a dynamic, the family dynamic repeating itself madly: it must stop I think, we must deal with the simple here and now of Mother's health, her safety, her freedom. Get the nursing notes to everyone before the conference call, make them understand the risks, the dangers; pull it all together and keep the peace. St. Anne's Home will be ruled out altogether; meanwhile file the objection to their inflated charges and do not pay the bill.

Imagine my surprise two days later to hear that Sally had volunteered to pay the entire sum of St. Anne's claims, has in fact written a check on Mother's account for no less than $2,300. Not the minimal rate, not $55 a day or even $85, but $122 a day, the "H" behavioral problem rate for all the nineteen days she never even lived there. But why? Why pay before the dispute is settled? Why—unless one wants the doors of St. Anne's Home to remain open.

I learn all this almost by accident: the Home telephones to recall a check they have written refunding Mother's spending money: $150 minus a $7 haircut. They want this back, they should never have issued it, Mother's bill has been paid in full except for this sum: if it is returned to them her account will be closed. They have received a check for $2,300 from Sally, and wish to deposit it. I would like to stop the check, thunderstruck that it was ever written: wasn't it our policy to pay after the dispute was settled? I must straighten this out, it's a mistake: if we win and the state decides on a lower fee we save Mother a thousand dollars. Will Sally give me permission to stop the check? But Sal is no longer quite speaking to me. She has a client in her office and cannot talk to me, her voice strained, angry, but nevertheless entirely confident that the money will be returned if our claim is honored.

But it's Mother's money, Mother who lay back in her chair when she heard and permitted herself an ironic observation on letting others put her in the poorhouse. Or back in St. Anne's, I think, afraid of the consequences of paying what does not yet need to be paid, propitiating this institution. Against Sal's lawyer voice my own is crunched, intimidated, incompetent. But I am Mother's advocate now and feel its responsibility, in dread for her future.

I remember the last phone call, Sal's "Fuck you" like a blow, her pitiful accusation, tears in her voice, that I had undermined Mother's trust in her. "No, stop don't hang up I just want to be sure Mother is safe—wait." Wanting to call back, afraid to, pissed off myself, then sorry, ready to apologize, to put myself in the wrong, be yelled at—anything to be sisters again.

But for the moment we cannot be sisters. The knowledge is hard and real. I cannot stop the check, I cannot bring about amity either. But I must continue to be an advocate and find help and support outside the family and its angers and impulses. For the moment, Sally and Steven too, have got to understand that Mother is a separate being with a civil existence which is quite apart from the wonderful circumstance of being their relative.

Mother cannot risk her freedom on that circumstance, trust everything, surrender entirely. Once yes, but experience has provided a warning that this was an insufficient guarantee against institutional force and in practice a dangerous policy. In view of events, one must now be more wary, circumspect. However innocently and with what good intentions Mother was committed into the hands of St. Anne's Home, once there, she had no recourse or rescue. But for the accident of my arrival and my amateur, even ambivalent efforts, she might still be there, might well be there forever, prey to any evil that might be practiced upon her, and we see now that there could be many. We did not protect, we did not even understand the dangers to which we subjected her, the dreadful hours of possible captivity she might experience there, a possibility becoming probability as events took their course. All because we didn't know. Ignorance may be a poor excuse, but it is no remedy in need.

What Mother needs is something better than me, she needs a real advocate, a bunch of them, a system which really protects the aged. Not presently in place, and so I must improvise, as frustrated and angry at the private-solution character of it as I will be grateful if I can just put anything in place. Running through whole afternoons in the social services bureaucracy, chasing after legal remedies and protections, my telephone persona like some animated comic strip figure sailing down one chute into another, flying from reference to reference, flunking out at answering machines for pilot programs which are open only three hours a week and serve a clientele who are required first of all to be destitute.

I don't get very far very fast. I discover that people in offices, the people I reach on the phone, do not fall over in shock at the vulnerability of the elderly. In fact they accept the inequities facing the aged with a commendable calm. The deprivations of the institutionalized are plain enough to social workers but they have no legal muscle and the law looks on misery and is completely undisturbed. I should have known, having watched the ACLU fail the "mad" for decades: the old are another category that fall through the cracks. Equal protection before the law becomes a chimera.

After days of searching I reach my own old defender here, Donald

Heffernan, who won my "insanity" hearing once. He tries to recommend attorneys who could help, give advice, take an interest. But when I reach them they are elsewhere engaged, busy being pregnant, uninterested in this particular legal question, or inexperienced with the power of attorney. Everyone agrees in theory that no one is to be placed in a nursing home against their will, but no one can explain in practice just how that can be prevented. There are procedures, they claim, the authorities would have to send someone out to inform your Mother, they say. By the time they are sent she has already lost her credibility I argue. No, they assure me, a health worker would visit, a doctor would have to attest that she is no longer mentally competent.

Surely that is not insuperable, I think, a frightened old woman answering the door to someone carefully prepared to find her senile, after most such reports the doctor's concurrence would be routine. Perhaps it would begin with the doctor: family members appealing to him to protect the elderly parent by placement; for her own good. It is always the word of the younger against the older, their credibility and energy, their civic status, their ability to construe senility whenever they choose. The family, the wishes of the family.

Finally I find a young turk, a civil libertarian and hear him say what I would say if I were myself a lawyer and not merely a relative intent on pleasing other relatives and keeping the peace. Namely that Mother's safety and autonomy, physical liberty of person and absolute control over her own funds are the primary, indeed, the only issues. They should not be compromised under any circumstances, she would be wise to revoke any power of attorney others have over her, particularly if the exercise of this power appears to threaten in any way. Acting on Mother's behalf, Sally has used Mother's money to pay an exorbitant bill instead of waiting until the dispute over it is settled, which is the usual procedure. That is also what the ombudswoman for the aged had recommended yesterday. This young attorney fears that paying the bill could constitute a threat because it appears to placate the business office at St. Anne's in hope of placing Mother there again in the near future. I swallow, hearing my own fears put into words. But I don't want a fight with my sister or my nephew, what shall I do? I even refuse to divulge their names, protecting them from legal gossip. I will call him back, prevaricating, avoiding a showdown, trying for a peaceful solution, the hope that perhaps Lisa could mediate. Banking on my covering letter to win my case in time for a conference call.

I will keep such a straight shooter on my team. And keeping at it day after day, I find other allies. On my second call to Sally Schoephoerster, ombudswoman for the aged in nursing homes at the Minnesota Alliance for Health, I finally get her attention and interest. How wonderful that her name is Sally too, how magical a circumstance, an antidote, portent of possible harmony. So often I have not been able to elicit promises of help because social officials did not perceive this as an emergency, only planning for one. Also because I would not hear of guardianship or conservatorship, mechanisms to protect rights which begin by depriving one of them and investing the power of decision elsewhere . . . some legal representative, some wiser soul. No, I insist, explaining, I want to preserve and guarantee my Mother's own power to decide and run her life, to increase, insure and safeguard it, not relinquish it to anyone else, no matter how disinterested. I do not even want the power of attorney myself, which Steven had momentarily suggested, a suggestion he did not return to again, probably already foreseeing disagreements, one little piece of paper fighting another. Nor will it do to revoke all these powers and keep mum: surely this is duplicitous, would be rightly rejected. Steven may or may not limit his document as Mother suggests, but Sally is mad as the dickens as she has not yet received hers in the mail—what in hell will I do?

I have stirred up a hornet's nest, have made angry enemies of Sal and Steve, and having asked for an ally in Lisa I have only created an ambivalent mediator who sees me not as her grandmother's advocate in a question of rights for the aged, but as one party in a quarrel with her own mother and brother, someone whose position she must modify if mediation is to succeed. I now apologize to everyone and am shouted at fairly often. Steven shouts on the phone, Sal has gone past shouting.

I go about on the verge of tears, poisoned with the dislike I have suddenly attracted. Better me than Mom, but for all her pretended serenity and control, confidence and bravado as the matriarch, Mom feels the strain. It brings on exhaustion, all the hazards to her untroubled recovery which it is my role to absorb. How can she concentrate on her convalescence when her future is still at risk, what if she tried for and were cheated of her freedom, were dragged back to the place she is struggling to escape forever through her own hard-won fitness and competence?

Working a 24-hour job in rehab and home nursing I have gone and got myself into a legal jam and a family feud, outgunned on all sides: Sal, Steve, Lisa . . . everybody playing lawman. No one playing nurse or physical therapist, everyone quarreling over how and where Mother's life will be run for her. Since all assume it is only a matter of time before Mother loses all control over her life they are intent upon staking out the territory beforehand. We are looking forward to conference calls which might take place when Mother is napping or has already gone to bed, occasions when she could not even participate—she can scarcely hear over the telephone—as we discuss her fate.

The outside pressure gets crazier and crazier—can't we just leave her alone, I think, watching her struggle with the immediacy of here and now on a day that has been full of this tension. Tonight she is facing again the risk of taking her walker down to dinner rather than the wheelchair, her anxiety over such a step actually bringing on a nosebleed last night, the first night we tried to venture forth. She decided for the wheelchair then and I had to agree with her. But tonight she ignores the nosebleed and gallantly decides for the walker and the long pilgrimage it represents, the independence, the public image of herself as better, less helpless, a more acceptable Wellingtonian. All through dinner I see her checking the barely stanched blood with her Kleenex, trying to follow the conversation, smiling, keeping up her front. God she has guts, I think, treasuring her, full of tenderness and admiration.

How stupid the quarrels of my generation. And how dangerous. That the fate of our elders should ever be left in our hands. But I have allies now, days of phoning have built me a network: Sally the ombudswoman and a sympathetic woman at Catholic Charities. Her name is Jo and she got the point right away, is a real tiger for the rights of the aged, and brings with her to Mother's side all the power of the diocese, the authority of the Church, the public face of the faith, St. Paul respectability: you don't mess with this woman. Moreover, she has offered to come out to the Wellington, assure Mother of her rights in person. Jo is much more persuasive and convincing than I am with my victim's paranoia, my activist's rhetoric and unsure data, my amateur standing and my out-of-town address.

Mother now has allies on the spot, titled and trained. Sally Schoephoerster has offered to deal with any family member, lay or lawyer, who questions Mother's choices of where and how to live. She will have a file on Mother, will represent her in the case of a disagreement: so will Jo. So too will our new case-worker from Optional Care, Deborah, who has looked over Mother's plan of care and array of allies and pronounced it the best she has ever seen. The allies go very far to solve the problem. I have sent off the nursing notes and my covering letter to Sal and Lisa and the others, and made my stand.

~

But the real solution was Ann. At first it didn't seem that way. At first, while it seemed miraculous that Sally would telephone at all, was speaking to me again, this woman, Ann, the reason for her call seemed like an order imposed: hire this woman. Ann seemed Sally's idea entirely. My amour-propre was offended, here was the caretaker who would solve all our troubles, perfection itself, the "answer to a maiden's prayer," in Sal's ironic phrase. "Hadn't she taken care of Aunt Mary in her last months, hadn't she been a companion to Cousin Rosellen's own friend Murilla: they went everywhere, used to hang out at the country club—this woman Ann is absolutely sensational." Sally leans into her sales pitch, by the time she has Mother on the line she has begun enacting promises from Mother that she'll hire Ann.

Of course Mother's delighted to hear Sal in a good mood, but Ann has stipulated that she will not take a job with Mother for less than forty hours a week: even at her extremely modest rate of $7 an hour, this comes to $1,120 a month. It's a little confusing as well; I was never given permission to employ anyone as many as forty hours a week—I was trying to get by with Vera for an hour in the morning, an hour around dinner and bedtime, covering lunch with "Meals on Wheels." Given a tight budget, I was told to arrange for a minimal schedule of personal care, one that was skimpy and would leave Mother alone for long stretches once I was gone, one that seemed inadequate, and I have stayed on here simply to fill it out till Mother was stronger, substituting myself for what I did not feel entitled to spend. Now suddenly someone may be here ten hours a day, four days a week—why not eight hours, five days a week? Clearly Ann's convenience is to make her money in as few days as possible. I have friends who do this kind of work: I've heard the chit-chat and the angles, discussions of cushy jobs and minimal effort. If Mother requires ten hours of care on four days a week, why not ten hours on the other three? I wonder.

But clearly it is simply the excellence of the caretaker that is at issue, the fact that Sal knows and trusts her. Mallory too, it appears. Cousin Joannie as well, who calls to second Sal's suggestion. I feel we are under pressure now; how could Mother fail to hire this person without offending everyone? Ann happens to be free just now and called Sally, offered her services. And Mother, who knows and likes Ann, appears delighted at the prospect. The spoiler, I worry over several aspects of this. The expense of this large number of hours, since Ann wants only one client and must do forty hours.

The dependency all this represents for both of them. Mother would be Ann's main source of support; Mother might be acquiring a total dependant. This might have complex effects: how much would it be in Ann's interest for Mother to get better, to get well enough to dispense with her services altogether? Were Ann then to transform herself from nurse to companion would Mother strike her as good material for a companion? Can Mother afford a paid companion, would she not simply fritter away a great deal on someone she may not really need, money she might require later merely to survive?

My greater concern is with the other possible dependency: what would happen to the entire project of Mother's recovery, her physical therapy, her return to absolute self-sufficiency? What caretaker, dependent upon Mother's own invalidism, would not be tempted to foster it, to subvert rather than join the crusade for fitness and autonomy, to permit her to beg off, decide she isn't up to walking the halls with her walker today? Physical therapists like Nancy and Maggie and Dave demand Mother work hard. How long would Nancy Kasa keep coming if Mother did not make the significant improvement Medicare demands? I would almost rather see money spent on a private therapist Mother had to pay herself in real dollars than guarantee the sum of $1,100 a month to a babysitter. However attractive Ann may be for Mother's relatives, is it possible that she may not have the passion and will to bring about Mother's rehabilitation?

On the other hand, Mother would at least be safe. Without someone like Ann how could you dare leave her, staying here week after week, hanging on not only for the payoff and excitement of watching her heal, but because you are still deeply afraid of what would become of her if she were alone.

I am frank about my doubts and questions to Mother, anxious that she may be spending too much not only for Ann, but for the combination of Ann and Vera, whom she will still need to hire since Ann does not work on weekends and, if she comes in the morning early enough to dress Mother, she will not be staying late enough to put her to bed. We add it up; between the two caretakers Mother will be spending about $1,500 a month. Is this essential expense or is it merely Ann's stated terms? Will she spend and be temporarily convenienced but not profit in the long run, I wonder, deeply protective of the program of rehabilitation for which I have finally wrangled her cooperation? How long would Mother qualify for physical therapy if I were gone and my substitute only luke-warm in this, without my conviction that Mother must be independent if she is to be safe? Ann may quit or move away. Mother must not entrust herself to someone who seduces her into slackness and then deserts her, leaving her open to another family assessment of incompetence and a final institutionalization.

"We will have to make Ann into Kate. You will have to convert her," Mother laughs. The interview begins and I start off calmly enough, explaining Mother's medical history to Ann, whom I like at once, for all my trepidations. Ann is a Mexican woman with a beautiful face and a generous figure, a lovely voice and an impressive manner, proud, dignified and very warm. In no time, the very generosity and sympathy with which she listens, has led me into turbulent feelings—in no time I sound like Mother's cheerleader, a shameless proponent of her freedom. "She didn't come here to watch you cry," Mother points out laconically, always an enemy to overstatement.

I must be sure of this woman, sure she is on Mother's side and not an agent of family interests and institutions—there is still St. Anne's to watch out for. Ann has lost clients to nursing homes, speaks of them shortly and sharply and without illusion, she has worked in them herself when younger.

She takes her work very seriously, she says simply but with great conviction; she would take the challenge of Mother's therapy and rehabilitation very seriously indeed. Go for it, I think; Ann could be the best ally of all. Mother thinks so and Mother is the boss, hires, fires and pays. Within an hour I have orders to call Ann back and ask if she would agree to start on Monday. I would stay on till the middle of November, that would give us two weeks to work together and to pass on what I know.

~

Ann's entrance ended the family quarrel, created a bridge, the one agreed-upon element of safety. For me, she stands for Mother's independence and the right to live at home; for Sally and everyone else Ann represents security and reliability, a known and proven caretaker, nearly a family retainer, absolute trustworthiness. Distrust vanishes from both sides, there is faith again. And the circle of Mother's outside allies have given her a status she did not have before, there is a civil and public space between her and her protective relatives which guarantees her the efficacy of her decisions and that her wishes will be honored, her independence assured. The Twins play for the pennant and we are a family of friends again.

Now that Ann is with Mother, my next assignment is to research the "next step," some future place of care when such was needed, when Mother couldn't live at home anymore, it being assumed that this was necessary. Not a nursing home, not Mallory's or my home, but some form of what the current jargon terms "assisted living." By the time Deborah had assessed our plan at the Wellington, she could approve it not only for the present, but for the future as well, suggesting that the Wellington itself has everything one finds in other plans and places—she has seen them all.

But following orders and preparing for future eventualities, I spend a day in a blizzard, exploring a place called Joanna's Shores, a Presbyterian complex for the aged on the banks of Lake Joanna: a model institution, swank, "state of the art," inconveniently distant from town but with twenty-seven acres of birches and a whole lake to look at. Unfortunately the lake looks desolate in the snow, lonely, and cold. The twenty-seven acres are inaccessible to Mother. The place is a paradise compared to St. Anne's, has privacy and luxury, is full of privilege, services, programs, plays and concerts, but not homey like the Wellington. There is a vast and energetic section for the bedridden, there are probably greater liberties and less constraint. The woman who conducted me through did refer to a ward I was not shown for the "absent-minded." One is led to presume the senile might be on a locked ward, as usual for their own good; physical restraint might not be an impossibility here either. And though the atmosphere is pleasant, almost hedonistic—a great formal dining room, stately and upper middle class—the dining room has a dour quality and a formal staircase; Mother might have to rent an attendant's services just to get to meals.

When I see the little room where Mother would live, it is so cold and sad it shrivels my heart: outside the lake in winter, lonely and forlorn, inside a hideous bile green carpet. Sure, you could change it but the very walls scream temporary: a motel room waiting for death. The place is princely by comparison to St. Anne's but Joanna's Shores' sparkling glass health center for the bedridden seems open and exposed.

I keep thinking of the motel room on the lake: why trade this ugly chilly utterly temporary room for her good big solid apartment at the Wellington, which is already home? Why live like a gypsy or a vagrant with too much furniture piled into one room, when she could simply stay home? I ask my guide if Mother could have Ann with her; she allows the possibility. But imagining the two of them bored through afternoons in this waiting room of a room, the idea fails to cheer: wouldn't they be better off at the Wellington, after all?

Everything is different now that there is Ann, a resident in charge of the plan, Mother's comfort, the ally of all allies. I type up lists for Ann with headings like "Mother's world," every friend and relative and phone number, another one entitled "Allies against institutionalization" with Jo and Sally the ombudswoman, Deborah and Mike Wolfe the scrappy lawyer, the social worker Shirley Welch who started it all. Ann and I become chums and cronies, we talk our heads off, we share our politics, we eat tostadas for lunch and bitch at George Bush, bemoan the recession, trade horror stories from geriatric wards where we've worked. She's solid,

I can leave Mother with this woman and go back to New York and still sleep at night.

Ann was the bridge that knit us all back together, since Ann was Sally's find, Sally's idea, Sally's sense of security. I would have left Mother entirely in Vera's good natured but possibly insufficient care. Sally is right, Mother has someone who will not just see her through a meal, but really oversee a course of rehabilitation.

Mother is fond of Ann, already they have set up their own particular lines of communication, the lines of relatives and children, Ann's sons, Mother's daughters. They like the same television programs, I come home from errands to find them watching "Oprah" in delight.

This does not entirely delight me, the egghead from New York: I like "Oprah" too, but I dislike long television afternoons, worry that Mother is spending money on mere care-taking. Ann watched television while Mother napped today, harmless. Harmless too that she spends such time reading magazines, there is nothing else for her to do at such moments, but it galls me that one pays another person so much per hour to watch TV or read *Newsweek*. I had the same reaction when I'd asked Vera to stay with Mom an hour so I could pick up the Lifeline downtown. I left Vera watching television and seeming to ignore Mother. All the way downtown I felt a sense of outrage at the idea of being so old or helpless or ill and needing human care so badly that you were reduced to paying someone to watch television at your expense, to entertain or distract themselves staring mindlessly at vapid programming. I remembered my own babysitting days when I was being paid merely to be present: I didn't mind accepting that money, but I find I care very much that Mother's money isn't wasted. Later Vera told me she turned to television on purpose since it would make Mother uneasy to be watched while she ate. I was impressed by her tact. Today I am aware that Ann is keeping Mother company in a companionable way. Mother vomited again during therapy today, has rested all afternoon in exhaustion and discouragement. Later I wondered if I were not a little envious of their bond in popular Americana. I have spent the afternoon doing something entirely different, creating a musical diversion for Mother that I'm anxious to try out. I have one of Kristen's tapes and have just bought a Walkman across the street, together with a set of earphones. Mother will be able to hear her granddaughter's own music: Kristen is a favorite, a special treasure, the genius offspring who was first a child actress and is now a rock and roll star with radio play and excellent reviews. I foresee that although Kristen is adored and stalwartly loves her grandmother—she came for Mother's surgery, arriving out of the blue for three days and disappeared back into it, her world a mystery even to me—her music, however, may not be Mother's "thing" at all. So I have taken the precaution of printing out the words as well, blowing up the tiny line notes that came with the cassette into huge type, with the help of the xerox store, making a regular book out of it. Kristen has written some of these songs, they are her poems, she too is a writer in our tribe, a fellow artist; I'm eager, even a little desperate that Mother hear and love what this youngster has made, the same old desperate urgency I have felt with my own art. Bringing one's life-blood home to St. Paul, into the different light of bourgeois existence, tends to shrink one's stuff, cause it to fade and look strange.

And still we try, for this is home and where we started out, leaving these people and this place just to return someday with the fresh meat of your achievement in hand—to show them: look, I went out and foraged and ran and hid and starved and was nearly destroyed but I have brought this back for you to see—I made it, stole it, wrung it out of my hardest moments, bitterest defeats, the emptiest weekends of my intolerable loneliness. Mallory must feel this as well, showing Mother a videotape of her performance of Jean Cocteau's *The Human Voice*.

Ann turns off the television, we prepare for a treat. Here is something enormously precious I say to Mother, carried away: see what it can give her, here is her own granddaughter's first music, her poems, those she has written herself as well as those of others which she has chosen to interpret.

"You'll be able to hear every note on these headphones, and you won't miss a word if you follow the text. I'll turn it on—just enjoy it." Ann and I sit back to watch her happiness. It never materializes. She cannot hear the music through the headphones, nothing comes, only vibrations that hurt. It must be too loud, it must be the amplification of the hearing aid—we try it softer, with and without the other device in place—nothing works.

Mother looks on the lyrics and feels stupid, I feel wretched and cross, convinced that Mother is not trying, simply dislikes the drumbeat, the rock and roll volume, disapproves of the blues—wasn't it a miracle that she could never understand the Bessie Smith lyrics I lived by in adolescence? And hasn't Mother always been obtuse about pictures and music, nothing but writing ever got through to her. Yet she will not pay homage to Kristen's language on the page either: she has to hear the song with its words. And she cannot hear. "Waste your life in American television then, for Christ's sake, spend your afternoons hearing about diets," I rail, my great surprise a failure. Will she ever hear Kristen in this life, I wonder, furious and near tears out the door to smoke a cigarette in the hall.

That evening Ann called to quit. Or, as she put it, she felt that perhaps she was "not the right person after all to oversee my mother's rehabilitation." "Why not?" I begged, terrified of losing her. "Because I hate to see your mother pushed so hard." When Mother vomited today it was after a long walk in the hall with Ann. But that's not it, Ann knows she doesn't push Mother too hard—I do. "You're right Ann, slow me down if you feel the program demands too much, you're a better judge of the pace than I am." She has also resented my remarks about watching television. "I think you were right there too, Ann: Mother needed Oprah to relax with far more than she needed me rubbing her nose in rock and roll. For some reason the earphones don't work, let's try regular speakers; after all, Mother hears the television's audio perfectly." It is not enough. Ann is not sure if she will stay past Friday, but she will finish the week.

My heart sinks—I have screwed this up, lost Mother her best hope.

"Remember, I'll be gone in ten days Ann. You could love this job, don't blame my mistakes on Mother, she needs you." "I've got to think it over," Ann says quietly, "I take my work very seriously." I love those words, am deeply moved by her integrity. Ann is not a babysitter, but a licensed practical nurse, a professional—she honestly wishes for Mother's recovery, in fact she is the perfect overseer of Mother's rehabilitation, wiser and gentler and less obsessive than I. I have hurt her beautiful pride and dignity, that honor and excellence I perceive most entirely at the moment I may have lost her. All through the evening I feel like one condemned. Of course Ann was right, I was wrong—but will she forgive?

In the morning I'm drinking coffee in the hall when Ann comes in, having laid in wait for her, having worried since six, smoked five cigarettes in fear, dreading the sight of her coming down the hall almost as much as I yearn for it. She approaches with a grin: she's thought it over, she'll stay. "I like Helen," she chuckles, we both understand how marginal and temporary I am. I relinquish a great deal at this point; Ann is now in charge. In someone else, this could be disastrous, this entirety of trust: with Ann one is fortunate. I retire my doubts and fears, they were well meant, necessary defenses against Mother's vulnerability, but unnecessary in this case.

Ann the peacemaker and the bridge—with Sally, Joannie, Mallory, Steven. We have weathered every snag and hazard now; much as I exasperated Ann this one occasion, how fortunate that she remembered she worked for Mother and not for me.

~

I imagine a bed of my own sometimes, I imagine living in my loft on the Bowery again—if ever. For it seems forever away, my own life. Relinquished, at times painfully—the trip to Europe; at times gratefully—since the here and now is so much less complicated than my own life: writing or the Farm. Ten times a day Mother and I thank my friend L.K. for being at the Farm in my stead, managing the place, making all this possible. Now that she types again Mother looks forward to typing thank-you letters "To L.K. the Manager."

Sometimes in wonderment I remember the fall I had planned, a few weeks at the Farm printing silkscreens and just enjoying the place, lazy almost after the rush of the summer farming and building, getting ready for shows: Michigan, then Provincetown. There would only be a few resident artists there in the fall, the off season, my favorite time of year, mellow weather, the leaves, drinks by the pond. Then when I had really cleaned up the studio, put everything to rights there and in my room upstairs, we'd pack the truck and get me down to town, the Bowery loft waiting, solitude and beauty, the floor waxed as only Naomi can wax it when she gives it back to me every fall. Then off to Europe: a little glory, dinners in Paris with my buddies, a chance to see Spain again and from the inside, with friendly feminist publishers, even Ireland once more, not this time a prisoner in a West County lunatic asylum but invited to rave on television. Such fun.

No emergency, no hurry, no living out of one checkbook and calling in transfers apologetically to the bank, covering the rent, running pell-mell after unpaid bills, furtive trips to the grocery cash machine, endless trips to the folks who wash my three shirts but take a week to do it, no awkward dinners in the same funny clothes among the Wellington smart set who come gussied up each evening. No longer a shabby bohemian stranger who causes her own mother a mild tremor of embarrassment. No longer running scared.

But of course if I were to live my own life I would have to write and like every writer I am always looking for respite from the endless possibilities for error in writing, getting it wrong or slanted, leaving important things out or putting in the extraneous. Now I have done something even worse: I am not only failing to finish the book on torture, my assignment all these years, I am full of the unplanned pregnancy of a book on Mother, expanding the three small pieces I did last spring, fugitive texts entirely for my own satisfaction or compulsion but not anything really. Now this digression might be prolonged by the press of real events to encompass the escape from the nursing home, the wars of rehabilitation, even the family disagreements—good God you can't write about all that—wasn't *The Loony Bin Trip* a sufficient invasion of family privacy, still resented.

Who would have thought Mother herself would require rescue from institutional captivity: you have now taken on the trials of the aged as well—will you never stop appropriating causes? But the image of Mother—or anyone—anyone's mother, anyone at all, any being tied to a bed and drugged . . . And it is not just anyone lying tied and drugged—that is a cause. It's your own Mother, immediate, insupportable. Of course you cannot rescue the women watching television but eyeing you too somehow as you left St. Anne's, nor the women you left behind in the loony bin at Ennis in Clare in Ireland. You go free and you leave them behind inside, even if you fight for them by writing or speaking out, your "activism."

But for Mother it came to the test, testing the rhetoric in one of your Provincetown drawings, words that scared you even then: "If they restrain you I will untie your hands." How could I carry that out, I thought, even as I wrote it down, how would you ever realize such a boast. Not just in terms of the powers that be—they have ways of dealing with enthusiasts like you—but in terms of putting yourself on the line, because what do you do for a captive once you've untied them? Now I know.

Keeping my own notes I can see that Mother slept six hours straight without recourse to the commode last night. That she has progressed from the plastic bottle with a built-in plastic straw that does not spill, her "sports bottle" a gift from Sally, to drinking from a glass. She has vomited only twice this week, is making a slow but still discernable progress with handwriting, a slow and faltering progress in recovering the ability to typewrite. There are days she refuses to copy out on the typewriter whatever foolishness in large type I have gathered from advertisements for Ford Cars and other junk mail. There are days when she gets mad at the whole project and quits after a row of commas and exclamation marks. But today we sent off a letter of congratulation to Lisa over her new baby whom we have already seen on videotape. Mother of course would not give house room to a VCR so I rented one and cursed my way through the hookup—but got it to work finally and Mother could see another great-grandchild through photography, this one in action and sound sync.

Mother goes through a book every other day now, the library will even bring her things at home through a program of volunteers. She goes to dinner in her walker and is congratulated by the whole crowd, having earned their respect. We now have a speech therapist named Tracy who sat through dinner and observed the social politics so that she can coach Mother in lip reading. Ann and I pushed Mother's wheelchair through the snow so that she could vote for gay rights, all three of us laughing at her civil enthusiasm: the measure won, righting an old wrong. At Jo's suggestion Mother, aware of her rights and secure in them now has made a statement: "I would like to make my wishes clear. I did not like St. Anne's Home and have no desire to return there or to go into any other nursing home either. I am happy in my own home at the Wellington and wish to continue here." Signed and dated.

I see all the hope of my late night prowls fulfilled in the reorganized apartment, the commode and the grab bars. We watch the Twins win again and again, going from the playoffs to the series, having hitched our star to them, Mother having done so as a true fan, I having done so out of sheer superstition—if they win, we do. But what if they lose? There is also the possibility that some form of outside interference or maybe just bad luck might break up Mother's fragile hold over her own life and apartment. Last Saturday while I was running errands Ollie vacuumed up the pull cord for emergency assistance and set off the alarm in the office downstairs. I never even had time to panic since Dell and Edith told me the story as a joke as I walked in the front door. Edith then told me the story of an old man, a neighbor of hers when she first married. He was ninety and lived alone and loved it, completely independent and self-sufficient. He even drove a car. Then he had a heart attack. When he was ready to be discharged from the hospital they wouldn't let him live alone, he was forced into an old age home where he lived only two weeks. "You know, he could have gone home—and lived in peace. My little girl wanted me to rescue him, to adopt him. I had my hands full, I couldn't do it. But I vowed then that I'd never put my mother away. And look at the direction my own life has taken: here I am working with the aged."

Cheering for baseball as well: Edith wears a Twins sweatsuit and conducts baseball parties after dinner. This is partly in earnest and partly to entertain the residents with the extravagance of her enthusiasm. It is undeniable that she lives in a fever of season tickets, even goes to the airport to greet the team when they arrive home as the champions of the American league, Western division. As the Wellington's leading fan, here where everyone is a fan, where baseball has become a kind of religion, Edith has made it a source of collective excitement and partying as well: the baseball parties take place downstairs every night now before a huge screen: there is popcorn, cookies, root beer floats. After a while we no longer depend on the management for treats but begin bringing our own, everyone chipping in and showing off. Of course each individual who lives at the Wellington has a television in his or her apartment but it is far more fun to watch together, to groan and rejoice together, even to accept defeat together. I have become, without quite noticing it, addicted to the Twins and the one night I was invited out for dinner with two professors from the University, perfectly nice women who share my age and interests, I felt an odd twinge at the thought that I would not be sitting next to Mother, surrounded by Mary Sheahy and Izzy and Marjorie Bordenave and taking cigarette breaks with Vera outside the building between innings and during ads. Tonight I was supposed to read in Paris at the Village Voice bookstore: there are times I come to and wonder.

Looking at the little collection of my clothes huddled into Mother's tiny spare closet I have an unexpected recall of my old Mother—the one of visits past: boring and evasive, the claustrophobia of those visits home to St. Paul, her endless ordering me about, criticizing me. Her look of horror for everything I represented; my own condescension toward her milieu. It is another Mother now and I am like someone "in love" with her, ready to lay everything down as for a lover. Of course not the momentous and wonderful silliness of my lifetime of love affairs, not love in the meaning it used to have for me, but deeply loving this small creature with an overmastering tenderness, a closeness I would never have believed possible. So that these days are a miracle and a grace, a gift.

Loving now as parents must love children where the term sacrifice has no meaning at all; being here is nothing less than a stroke of good luck, something I might so easily never have had, this unlooked-for long visit with her before her death and while she was still alive, the time most people miss and never get, running to deathbeds too late. If it were not for this accident, I would never have had the length and depth of time, the weeks and months, our communion would have never been longer than the week stolen from New York or the Farm, my busy, self-important life. If I had not "laid down the time" as Shirley Welch put it, I would never have gained this magnificent experience of affection, this strange late love.

And I will be back again soon: we have made an arrangement now, the four of us. Mother will have one of her three daughters now for a week of every month, the twelve months divided by three or four visits a year, Sal for December, Mallory for January—I will have February. No one will have to come running, we will know ahead of time, can arrange our lives: Mallory can book train tickets since she is afraid to fly, I can plan gigs. Mallory and I might buy an old car together to keep here for our visits; this year alone I gave Hertz $1,700—at that rate I could have bought two cars, the kind of car I go in for, something like the little old red Toyota that did the Farm errands.

There is the future, there is even a present still full of magic and surprise. There has been a great snowstorm and all our appointments have been canceled this weekend. The world is hushed and white, I cleaned off the car and went shopping, came across Joannie and Helen Ann and Rosellen at the supermarket, all three of Mother's nieces, their lives seeming sad and constrained: Rosellen's husband Harold has had another heart attack. There is something so curtailed about them this morning, so discouraged: age and illness closing in. I feel a great compassion but helpless too. We were to go out to Jim and Laurie's on the St. Croix today, but with twenty-six inches of snow it is impossible. All prospects seem defeated and deferred, a great dissatisfaction. A restlessness seizes me, I come home longing for adventure and suggest that at last we venture out into the big snow and see "The Emperor's Clothes," a fabulous exhibition at the Minneapolis Art Institute we have been planning to go to —that we go even despite the snow.

It's crazy, but let's do it. The posters are all over town, there are experts on the radio describing the treasures, these are all the silks of the last dynasty of China, we have set our hearts on it. Since it is costume it is the kind of art Mother likes best. Sometime today or this evening the conference call is supposed to come, the wrangling over Mother's fate, possible argument, managing voices managing what has already been solved. We could accept this and wait passively, or we could take life in our hands. "Would it be crazy?" I ask, thinking of what the family would say to such an outing. This is the biggest snowfall in a hundred years.

"If we have to turn back, we tried," Mother says. Like a pair of delinquents we prepare for the escapade. The roads are treacherous, there are several inches of packed snow, we don't dare Snelling Avenue but go the long slow way across Cleveland to Summit, Summit to Lexington and then Highway 94 over to Minneapolis: ten miles on roads that have not been ploughed yet, the world silent and white and beautiful and perilous. All to see an art show, all to go to a museum, all to find China in the Midwest. The museum's directions are excellent, here is the great neoclassical building,

Mother snug inside in her wheelchair in charge of the staff while I park the car. There is a black woman in gold shoes and furs at the entrance, like an apparition, as impractical as we are.

We take the intermediate rooms at a fast clip, the Romans, the Greeks, the Japanese, the Moderns—I would love to linger but must save Mother's energy—we are here for one thing only. Still there is Marisol's *Cocktail Party* and Mother likes it too. Then we start on the Emperor's clothes, the rooms very dim so that the ancient fabric is not harmed by exposure to artificial light. You must look very carefully, the few visitors are extremely quiet. The strange garments of the court, the outlandish display of wealth, the corruption of silk and gold, the luxury and excess of it, the colors, the embroidery. All this in the quiet and the unnatural semi-darkness, the golds and reds gleaming, the purples and yellows inside these rooms. And outside the snow. Yeats's golden bird in Byzantium, the artifice of eternity, singing of what is past and passing or to come. We explore in reverence. Mother finds it beautiful. We are in rapture at the impossible beauty of Chinese civilization. Wonderment at what is so foreign, exotic, useless and gorgeous. A great sense of triumph overcomes us, simply that we did it, got there, are seeing this, have dared to use the time this way.

We could have stayed home and waited for the conference call, which still hasn't come through, or we could steal a march and see the woman in the golden shoes leaving just as we do, both of us conscious that this is a high point of our time together, our adventure, her recovery, the satisfaction of success. The way home is a little blurry, we miss a turn, become involved with football traffic from the Metrodome, but Mother takes charge, is cool and sure and gives all the directions. She used to drive Highway 94 every day. On our trips to the ball games in the last months she was passive, today she is competent, sure with a new confidence. "We have been to see the Emperor's clothes," Mother announces to an astonished elderly woman in the elevator.

We return home safely to soup and shrimp, *Sixty Minutes* and *Murder*

She Wrote, gratified with our day. The conference call dwindles to a simple conversation with Sally and Lisa where I spell out the allies and Sally agrees to remove Mother's name from the waiting list at St. Anne's. We have solved thereby the problem of the power of attorney. Mother is asleep. We are all excited by the accord we have arrived at, our general satisfaction over Ann and the whole program of Mother's recovery and progress, I even try to explain about the Emperor's clothes, what it meant to both of us to get there; they are only puzzled.

~

I take a cookie out of the jar. Life is normal. Mother sleeps in her room. She is not dying, she is not a helpless bundle it could have been a tragic error to rescue. She is herself again. And I am her daughter staying up too late and smoking cigarettes and reading the wrong kinds of books.

We have succeeded. And in succeeding I have turned back time. I remember the nursing supervisor at St. Anne's, her strange remark that she and her siblings were "not ready to let go of Mom yet," so they did not put their mother into a home, but cared for her themselves. A remark which at the time seemed like new age folly, something in it even cruel and stupid—as if mothers were a commodity one could let go of. Instead we have given Mother her own life back, an acceptable life compared to the despair and quick death at St. Anne's. But in restoring Mother's life, something of mine is restored as well. As if I have prolonged my own youth, assured I would continue as a daughter not an orphan: an orphan riddled with guilt and a despairing conviction that life is a cheat you pay for, as much as thirty grand a year to dwindle in bondage. That life itself is a sentence.

Tonight, in a carefree moment, I am just another St. Paul kid eating chocolate chips and looking forward to getting out of here and back to the real party in New York, still having a home to run away from, a place I came from but have never found again as an adult. She is home, it is just her. My home breathing serenely in the next room, still alive and independent and an example. So then I can still experiment with life, come and go from my sought-out existence back into the certitude and repression I escaped, the goodness and common sense and limitations I left behind but can still touch down on every now and then, the heartland, the reality behind art and illusion and the tricks of the market—the actuality at the bottom of the cake pan, the wheatfields and cornstubble, the River when you see it from the airplane, holding Trumbell's biography of Fitzgerald, seeing it through tears, never really sure if all your emotion and self-generated sentimentality is directed at the Minnesota, the Mississippi or the St. Croix.

Because you come from here but left so long ago it's a blur and you couldn't do the street names from Randolph to Summit in the correct order if your life depended on it and even bought a map to take back with you to New York. Maybe it doesn't matter, maybe what matters most is how each landmark still works, still lives, still beckons mysteriously. Each street as you drive by is full of recollections, full of kids who have vanished, full of traumas or ideas or exaltations—vague unexplored memories or intuitions, catalysts or impressions that end up incongruously being the scenes of rebellions or peace treaties or novels really set in France—where they would never have a playground like the Groveland Park School's or a pillared house like the one on Cleveland between Grand and St. Clair. But the real scene suggested the imagined one because of the accident of the physical placement of space, an arrangement of houses. Or something further back, a kind of archetypal mental photograph or diagram of mood occasionally discovered when one pursued the image at the edge of the mind while reading or fantasizing. Something must have happened to me at that alley along Dayton that I position a spy novel there or subliminally recall another down by the river when I read about the African National Congress. A graveyard of unexplored and unresolved pre-ideation that still must have a use and a source, like the irrational little skits and pictures I sometimes experience just as I fall asleep, illogical events I used to disavow in uneasiness—but perhaps just as fertile.

The seeds are here. Of everything that ever followed. They do not always germinate but are frozen, stored, as agricultural historians preserve species, just because someday they may come in handy in cross-breeding, even and just because these grains existed once and can again. They are always potential. So is this place, as long as she is here and alive—my own potentiality, youth, promise, choice, option—the life that still affords scope for excellence and the careful exercise of powers. Any and all I can script. I am not looking at the end and deciding to limit my energy to books rather than art. I am not in the home stretch but still starting out; with each start from here. From her who is my here.

Maybe while she is still here, I can reach around her enormous demand and lay some of the place and its people in store for other times, when she can spare me, need me less. I always think so when I come, yet it never happens. I failed again this time to make contacts. And I fear that were she gone from here in death I could never come here again, never set foot in this town again, never touch down, not even as a stranger making a speech in some strange burg.

She is this place. To see it without her would be pointless, painful, obscene. I would be deracinated, a person without a hometown or a childhood. What remains of then is in her, she is the here of here.

When she goes, it does? Without her, and except for her, I never found the place, in all my trips. I thought to come back with the idea of a landing at the St. Croix, a tribal home, but when it failed with Jim and Laura and the St. Croix, it failed permanently perhaps, which is hard to write down and even doing so I wish it could be changed. I have asked Laura to look again, but it is hard enough to hold reunions at the Farm. So it is Mother then, she is everything here. I can imagine her reading this and calling it "poppycock." But tonight her sleeping form is that entirety still, that comforting and complete. She is it: the town, the place, the land, home itself.

Birthplace. While that thread holds . . .

Eulogy

Crossing the ocean, coming home to her funeral, I realize her suddenly. Mother, childhood, tomato soup and the kitchen chairs with round backs we called "peanut butter" chairs. Every inch of the house on Selby Avenue clear and felt. Riding to America on Aer Lingus only hours away from the phone call in the middle of the night. Surrounded by this catastrophe; so long awaited, so unprepared for. Seven hours with nothing to read, no escape valve, no distraction. Only this bewilderment in a crowded cabin over water, the sound of the engine, the pain a constant and obdurate force around this chair suspended in nothingness. Relentless and pushing to a crescendo. Words come and with them tears. Words themselves, she gave me language. How much she taught me of literature, Shakespeare and Synge and Shaw, of the role of speech, the ring of a line, how a word could hit the mark, the success of it.

And people and judgment. And kindness, the tact that averts a quarrel, gentleness, the habit of peace. And determination when propitiation wouldn't do finally and you had to go back to principle and speak up. Courage and toleration and fairness. The fact that she once expelled a wedding guest from her house in the midst of his own festivities for a joke she regarded as anti-Semitic. I know Martin Luther King and Gandhi through her. And Richard Wright and the *Death of a Salesman*. And *Riders to the Sea*. Also her deliberate and lady-like honesty over money or the truth, the limits of a white lie or courtesy or charity. Suddenly I remember every callow remark and superior opinion of my own, how I carped and contradicted.

It is a long time since Helen Feely Millett has been as we once knew her. But then we knew her real self far longer, only in the last years have we had to watch the inches and inches giving way to death, to infirmity, our enemy the tumor paralyzing her. Our enemy age and frailty. Her strength, then surrender. In a sense we lost her even before we lose her now, the going from us gradual, as if we were being seasoned to bear it finally. Only by degrees having to take on that dreadful singular state in the world—motherlessness.

As I copy out these words Dvorak's "New World" Symphony is playing, one of her favorite pieces of music. She was our America, the daughter of immigrant farmers, Minnesota pioneers in Farmington. She was also our Ireland, its virtues and memories and landscape. She was, finally transcending the limitations and particulars of her early years, a wise internationalist with a vital and unfailing concern not only for business but politics and peace and justice. I explored the meaning of the 500th anniversary of Columbus and the European devastation of the Americas with her in the months following her surgery when I was able to care for her and teach her to walk again, safely restored to her beloved Wellington where she spent the last two years of her life. I was also able then to read her the first two chapters of *The Politics of Cruelty*, a book she encouraged and urged forward during the seven years of its composition, the wisdom of her world view being my reference point and beacon the long while I worked on this book. Hearing the sad news of how the gulag and the death camps had restored the practice of torture to the modern world, she sighed,

"I'm not sure I wanted to know this much before I died . . . but then, imagine what they knew."

I see her now as a pioneer, a brave and lonely groundbreaker in her time and place; troubled, afraid but having to be brave and finally triumphant in her integrity. It stands before us now as a challenge, daunting in its example, radiant and complete now entirely visible.

I want to say that we do not lose the ones we love in death, we incorporate them. If we have imagination we absorb the dead rather than relinquish them. One need hardly assume the leap of faith into a hereafter. Here and now as long as I live I will bear her with me, not a voice from outside my mind but from within it. Helen Millett—that soul, its fallibility as well as its grandeur—surer now, less timid and uncertain than in life, less harried, even braver than her familiar courage and certainty—quicker on the draw—surer now for being an extract, a concentrate, that essence, that bullion cube of rectitude and common sense.

A small woman in a little woman's body, that frail and vulnerable being. That figure habitually ignored or derided and passed over, incarnate in human flesh—it is this I celebrate as a tower of integrity, a conscience and a will. Imperishable bone—flesh of her blood in all I do hereafter, remembering her, becoming her.

My sisters too and all their progeny—all who through kinship or contact—she made us. Carefully and deliberately, no maker of souls worked more consciously in her creation. And we must cleave together agreeing and disagreeing, even agreeing to disagree, separate but individual—this above all was her wish. That we remain in love in fellowship, in harmony and continuation. That what she held together never be sundered by her transformation into spirit.

Ashes to ashes—we are all on our way to death—we are all going there . . . and know better now that it is what we bring with us, what knowledge we acquire along the way, that matters. A terrible solitude is still before me and will last all the days of my life. But having assumed her one can endure for she is not departed but present. She enters and dwells within, as time passes more and more comfortably, transformed and transforming energy and spirit. So that we need not say hail and farewell . . . but welcome.